Trade Financial Markets Like The Pros

Simon Watkins

Copyright © 2016 Simon Watkins
All rights reserved.
ISBN: 1908756845
ISBN-13: 978-1908756848 (ADVFN Books)

ADVFN BOOKS

Trade Financial Markets Like The Pros

This book is dedicated to my son, James Harper-Watkins, and my partner, Kate Baics

Contents

A New Trading Environment	1
The Risk/Reward Balance	3
Credit Ratings	4
The Big Lie Behind Ratings	6
Local Currency Vs. Foreign Currency Ratings	8
The Seismic Shift In Global Interest Rate Policy	9
The Importance Of International Bond Markets	13
Quantitative Easing Has Changed Bond Market Dynamics	16
The Importance Of Central Bank Comments	21
Risk-On/Risk-Off And Other Correlations	25
Long-Term Economic Patterns	28
The Kondratieff Wave	28
The Business Cycle	31
The Minsky Cycle	33
Changing Bond And Equity Correlations	36
Equities Trading In A Rising US Interest Rates Scenario	45
Oil And Metals In The Correlations Mix	52
The Current Saudi Oil Price Fix	57
Trading Strategies Off The Current Saudi Fix	57
Short Oil	61
Short Middle East Hydrocarbons Producers' Stock Markets	65
Short Canada	71
Long USD	71
Short Emerging Markets FX	73
Short European And US Banks With Significant Energy Exposure	78
Long Gold	84
The Ghosts In The Machine	86
Oil	86
China	92
Changing Growth Model	92
Significant Danger Of A Major Banking Crisis	95
Japan	101

Shinzo Abe's Big Plan	101
'Abenomics' Hits Predictable Problems	106
Eurozone	108
Fundamental Flaws	108
Deteriorating Backdrop	111
The US	115
Emerging And Frontier Markets	118
Basic Convergence Premise	118
Euro-Convergence Template	121
Convergence-Driven Top-Down Trading	123
Further Convergence Criteria For EM Assets	127
Key Opportunity And Risk Factors For EM Assets Now	131
The US	131
China	132
Frontier To Emerging Market Can Offer Alpha Returns	134
Emerging To Developed Market Progress Is Rarer Than Thought	134
Spotting Paradigmatic Shifts In Frontier Markets Is The Key	137
Technical Analysis	148
Candlesticks	148
Resistance And Support Levels	154
Fibonacci Levels	157
Moving Averages	158
Relative Strength Index (RSI)	165
Bollinger Bands	168
Elliott Wave Theory	170
Continuation Patterns	173
Ascending And Descending Triangles	174
Flags	176
Trend Reversals	178
Double Top And Double Bottom	178
Risk/Reward Management And Hedging	181
The Nature Of Risk	181
The Risk Curve	182
Risk/Reward Ratios And Effective Order Management	183
Net Margin/Trading Requirement (NMR/NTR)	185
Account Size And Setting Targets	186
Straight Averaging Up	188
Layered Averaging Up	190

Value Averaging	191
Trailing Stops	191
Hedging	192
Cross-Currency Hedging	192
Cross-Asset Hedging	197
Cross-Sovereign/Credit Rating Hedging	198
Options	199
Key Types	199
Key Terms	200
Key Legislation	202
Basic Structures	203
About the Author	207
Also by Simon Watkins	209
More books from ADVFN	215

A New Trading Environment

There has never been a more difficult time to make money from trading the markets than now, with all of the long-standing foundation stones of the global financial system in a state of flux: engines of growth, monetary policies and the correlation dynamics between asset classes, to name but three.

In all previous difficult trading eras, many of these relationships held good. During the **Great Depression**, for example, initially shorting equities and then looking for value buys across asset classes based on alpha growth prospects was a very profitable strategy, as was buying selected commodities. In the lead-up to the **Global Financial Crisis**, convergence trades offered huge returns, particularly for EU accession states and some major Asian economies, based on the notion that they would soon morph into 'developed markets' rather than 'emerging' ones. Even when the Crisis hit, there were clear pockets of value to be exploited, based predominantly on future economic prospects, most notably in China.

Now, though, there is a huge question about where global growth will come from, as each of the four core regional growth engines around the world faces its own set of problems. The Eurozone continues to record dismal GDP numbers, the US has begun an interest rate hiking cycle even though its growth trajectory remains fragile, Japan continues to teeter on the edge of further recession and China itself moves from a manufacturing-led economy to a consumer-led one, recording ever-lower GDP growth figures in the process.

As a result of these factors, the long-running commodities super-cycle has come to an end as manufacturing-led growth in emerging markets especially is waning from the peak point, convergence trade opportunities are limited to much higher-

risk areas than before, and many of the historic relationships between stocks, bonds and currencies have broken down. As such, countries are looking to secure their piece of a global economic pie that is failing to grow in any meaningful way.

This will lead to a broadening out of the type of extremely volatile and seemingly unpredictable activity that we have seen most notably in the past year or so in the oil (and other hydrocarbons products) pricing complex, which has seesawed dramatically as a result of Saudi Arabia seeking to hold onto its market share in the face of a new threat from the nascent shale energy sector by continuing to over-produce. The same dealing pattern was seen towards the end of 2015 in the euro, as it appeared finally to be trading in a 'sensible' devaluation pattern before the most dramatic reversal in recent trading history wiped out short positions.

Exactly the same basic policy – engaging in strategies based on ultra-self-interest that may, only in theory, be in a state's long-term interest, even at the expense of massive short-term pain both for it and other states with similar economic dynamics – can be expected going forward, as **new currency wars are likely to gather pace, with concomitant effects on the global equities, bond and commodities markets.**

Given this backdrop, **it is more important than ever that traders manage and exploit the few remaining factors in global markets that hold good, and this is what this book is about: knowing what these are, exploiting them and banking the profits in a risk/reward efficient manner.**

The Risk/Reward Balance

Money held anywhere around the world for investment purposes will ultimately flow to wherever it is best rewarded, given the corollary risks involved. This forms the absolute basis of all investment approaches taken by the world's top fund managers and should do the same for retail investors as well. This maxim has always ultimately held good under all circumstances, regardless of asset class, geography, politics and legal strictures, and always will, even in the current market environment that is struggling to find which of its previously understood relationships still hold good.

Retail traders who do not want to be one of the 90% of all such investors who lose all of their investable funds within the first 90 days of starting to trade need to understand as many of the dynamics of the FX, equities, commodities and bond markets as they can, together with the prevailing political climates in all traded economies across the globe in order to tip the risk/reward balance firmly in their favour. This is especially true in markets as seemingly disordered as the current ones (see *The Ghosts In The Machine* section).

It is all very well to believe that focussing on one asset class or one country's markets will provide a trading edge, but any success from this approach will be transitory at best.

This book, then, will look in depth at each of the key asset classes, the principal market types, key economic and political drivers, technical analytical factors (see *Technical Analysis* section), and the ways in which they interact on asset pricing, enabling investors to make optimal trading decisions ahead of major moves across all markets, all within the context of investment structures that allow for optimally high returns to be generated from minimal risks taken (see *Risk/Reward Management And Hedging* section).

Credit Ratings

The most obvious reward for investable funds lies in the interest rate it can garner over time, but this needs to be balanced against the risks inherent in the asset and the country in which the interest rate is on offer. **This latter factor can be gauged in the most basic terms from averaging out the foreign currency-denominated sovereign bond credit ratings of the leading two global ratings agencies – Standard & Poor's (S&P) and Moody's – and also looking at what Fitch Ratings has to say.**

The reason for looking at the first two is that these are the ratings that all major investors – hedge funds and 'real money' funds (pension funds, insurance companies and similar long-term horizon players) – look at in determining their broad investment risk parameters and consequent approaches. For example, as a rule of thumb, the real money funds will be working under the auspices of an overarching investment mandate that governs all of their investment decisions, typically including provisions that allow them only to invest in assets that have a minimum (and high) credit rating, such as AA and upwards.

Credit Ratings Risk Profiles

Moody's		S&P		Fitch		
Long-term	Short-term	Long-term	Short-term	Long-term	Short-term	
Aaa		AAA		AAA		Prime
Aa1		AA+	A-1+	AA+	F1+	High grade
Aa2	P-1	AA		AA		
Aa3		AA-		AA-		
A1		A+	A-1	A+	F1	Upper medium grade
A2		A		A		
A3	P-2	A-	A-2	A-	F2	
Baa1		BBB+		BBB+		
Baa2	P-3	BBB	A-3	BBB	F3	Lower medium grade
Baa3		BBB-		BBB-		
Ba1		BB+		BB+		Non-investment grade speculative
Ba2		BB		BB		
Ba3		BB-	B	BB-	B	
B1		B+		B+		
B2		B		B		Highly speculative
B3		B-		B-		
Caa1	Not prime	CCC+				Substantial risks
Caa2		CCC				Extremely speculative
Caa3		CCC-	C	CCC	C	In default with little prospect for recovery
Ca		CC				
		C				
C		D	/	DDD	/	In default
/				DD		

The practical effect of this is broadly threefold. First, these trades will be fairly crowded, as there is a lot of money held in **real money funds** that have to find sufficiently well-rated assets in which to park their money. Second, these trades will tend to be priced to the high side, for the supply and demand reason just outlined. And third, they are usually less prone to quick, large moves (i.e. exceptional volatility), as the investors in them are not of the 'cut and run, churn and burn' variety.

This type of move is more associated with **hedge funds**, and for good reason. A large part of their returns are generated from big price swings, which often occur when an asset suddenly appears to be incorrectly rated (this relates to all asset markets, including currencies, although in this latter regard the 'rating' is not of the official variety, but rather of the 'market perception' one). Often, hedge funds will be instrumental in causing a run on a particular asset, either by being nimble enough to invest quickly in an asset that is genuinely under- or over-valued and being the first ones in the trade in size, or simply by spooking the broader market into a trade that the hedge funds want simply by massive leveraged buying or selling of that asset, irrespective of the fundamental merits of the trade.

So, **knowing what the 'Big Two' ratings are and, more importantly, being cognisant of potential changes to them (all ratings agencies will broadcast, usually a relatively long time in advance, whether or not a rating is 'Under Review' and whether that is for a possible upgrade or downgrade), is a key to knowing what sort of money is likely to be the dominant investment in the asset and consequently how vulnerable it is to sudden shocks and how quickly it will move based on these.**

Looking at Fitch's ratings is an important auxiliary to the Big Two as this agency has always tended towards taking a more realistic view towards its analysis of assets and countries than the others, for reasons outlined immediately below.

The Big Lie Behind Ratings

Knowing what the ratings are is one thing – it is necessary in understanding how the institutional money is likely to be positioned in any asset, as mentioned – but **knowing that ratings are in reality often completely inaccurate is another, as this allows the investor to act in the same manner as a hedge fund, pre-empting corrections in an asset's value based on reality hitting perception.**

In this context, it is absolutely essential to know that – unbelievably to most people, whether a professional bank or fund trader or a retail one – **it is the owner of the asset that almost always pays the ratings agencies to rate the asset! Each of the** two big ratings agencies know that if they do not give the owner of the asset a rating that is in line with the owner's belief of what it should be then the owner will simply go to the other one and negotiate for a better rating. More broadly, if one of the big two ratings agencies gets a reputation for 'being tough on ratings awards' then it will quite simply go out of business, as no asset owner will employ it to rate their products.

This, by the way, was told to me by a very senior ratings person at one of the big two agencies some time before the Global Financial Crisis hit in 2007/08, and prompted me to short anything highly rated that I could find, including bonds, stocks and the currencies of 'better rated than they should be' sovereigns. Finally, when the Crisis did hit – itself triggered by the inability of banks to pay margin calls on credit default swaps (the likelihood of a company or country defaulting on a debt obligation, the probability of which is determined by credit ratings) – the Big Two credit ratings agencies were shown to be incompetent, at best, and collusive at worst. Indeed, just prior to the Crisis, the Big Two agencies were still rating the big investment banks – for example Lehman Brothers and Bear Stearns – as AA or better, even as they were going bust. Even on a sovereign level, they continued to play the tune of the guys paying the piper, continuing to rate Iceland as a prime credit, even as its entire financial system unravelled.

The point here is that **being aware of the ratings of the Big Two is essential, as is knowledge that they are in many key cases fundamentally flawed and incorrect, as neither of them have changed their business procedures since the Crisis: their businesses still largely depend on being paid for ratings by the people who want the ratings.**

Local Currency Vs. Foreign Currency Ratings

Even worse than standard credit ratings are local currency-denominated bond ratings, which are completely irrelevant for shrewd investors as, in practice, a country can simply print more of its own currency when required ('quantitative easing' is effectively the same thing, but sounds less alarming to the public). It cannot, though, print more foreign currency to meet its foreign obligations as it cannot simply instruct another country's central bank to do its bidding, so foreign currency-denominated bond ratings are the ones to watch, albeit with the same caveats as mentioned above.

The major global exception to the first point here is for the constituent countries of the Eurozone, which are dependent on the European Central Bank (ECB) for printing money. This dependence on a non-indigenous central bank, together with the fact that the euro's value does not reflect the inherent state of an individual member's economy in the same way that its former currency could, is at the heart of the essential problem in the alliance.

Generally speaking, though, it is much less likely that a country can fudge its credit worthiness as spectacularly as individual corporates and, in broad terms, the better the credit rating grade (as shown below) the better a country's foreign currency-denominated debt obligations (bonds) and therefore its currency will be supported (as in order to buy a bond an investor has to buy the relevant currency as well and vice-versa if selling the bond).

Again, though, **the ratings should be regarded much more simply as starting points from which the individual investor can use their market knowledge to determine how far these ratings are in practical terms and to buy/sell/abstain accordingly: in short, every investor should be their own credit ratings agency.**

The Seismic Shift In Global Interest Rate Policy

In general terms, the Global Financial Crisis prompted a huge economic contraction around the world, and policy makers took a number of approaches to counteract this, to boost economic expansion once again. **Some chose to pump money into their financial systems through quantitative easing (QE) of one sort of another, some chose to effectively devalue their currencies, some chose to cut interest rates and some chose a combination thereof.**

The **problem now facing many economies is that, even having engaged these dramatic policy interventions, meaningful economic growth has still not returned, but the feasibility of continuing with some of the aforementioned policies is nil.** There is a limit to how much a country can expand its central bank balance sheet (QE) without causing long-term damage (through spiralling inflation, for example), and there is only so much that it can devalue its currency to gain a competitive export advantage before its competitors do the same and nullify the effect. It was thought that there was only so far that countries could go in cutting interest rates but, in fact, with no other realistic monetary or fiscal tools available to them, **some governments around the world have cut interest rates into negative territory, with others set to follow and no end in sight for a return to positive territory. The most notable of these, on global economic terms, are the Eurozone and Japan, but Switzerland, Sweden and Denmark are also trusting in this policy.**

The expected effects of cutting interest rates are: first, that companies can borrow at lower rates and the lower cost of capital can translate either into expansion plans or to lower prices for products and services (by investing in more economic processes); second, the populace can spend more; and third – and historically always a neat side-effect of cutting interest rates – the cutting country's currency will devalue as well, even more so than as a function of direct central bank intervention to sell the currency. Indeed, Sweden's Riksbank and Switzerland's National Bank have made no secret of their desire to prevent currency strength, and negative rates have become a key part of their policy arsenal in this respect. In the Eurozone, a stronger EUR provoked a fresh promise of action at the March 2016 ECB meeting, and in Japan the decision to adopt negative interest rates coincided with a bout of JPY strength that threatened to derail at least some of the gains from the currency's QE-driven depreciation.

The **problem is with those countries that have already sent their rates into negative territory – most notably the Eurozone and Japan, but also Switzerland, Sweden and Denmark – the positive effects on a lower cost of capital and on consumer spending have been extremely limited, if any, whilst those on the currency have been nil.** This latter point has militated into the looping effect that has called into question the likely upside of the policy in general on engendering greater economic growth, which in turn has fed back into the currency, and so it goes on. **More specifically, the problem of negative rates feeding through into a virtuous loop that promotes greater economic growth, in part driven by currency devaluation, is twofold: one, the FX markets look at the interest rate gap, not specific levels of interest rates; and, two, negative rates in and of themselves smack of utter policy desperation.**

Looking more closely at the first point, to begin with, the basic idea is that imposing negative rates is supposed to have a strong influence on behaviour (the 'fear of losses outweighing the greed for gains' concept). The point that has been lost on central bankers is that for FX dealers the absolute level of rates is immaterial; rather, it is the interest rate differential between two currencies which is significant. It is true that, all else being equal, dealers prefer trading positions which come with positive carry (whenever a dealer sells a high-yielding currency against a low-yielding currency he has to pay this negative carry), but if they have conviction in a view that comes with negative carry then they will not hesitate to enter such a trade, and negative carry in this regard is just a part of the game. This has been seen for some time now in the long JPY/short EM trades, for example. Additionally, market volatility needs to be factored into the equation: for example, the Bank of Japan (BOJ) cutting rates by 10 basis points (bps) is miniscule in dealers' minds when compared to the market volatility (in pips) at the time.

This feeds into, and feeds off, the second point, which is that cutting interest rates into negative territory just smacks of weakness, upon which the markets love to pounce. An absolute sparkling example of this is in the Eurozone, which has seen anaemic growth for a very long period and an uninspiring central bank (ECB) chief in Mario Draghi. Prior to December 2015's cut, taking rates further into negative territory, implementation of a EUR60 billion/month QE programme had seen the EUR plummet against the USD. Even after the anticipation and announcement of QE had already driven EURUSD down from around 1.40 to 1.14, implementation of the programme provoked a further 5% move lower in March 2015, this showing that, in some cases, FX was still responding as expected to QE initiatives. But the point is that QE was required at all when deposit rates were already negative in the Eurozone, implying that negative rates had already failed. June's cut in 2014 to -10bp had no discernible impact on the EUR, and September's follow-up to -20bp saw EURUSD fall only 1.5% on the day. Further negative rates failed again a year later. Moreover, despite another 10bp easing to -30bp on 3 December 2015, EURUSD actually appreciated by 3%: the biggest one-day move of the year.

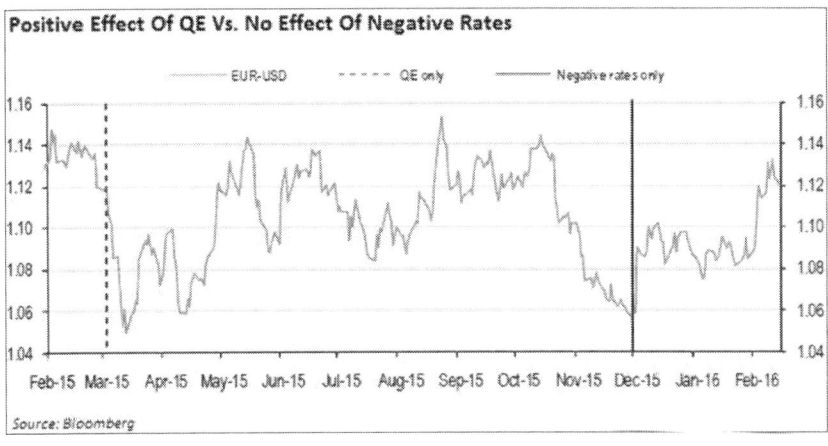

The same pattern is reflected in the BOJ's activities in recent years. **It had been using QE long before the ECB and for the most part enjoyed the same success.** However, it had faced a problem in that the run-rate of bond purchases was likely to hit constraints before the end of 2015 (they would run out of bonds to buy), so **it opted for a shift in strategy to negative rates, with the same dismal lack of success as the ECB has seen.** All that the market saw in the cut was an inability on the BOJ's part to do anything more meaningful.

In both of these cases, and indeed to a greater or lesser degree in the others that are using a negative rates only policy, all that happens when such a policy is used is that markets see weakness, This creates the negative feedback loop mentioned earlier, and the fleeting negative impact on currencies have reinforced this fear. This fear, in turn, has engendered cyclical 'risk-off' moves (see next section on *RORO*) that have occurred with much greater regularity than used to occur in the markets. Worse still is that both the JPY and the EUR have now taken on safe-haven qualities, in part precisely because traders believe that they may only appreciate from any further such dips in interest rates, more than nullifying any impact of negative rates.

The Importance Of International Bond Markets

In theory, **the least risky of the major traded asset classes is the foreign currency-denominated international sovereign bond market, as bonds are the closest asset to straight cash, and the least risky of these are the bonds of the countries with the highest credit ratings.** Given this, foreign currency-denominated international sovereign bonds are the foundation stone of many portfolios and, partly as an extension to this prevalence among investors and partly as a function of two other characteristics of the bonds, their relative performance has a major impact on the global equities and FX markets.

The first characteristic is that, as highlighted below, **bonds are in one sense simple expressions of interest rates. As such, as a rule of thumb, when interest rates rise equities fall, and when they fall equities rise.** The key reason why this relationship mostly holds good is a function of the maxim that money always goes to where it is best rewarded, given the corollary risks involved. That is, the static reward of holding shares is the dividend payment (a percentage of the share price, in effect an interest rate), over and above any dynamic capital gain or loss from price fluctuations, so if a benchmark government bond starts to pay an interest rate equal to the average dividend gains of a benchmark stock index then investors will prefer the bond, as it has less risk attached (through price fluctuations) for the same reward. An additional factor is that when a country's interest rates go up (reflected in its bonds) then borrowing for its companies becomes more expensive, negatively affecting profitability and also its ability to expand its business.

The second characteristic comes from the fact that this type of bond is denominated in a particular currency, so it is in many ways **a proxy FX instrument**: that is, if you buy 30 Year US Treasury bonds (a key benchmark of the international bond market, as the US is always well-rated and this duration is long and consequently less prone in theory to short-term market movements) then you need US dollars to do so and, in any event, you are buying the US sovereign risk. As can be seen in the charts below, when yields of benchmark US bonds began to rise markedly last year, itself a move that attracted more buyers, so the US dollar strengthened at a heightened pace, and when the yields began to fall, so did the US dollar.

In purely mathematical terms, bond prices are very easy to understand, as **the traded interest rate (yield) is a function of the nominal price of the bond (always 100) minus the traded price of the bond in the market; or to put it another way, 100 minus the traded interest rate (called the coupon) of the bond equals the price.** So, for example, a 30 year US Treasury bond with a coupon of 10% (it will be referred to as 'the 30 Year 10% US Treasury'), will have a price of 90 (100 – the 10% coupon). In theory – that is without any speculative activity whatsoever – the traded interest rate of a bond would be exactly that, over time, as the printed interest rate on the bond. Factoring in speculative activity, though, alters this straightforward calculation: so, if the price at the end of a particular day is 88.50, for instance, then the owner of the bond will accrue 11.5% for as long as that price holds (100 – 88.50 traded price = 11.5% interest rate). **Naturally, the more risky the profile of the country issuing the bond, the higher the interest rate that will be required to compensate investors for the incrementally higher risk and thus the lower the price of the bond.**

Because bonds are the least risky of the major asset classes, virtually every major investment firm in the world holds at least some, denominated in one currency or another. The benchmark long-term bond, as mentioned, is the US 30 year Treasury bond, but similarly well-rated long-term bonds issued by the governments of other developed market countries are also a staple of most investment companies around the globe.

As the investment mandate of an investment firm becomes more risk-taking (pension funds are theoretically the least risky of all investment funds, whilst hedge funds and similar are regarded as the most risk-taking, as highlighted) then bonds of less well-rated developed market countries will also be held and after that – in terms of going up the risk-curve – then bonds in emerging markets and then in frontier markets may also be held.

Due to their very direct link to interest rates, bond allocations tend to shift in big moves in a relatively short time, albeit not as quickly as often happens when a stock price rockets or plummets within a second or so of the release of major results, for example. As mentioned earlier, because there is a direct link between foreign currency-denominated bonds and FX, bond moves ripple through the FX market, sometimes with enormous effects that are, also, sometimes completely contradictory to what FX-only traders would normally expect.

Quantitative Easing Has Changed Bond Market Dynamics

As touched on earlier in examining the seismic shifts in interest rates policy around the globe, another reason why bond trading patterns in recent years have not resulted in the relatively straightforward historical trading correlations with FX counterparts, or equities ones, has been the unprecedented

degree of quantitative easing (QE) in global markets. This 'QE Effect' will continue to dominate trading patterns for some time to come – whether QE levels stay the same, increase or, most likely, diminish – and needs to be properly understood in order to make money going forward.

QE, in one form or another, has been the dominant weapon of choice for many major central banks to attempt to engineer some inflation-fires growth into their economies since the onset of the Global Financial Crisis began in 2007/2008. Last year, though, may be looked back on – perhaps – as being the peak of global QE, with the US having ceased its own programs and instead having begun to hike rates, although Japan continues it QE efforts and the EU resumed its own in earnest.

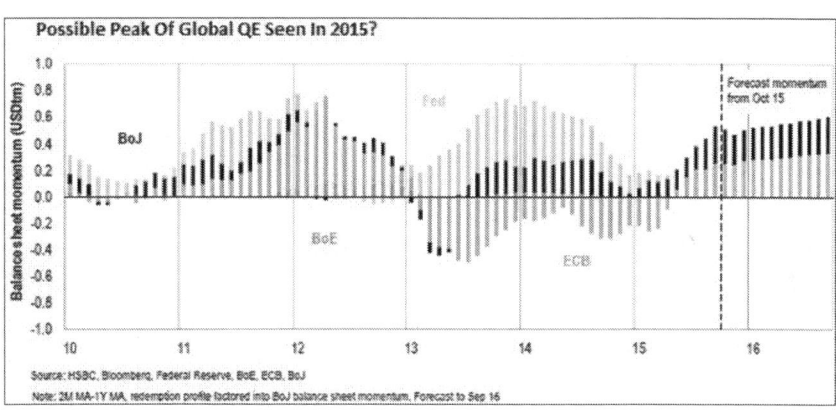

The vagaries of how much a country/region is already doing in QE terms and how much it will do down the line have led to very poor general market trading directions, which have then spectacularly reversed when errors in market views have belatedly been realised. In turn, large scale asset purchases (LSAPs), which were the key part of QE for the bond market, are a function of monetary conditions that are not just set by the short-term rate, but also by views on where that rate will be in the future. Various major bank studies have estimated that the US Fed's three QE programs reduced the level of 10-year yields by 60-100 basis points (bps) and it is intuitive to think that these LSAPs were instrumental in driving these yields lower. However, this happened over a much longer time period than many traders expected, as reflected in the discrepancy in the chart immediately below.

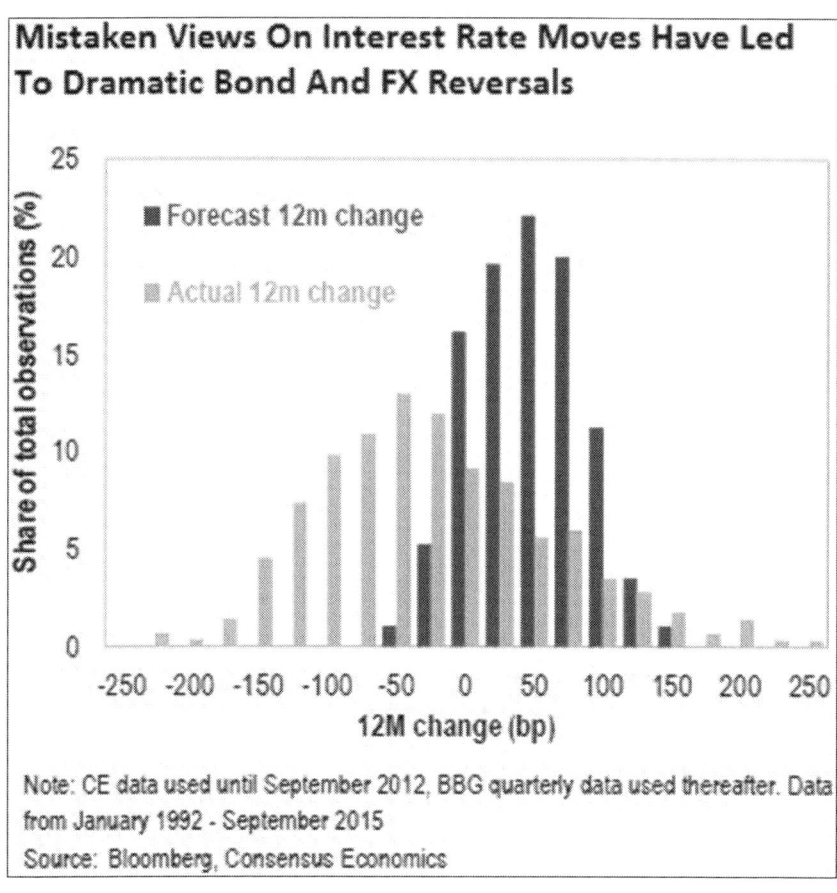

In fact, during heavy periods of QE, the yield curve went up, rather than flattening out, as the usual laws of supply and demand would dictate (i.e. more supply, lower value). This, then, is precisely what led to the whipsawing evident in many corollary investments such as FX and equities.

For example, the US bond curve during the extreme bond buying phases of the three QE programs notably steepened even as vast quantities of bonds were being sold in the market and new ones created, and it was only when this stopped that the curves actually flattened out, as shown below.

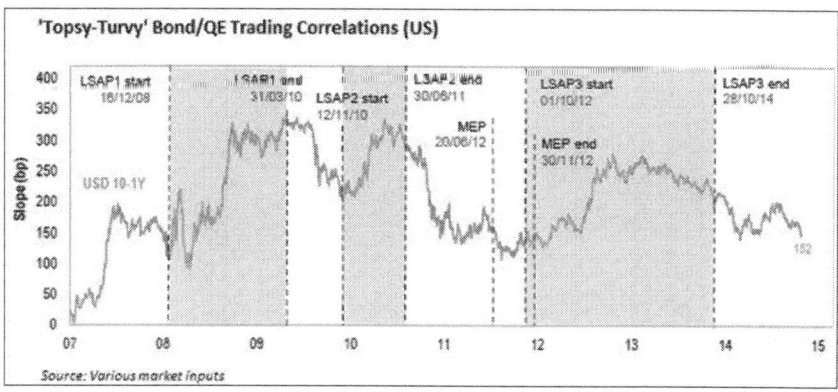

The reason that yield curves had a **counter-intuitive steepening bias at key points was a function of the two elements to the monetary policies involved: the size of reserves created under QE and the nature of the forward guidance given along the way.** In the former's case, vast amounts of new cash was pumped into the systems of the US, Japan and the Eurozone, with central bankers hoping that this would seep out into the broader economy, sparking business expansion, higher employment and the greater spending and export revenues that these factors would imply. Instead, to a very great degree – and exactly as happened in China's enormous fiscal stimulus packages over the past few years (see later) – **much of this newly created money wound up either being held onto by banks to bolster their capital adequacy ratios (in line with the tougher regulations on this prompted by the Global Financial Crisis), which ultimately wound up being invested in bonds and equities, creating asset price inflation.**

The fact that this new incremental demand for these assets was in great part a function of banks looking to bolster their capital adequacy ratios in a tighter regulatory regime meant that the demand for them often swung wildly, depending on how risky or not risky they were judged to be at any given point (see 'forward guidance' below), and this is why the 'Risk-On/Risk-Off' (RORO) market trading paradigm has become a dominant force in all global markets since around 2007/08. This is dealt with in full later on, but a snapshot can be seen below.

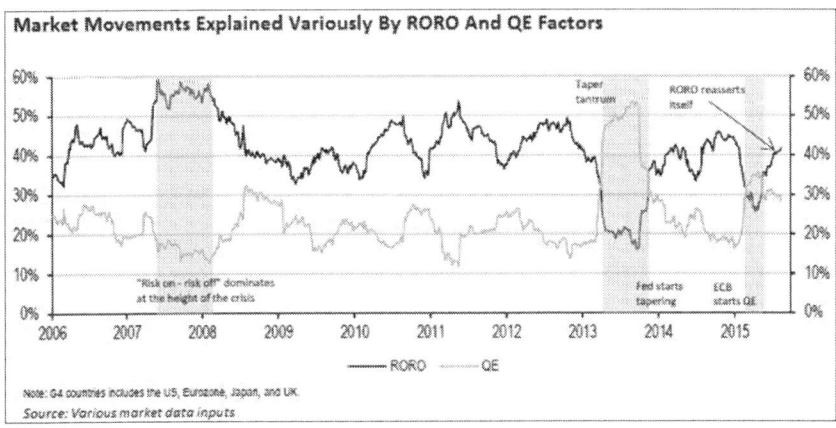

In the case of the second point – forward guidance – **the basic message was that central banks would keep interest rates lower for longer,** and this has certainly been the case for benchmark interest rates, creating a near zero interest rate policy (ZIRP) in all of the major continental economies. **Originally this guidance tended to be simply of the 'general statement' variety** – that is, a central bank governor would say, for example, that he/she expected interest rates to be held at the current rate for 'some considerable period' (a favourite of US Fed Chairman, Alan Greenspan) or similar broad-brush comment. **More latterly, though, this has been augmented by the 'data dependent' variety** – such as new Fed Chair Janet Yellen's comments that interest rates would not go up until unemployment was at or below 6.5% (the key consideration, in fact, for US interest rate hikes).

The Importance Of Central Bank Comments

The importance of staying up to date with such apparently mundane items as the minutes from central bank meetings and *ad hoc* statements from key central bankers was underlined after Yellen, in March 2014, implied that the Bank's long-held 6.5% jobless threshold for even considering hiking interest rates was to be discarded.

US financial policy makers had linked stimulus to employment and inflation for the first time in December 2012 and, with the target for US overnight interest rates having been 0-0.25% since December 2008, the long-anticipated 'USD uptrend theory' (the USD always moves in long-term cycles, see chart below) had been stuck in an environment where risk sentiment was not sufficiently buoyed by US growth to see inflows into US assets, but not sufficiently gloomy about an EM slowdown to see safe haven inflows either.

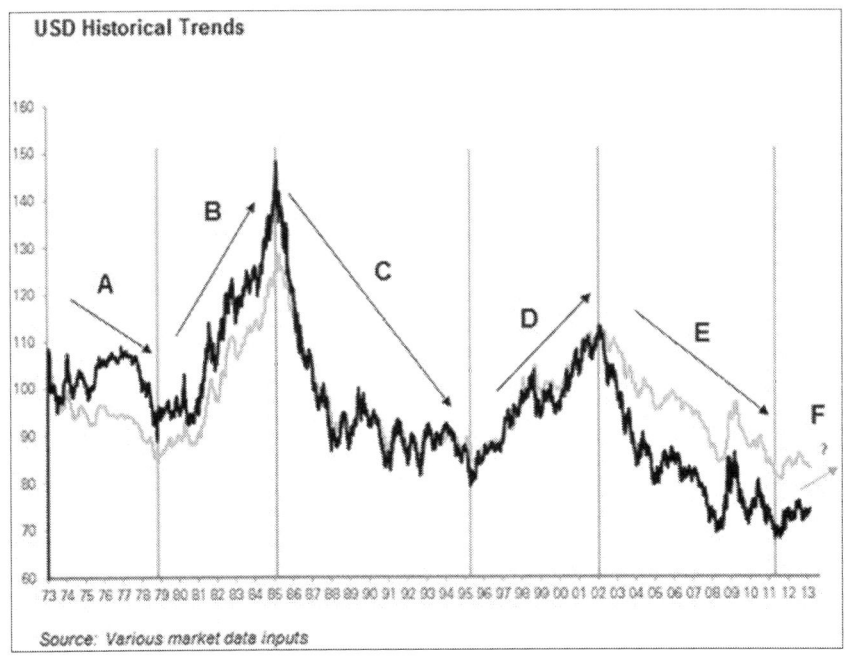

[Key:
Lines
Upper dark black from left to right = Nominal US dollar versus majors
Lower light black from left to right = Real broad US dollar
Vertical lines = Key trend turning points
Arrows From Left To Right
A = 6 years, down 18%
B = 6 years, up 67%
C = 10 years, down 46%
D = 7 years, up 43%
E = 9 years, down 40%
F = Next big trend?]

But it was not just the apparent abandonment of the jobless threshold (although in fact this still remained in reality) that lifted the USD Index from its previous four month lows but also Yellen's accompanying comment that the timing of the first hike after the end of the QE bond buying programme could well be even earlier than anybody had expected.

In practical terms, whether this was what Yellen intended to say or not – as she repeatedly stated that FOMC policy had not changed – the markets took the comments to suggest a greater Fed willingness to tighten than had earlier been expressed and the USD could not have asked for anything better than the prospect of a stiffening of two years' yields.

The convergence in terms of market importance of what a central bank does and what it says (which gives clues to future direction) can be seen in the market reaction to central bank meetings accompanied by press conferences. Sticking with the FOMC to illustrate the point, Fed meetings with press conferences have consistently generated large moves (volume, volatility and price) and much larger price changes than meetings without press conferences.

For example, as the chart below illustrates, in terms of volatility to begin with, USDJPY moves are consistently large on FOMC press conference days when compared with days when the FOMC finishes with only a regular statement.

The smallest absolute percentage change in USDJPY on an FOMC press conference day is 0.42%, which is the second largest absolute change on an FOMC day when only a statement is released. The same pattern is evident in EURUSD where the median of the absolute percentage change in EURUSD was 0.65% on press conference days and a very subdued 0.20% median on days when FOMC ended with no press conference. The above message was largely echoed in equities price action and slightly less so in Treasuries.

Median Of The Absolute 1 Day Change In Selected Asset Markets When The FOMC Does & Does Not Have A Press Conference						
	S&P 500 (% change)	2 yr yield (change in bps)	10 yr yield (change in bps)	USD/EUR (% change)	USD/JPY (% change)	USD/AUD (% change)
Press conference	0.94	2	6	0.65	0.91	0.54
No press conference	0.35	1	4	0.20	0.34	0.50

Source: EcoWin, Federal Reserve Board

As an adjunct to this, there is a strong bias for FOMC press conference days to result in higher 10-year yields and a very similar story of USDJPY going up. By contrast, the USD generally over the course of the first half of 2014 and the latter half of 2013 had a downward bias versus the EUR on press conference days, but showed no directional bias on non-press conference FOMC days.

The implication on the asset markets of these two factors – QE and changing forward guidance – was often to completely obscure any clear message to the markets at all (from the forward guidance element), resulting in periods of extraordinary volatility (along RORO principles and powered by the vast new QE funds). Oftentimes, various central bankers from the same bank would make comments on some aspect of monetary policy that would throw dealers into tumult, as they did not know whether these comments were statements sanctioned by the central bank itself or just personal ones, resulting in wild swings one way and then, when another different and opposite statement from another central banker came out, wild swings in the other direction. With the first of the US hikes having now been effected, though, and QE having been abandoned by it for the time being, some of this general uncertainty has been eliminated. However, growing uncertainties elsewhere still militate into a very choppy and challenging trading environment, and these uncertainties are analysed later on in depth. This is exacerbated by the ongoing QE still in operation in the Eurozone and Japan.

Risk-On/Risk-Off And Other Correlations

Even in a more 'normal' market environment – that is, one not torn in different directions by some major central banks continuing QE and some not, differing central bank emphasis on certain key economic data points rather than others and divergent inflation and interest rate paths for pivotal global economies – simply 'jobbing' in and out of an asset in isolation in search of a few pips here and there is almost certain to result in trading disaster. Indeed, **this style of dealing is the number one reason why 90% of retail traders lose all of their trading funds within 90 days of beginning to deal.** Not being one of these – and, rather, being one of those that makes life-changing serious money – requires self-discipline, knowledge of trading fundamentals (see later), a sound grasp of technical analysis and risk management (see later), extensive knowledge of risk management techniques (see later) and the ability to discern what patterns are in play across the global financial markets at any given point. This last point is what this section is about.

In general terms, the degree to which the price action of all major financial markets assets are correlated positively or negatively has varied since this phenomenon fully manifested itself after the collapse of Lehman Brothers in 2008. It is equally the case, though, that **these correlations, which are a function of the risk of systemic failure across the global financial system, remain a significant common price component of all assets in all regions across the world.**

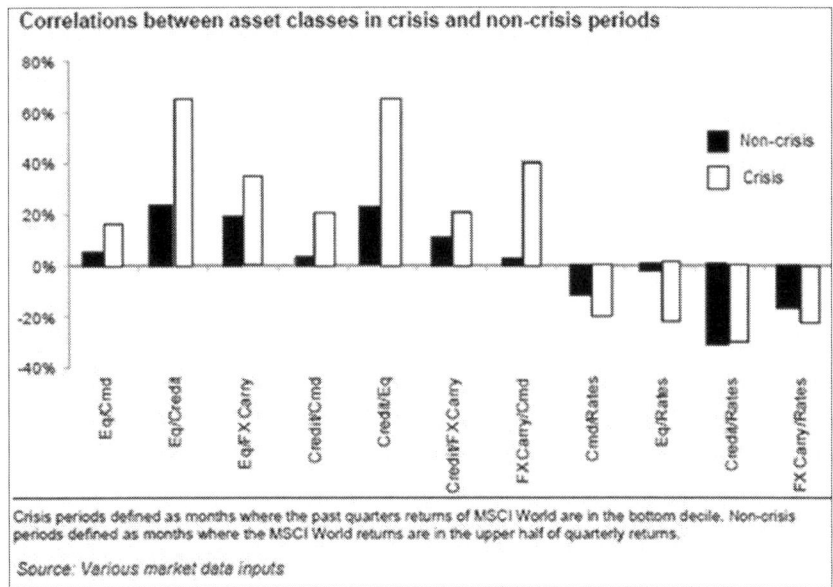

When the risk of this failure rises there is a shift towards less risk-exposed assets ('risk-off') and when it falls there is a move towards more risk-exposed assets ('risk-on'); both conditions together being acronymically termed 'RORO'.

As at the end of the first quarter of 2016, the RORO trading model was a dominant theme again (together with the more specific trading correlations mentioned earlier) as shown below.

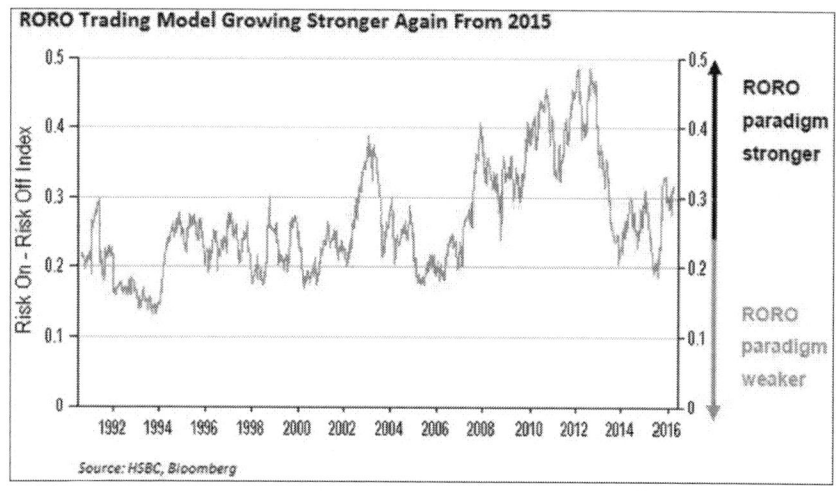

The fact that the prices of apparently disparate individual assets move in tandem (either positively correlated or inversely correlated) means that **classical methods of maximising returns whilst minimising risk will remain sidelined for the foreseeable future, calling for shrewder and nimbler investment approaches going forward** (currently, the RORO matrix is as laid out in the chart below).

This is even truer in periods when these correlations change on a proverbial dime, as they have been doing for some time now, although there are much longer-term cycles of which a trader must be aware in order to understand the base point from which they are operating, and these are identified immediately below.

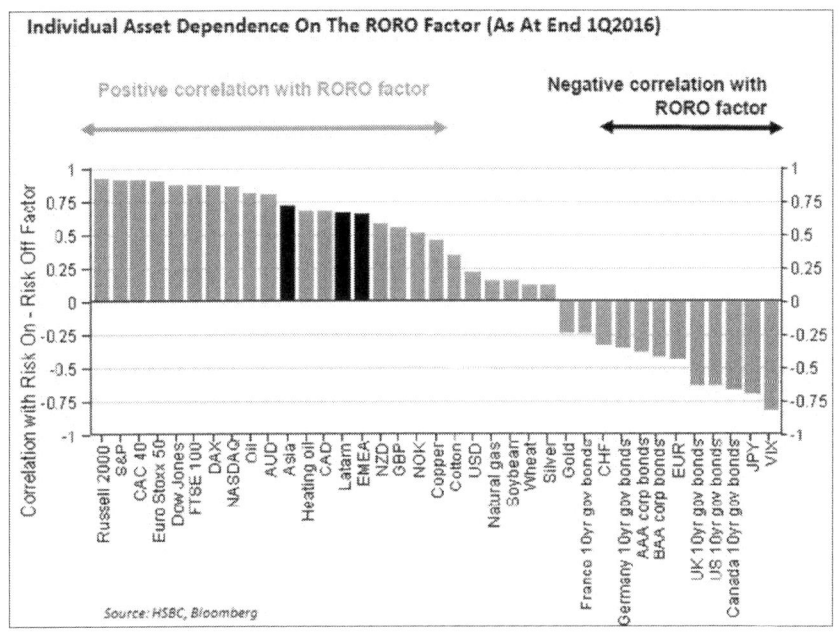

Long-Term Economic Patterns

There are broad-based long-term cycles that have important ramifications for overall portfolio structuring. They include the comparative weighting of different asset classes, the point of possible convergence of an economy from 'frontier' market status to 'emerging' and then to 'developed', and even for discerning very long-term patterns in technical analysis.

The Kondratieff Wave

In global terms (we will get to the specifics for regions and asset classes in a moment) to kick off with, the trader needs to be aware of the Kondratieff Wave ('K-Wave') – named after a Russian economist active in the 1920s named Nikolai Kondratieff – which seeks to show that **there are long-term cycles in the entire global capitalist economy of between 45 and 60 years – and even much longer –**

each that are self-correcting and evolving and are defined by the emergence of new industries in ongoing technological revolutions. As an adjunct of this, each major cycle involves the destruction of much of the past cycle and the concomitant evolution of new innovation.

Kondratieff's theory has been refined/distorted – however you want to look at it – by various people since, but the consensus of the major examples over the past few hundred years would be:

- 1770s – the Industrial Revolution
- 1820s – the Steam and Railways age beginning
- 1870s – the Steel and Heavy Engineering move
- 1900s – the era of Oil, Electricity, Automobiles and Mass Production
- 1970s – the shift to the age of Information and Telecommunications.

It is interesting to note at this point that – arguably, although not much – the world's most successful stock investor ever, Warren Buffett, bases his investment strategy on such fundamental paradigmatic shifts; seeking to identify the onset of a new cycle (or 'wave'), buying shares in as many solid new cycle-related businesses as he can and just sitting on them.

In any event, the correlations between the K-Waves and key asset markets are evident from the charts below.

US Government 10-Year Yields 1790 to 2015

Kondratieff Waves

1845 1896 1949

Source: Various market data inputs

US Stock Market In Gold Terms 1790-2015

Kondratieff Waves

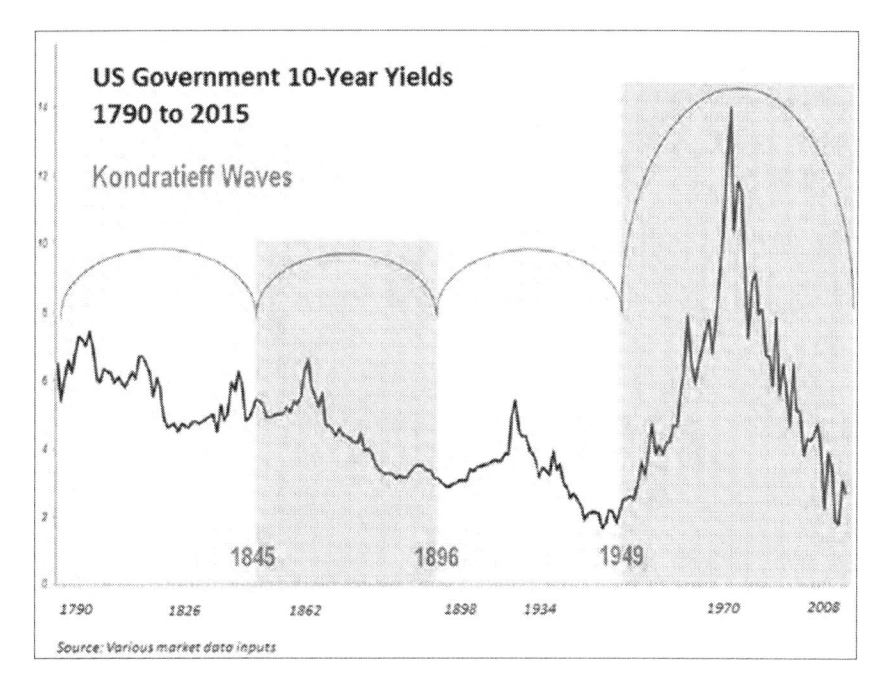

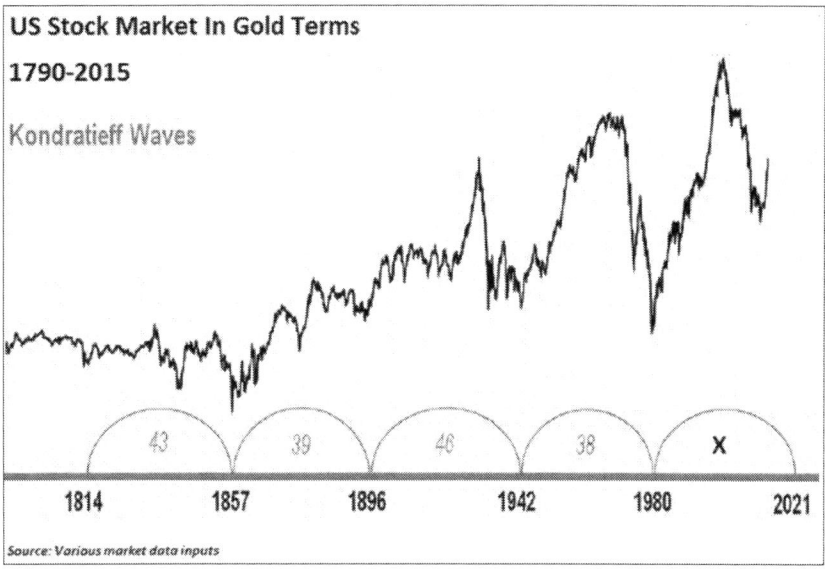

43 39 46 38 X

1814 1857 1896 1942 1980 2021

Source: Various market data inputs

In broad terms, there are four stages to the cycle described by the K-Wave:

1. At the onset of a long-term economic cycle there is likely to be a lack of confidence and a fear of falling back into slump or depression, before inflation, interest rates and credit slowly start to rise as confidence in the new age increases.
2. As the economy expands (indicated in this instance by inflation) and interest rates increase as an adjunct to this, then so business and consumer confidence grows further and credit is extended more.
3. As we enter into the final up-phase of the move, confidence levels morph into over-exuberance and extraordinary loose 'bubble-like' credit conditions, with interest rates also declining.
4. Finally, rising concerns over loose credit, inflationary upward spiral and bad debt causes business and consumer reticence to embark on new projects (in business terms, expansion, and in consumer terms, new purchases), default rates increase, credit is squeezed, the economic outlook turns negative, unemployment rises, disinflation turns into deflation and we have a negative world view.

The Business Cycle

Within these long cycles, though, there are other shorter-time patterns manifesting themselves in the classic business cycle, which is the recurrent level of business activity that changes in an economy over a period of time. Here again, there are four stages of a cycle (although some maintain that there are five): full scale recession, early recovery, late recovery and early recession.

Since the Second World War, most business cycles have lasted between three to five years from peak to peak, with the average duration of an expansion being nearly four years and the average length of a recession being just under a year, although as we have seen in the most recent recession (and in the Great Depression era) recessions can last a lot longer.

According to the USA's National Bureau of Economic Research (NBER), the US has experienced 12 recessions (including the most recent one) and 11 expansions since the end of the Second World War, as shown in the chart below.

US Business Cycles Since 1857 (NBER)

BUSINESS CYCLE REFERENCE DATES		DURATION IN MONTHS			
Peak	Trough	Contraction	Expansion	Cycle	
Quarterly dates are in parentheses		Peak to Trough	Previous trough to this peak	Trough from Previous Trough	Peak from Previous Peak
	December 1854 (IV)	--	--	--	--
June 1857(II)	December 1858 (IV)	18	30	48	--
October 1860(III)	June 1861 (III)	8	22	30	40
April 1865(I)	December 1867 (I)	32	46	78	54
June 1869(II)	December 1870 (IV)	18	18	36	50
October 1873(III)	March 1879 (I)	65	34	99	52
March 1882(I)	May 1885 (II)	38	36	74	101
March 1887(II)	April 1888 (I)	13	22	35	60
July 1890(III)	May 1891 (II)	10	27	37	40
January 1893(I)	June 1894 (II)	17	20	37	30
December 1895(IV)	June 1897 (II)	18	18	36	35
June 1899(III)	December 1900 (IV)	18	24	42	42
September 1902(IV)	August 1904 (III)	23	21	44	39
May 1907(II)	June 1908 (II)	13	33	46	56
January 1910(I)	January 1912 (IV)	24	19	43	32
January 1913(I)	December 1914 (IV)	23	12	35	36
August 1918(III)	March 1919 (I)	7	44	51	67
January 1920(I)	July 1921 (III)	18	10	28	17
May 1923(II)	July 1924 (III)	14	22	36	40
October 1926(III)	November 1927 (IV)	13	27	40	41
August 1929(III)	March 1933 (I)	43	21	64	34
May 1937(II)	June 1938 (II)	13	50	63	93
February 1945(I)	October 1945 (IV)	8	80	88	93
November 1948(IV)	October 1949 (IV)	11	37	48	45
July 1953(II)	May 1954 (II)	10	45	55	56
August 1957(III)	April 1958 (II)	8	39	47	49
April 1960(II)	February 1961 (I)	10	24	34	32
December 1969(IV)	November 1970 (IV)	11	106	117	116
November 1973(IV)	March 1975 (I)	16	36	52	47
January 1980(I)	July 1980 (III)	6	58	64	74
July 1981(III)	November 1982 (IV)	16	12	28	18
July 1990(III)	March 1991(I)	8	92	100	108
March 2001(I)	November 2001 (IV)	8	120	128	128
December 2007 (IV)	June 2009 (II)	18	73	91	81
Average, all cycles:					
1854-2009 (33 cycles)		17.5	38.7	56.2	56.4*
1854-1919 (16 cycles)		21.6	26.6	48.2	48.9**
1919-1945 (6 cycles)		18.2	35.0	53.2	53.0
1945-2009 (11 cycles)		11.1	58.4	69.5	68.5

* 32 cycles
** 15 cycles
Source: NBER

The Minsky Cycle

Within each of the two above cycles fits the 'Minsky Cycle' as another important element in the understanding of where one is in the overall global investment mix (which means, in practical terms, narrowing down the best trading options further).

The Minsky Cycle – coined around the time of the 1998 Russian financial crisis by a guy from PIMCO (Pacific Investment Management Company) – is a key part of the general psychology of trading (see later) and **seeks to chart the nature of the normal life cycle of an economy with particular reference to speculative investment bubbles.**

The idea here is that in times of prosperity, when the cashflow of banks and corporates moves to excess levels (over and above that which is needed simply to pay off debt), a 'speculative euphoria' develops, which soon exceeds that which borrowers can pay off, which, in turn leads to tighter credit conditions etc etc. It is the slow pace at which the financial system moves to at first realise this and then seek to accommodate it that produces a financial crisis; known as the 'Minsky Moment'.

It is interesting to note here that knowing where one is in the cycle is crucial to making long-term, informed and extremely profitable positions, as is illustrated below in the shift along the Minsky Curve of what is propitious and what is not.

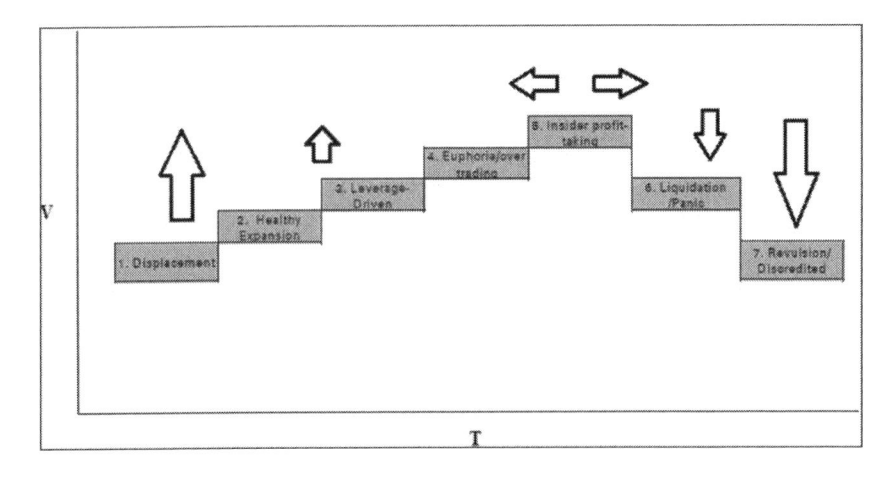

[Key:
V = Values, various assets
T = Time]

So, looking at the above chart, for example, **in the immediate 'displacement' aftermath of the Great Financial Crisis, in the middle or so of 2011, one might have identified nascent pockets of value in Asian FX as various of the countries continued to show exceptional performance**. As the cycle progressed, the major beneficiaries of leverage became certain high-yielding currencies (such as the AUD) and certain commodities (notably, gold).

As credit became easier, so investors became less discerning about the underlying fundamentals of the assets into which they invested, and in the 'euphoria/over-trading' phase, for example, money poured into various of the already over-performing equities markets (China springs to mind). As ever in the markets, key insiders began to twig that a new indiscriminate phase of investment had manifested itself (the "when my barber is talking to me about stocks then I know it's time to get out" concept), so liquidated out of things like Japanese government bonds and toppish currency positions. And, once this has occurred, of course, there is a much broader liquidation of assets (at this point it included things like selling USD and gold), which, given the need to make good on losses in margin calls, actually involves selling a much broader base of assets than would otherwise be merited.

Finally, the markets reach a point where investors are ultra-cautious in spending their money and regard any asset that is not seen as absolutely solid as being, in fact, abhorrent, with the main loser at the end of this particular cycle being the debt and other assets of Eurozone periphery countries (and there is an even larger corollary move into safe-haven assets at this point).

Looking at where we were in the middle of 2014, we can see that the displacement macro-shock had been negative rates announced by the ECB, the long and low easing policy of the US Fed appearing to be drawing to an end and a broad-based acceptance of an enduring economic slowdown in China gathering pace.

Within this, different asset classes are at different points along that cycle: for example, the USD may be entering a new long-term uptrend, as mentioned earlier; the JPY appears to be nearing the 'discredited' phase (as dealers cannot see what more can be done to weaken the currency, given what has already been implemented to do so); whilst there has been a generalised liquidation of being long volatility (volatility can be bought or sold, like any other aspect of the market, either directly – say through the VIX and similar indices – or indirectly through proxies).

Given such an identification of which part of the cycle forms the backdrop to your current investment environment, **there are some general inferences that you can take regarding which sectors within – specifically – stock markets may prove the most beneficial at a particular point in time,** as delineated below:

- *Full Scale Recession* (characterised by contracting GDP q-o-q, falling interest rates, increasing unemployment, declining consumer expectations, among others). Sectors that do well in this environment tend to be: **Cyclicals** (a company's revenues are generally higher in periods of economic prosperity and expansion and lower in periods of economic downturn and contraction, but they can cope easily by reducing wages and workforce during bad times and include companies that produce durable goods, such as raw materials and heavy equipment), **Transports, Technology and Industrials.**

- *Early Recovery* (consumer expectations are rising, unemployment is falling, industrial production is growing and interest rates have bottomed out): **Industrials, Basic materials industry and Energy firms.**
- *Late Recovery* (interest rates can be rising rapidly, consumer expectations are beginning to decline and industrial production is flat): **Energy, Staples and Services.**
- *Early Recession* (Consumer expectations are at their worst, industrial production is falling and interest rates are at their highest): **Services, Utilities, Cyclicals and Transports.**

Changing Bond And Equity Correlations

As mentioned earlier, there is a **general rule of thumb that early on in a market cycle when interest rates rise (or are expected to rise shortly) then bonds are bought and equities are sold. As the cycle progresses, then increased buying of bonds reduces the yield (the simple mathematical formula mentioned earlier) resulting in money then flowing back into equities.** Both of these phases have corollary effects on the FX and commodities asset classes (see later). Over the past few months in particular, though, there have been enormous swings in these movements, principally as a result of dramatically shifting market views on where interest rates will be in any of the major world economic groups (US, Eurozone and Japan), tempered by growth outlooks in these and in China, and by the relative position of each on the quantitative easing curve.

In broad terms, correlations heatmaps are a good starting point to see how the relationships between bonds and equities have changed over the relatively recent past, as shown in the following two charts.

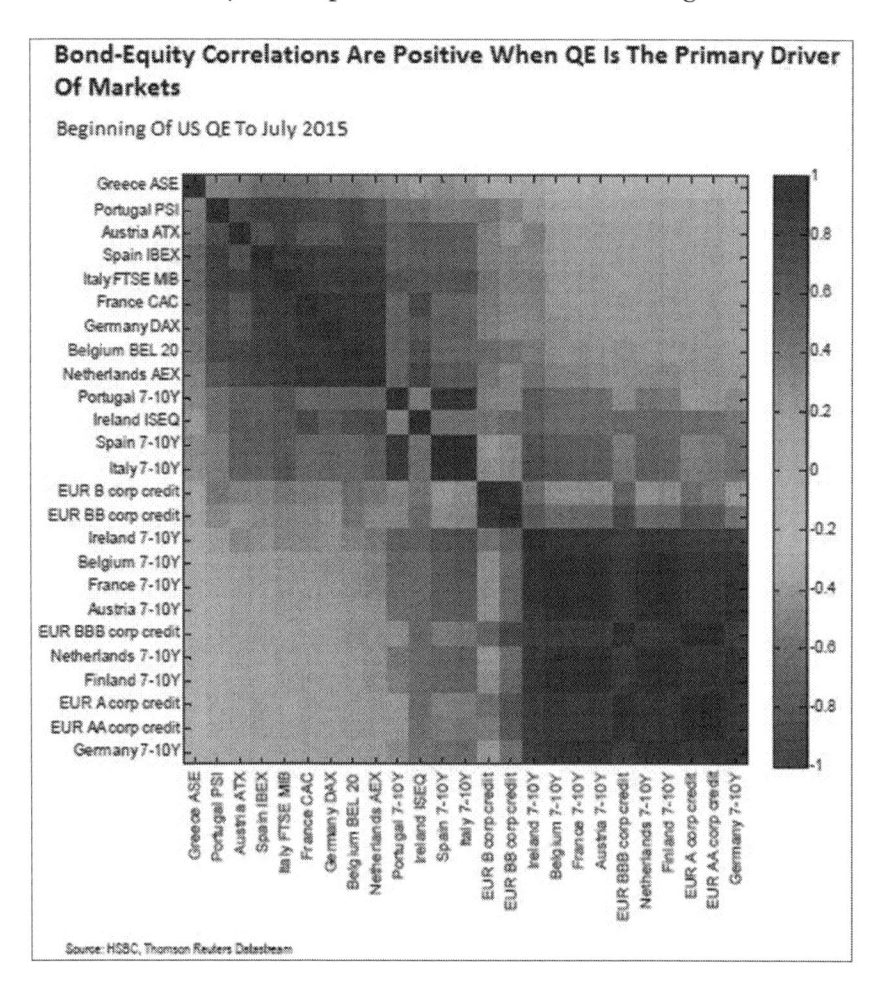

Bond-Equity Correlations Are Positive When QE Is The Primary Driver Of Markets

Beginning Of US QE To July 2015

[Heatmap showing correlations between European equity indices (Greece ASE, Portugal PSI, Austria ATX, Spain IBEX, Italy FTSE MIB, France CAC, Germany DAX, Belgium BEL 20, Netherlands AEX), sovereign bonds 7-10Y (Portugal, Ireland ISEQ, Spain, Italy), EUR B corp credit, EUR BB corp credit, Ireland 7-10Y, Belgium 7-10Y, France 7-10Y, Austria 7-10Y, EUR BBB corp credit, Netherlands 7-10Y, Finland 7-10Y, EUR A corp credit, EUR AA corp credit, Germany 7-10Y. Scale from -1 to 1.]

Source: HSBC, Thomson Reuters Datastream

Bond-Equity Correlations Are Negative When 'Risk-On Risk-Off' Is The Primary Driver Of The Markets

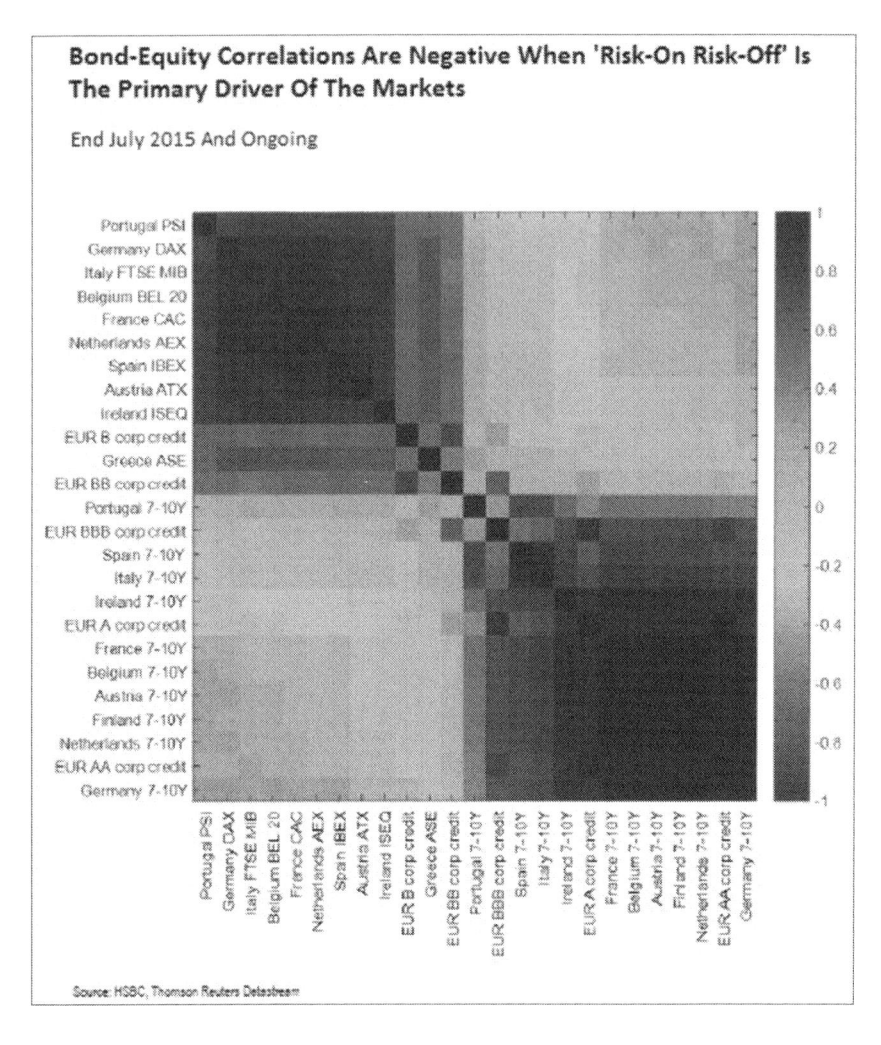

End July 2015 And Ongoing

Source: HSBC, Thomson Reuters Datastream

Risk-on risk-off is arguably easier to deal with in the overall bond-equity context because generally in this environment they do what they 'should' do, which is move in opposite directions. **When QE dominates, though, a wider range of assets rise and fall together.** In practice, both environments are difficult in this particular market paradigm because it can be difficult to discern at any given time which of the two trading key trading factors – QE or RORO – is prevalent and which will be prevalent within the next few hours even, depending on upcoming data releases or statements from central bankers or politicians.

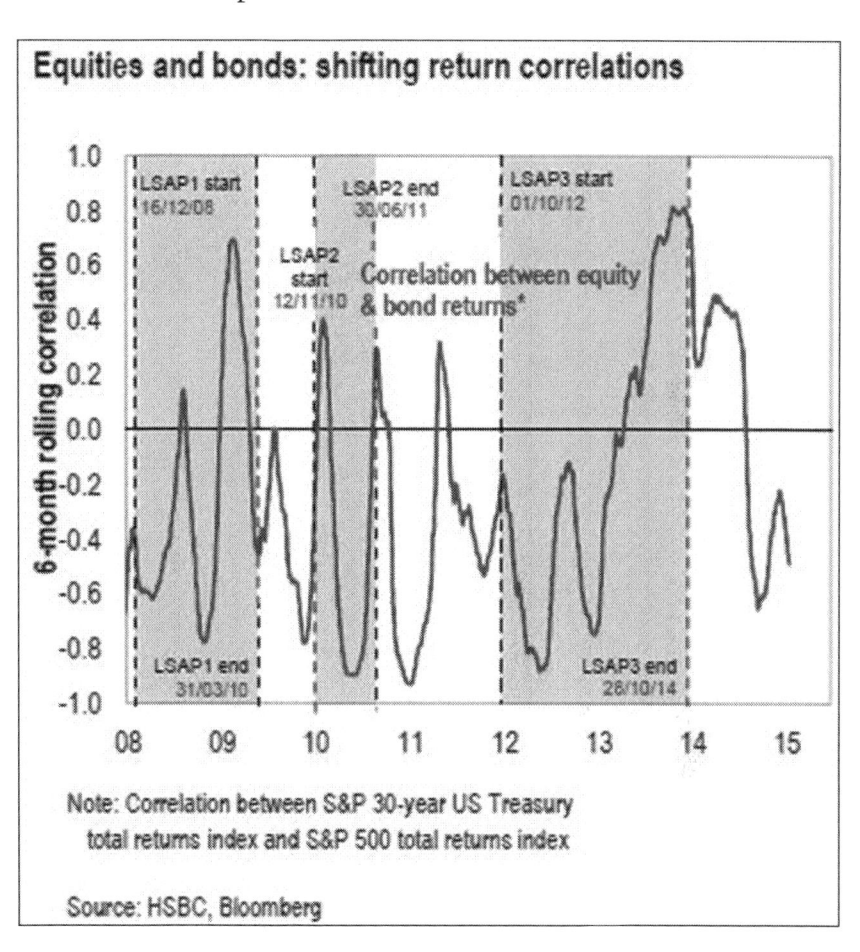

Equities and bonds: shifting return correlations

[Chart showing 6-month rolling correlation between S&P 30-year US Treasury total returns index and S&P 500 total returns index from 2008 to 2015, with markers for LSAP1 start (16/12/08), LSAP1 end (31/03/10), LSAP2 start (12/11/10), LSAP2 end (30/06/11), LSAP3 start (01/10/12), and LSAP3 end (28/10/14).]

Note: Correlation between S&P 30-year US Treasury total returns index and S&P 500 total returns index

Source: HSBC, Bloomberg

These changing relationships within financial markets are suggestive not only of recent regime shifts but of future ones that are imminent as well. In the early days of QE, benchmark bond curves (like US Treasuries and German bunds) would steepen and there was no discernible trend in inflation expectations. Now we have seen both a flatter curve and lower expectations, and this is essentially the market telling the central banks that recession risk has increased and the inflation target is less likely to be hit. Indeed, the past few months have already seen numerous radical policy shifts from central banks (from negative rates employed by the Swiss National Bank to changes in the renminbi currency regime by the People's Bank of China), and it is very likely that equally dramatic moves are on the cards for reasons outlined later.

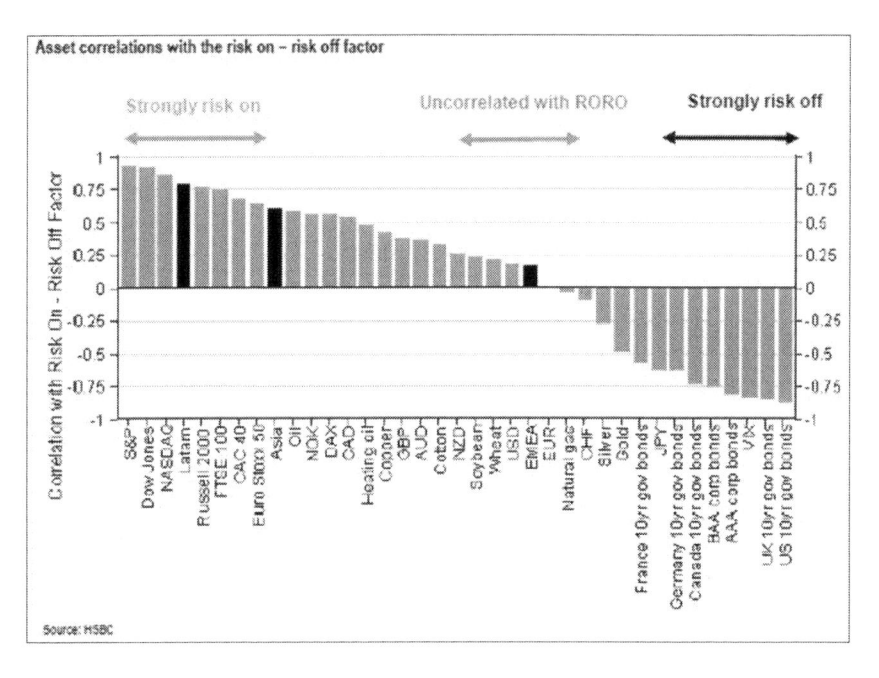

Looking only at what the recent shifting regimes has meant for the US markets, with knock-on effects elsewhere, of course, the reduction in USD holdings and Treasury sales, which could be regarded as a recycling operation between public and private sectors, has seen at least a USD2 trillion swing in foreign exchange flows. Whatever the state of play of QE now is – whether it is close to peak or not – a return to a more 'usual' market will not occur any time soon. It has taken the world's central banks around eight years to inflate and distort the globe's liquidity to where it is now and there is no reason to expect that it will not take another eight years for it to be unwound and normalised.

Having said all of this, it is possible to establish some key trading points dependent on which trading factor – QE or RORO – is dominant at any point (and working out which is dominant is discussed throughout this book). **Looking at shorter-term (15-day) correlations over the past two years, it is clear that bond yields (as opposed to prices) have been positively correlated with equities for most of the time.** This implies that it is primarily growth expectations as opposed to liquidity ones that has been driving the relationship, although there was a notable exception during 2013 with the 'Taper Tantrum' that was focussed on how much and when the US Fed would begin to wind down its QE. Aside from this period, generally inversions of this relationship tend to be brief, as equities initially pull back on the pure uncertainty fuelled by momentary bond market disorder but then (when dealers revert back to basics and are struck by the reality that strengthening reflationary demand remains intact) the correlation tends to revert to its normal negative value and equities are able to re-rate via a discounting of future growth expectations.

US short-term equity/bond price correlations

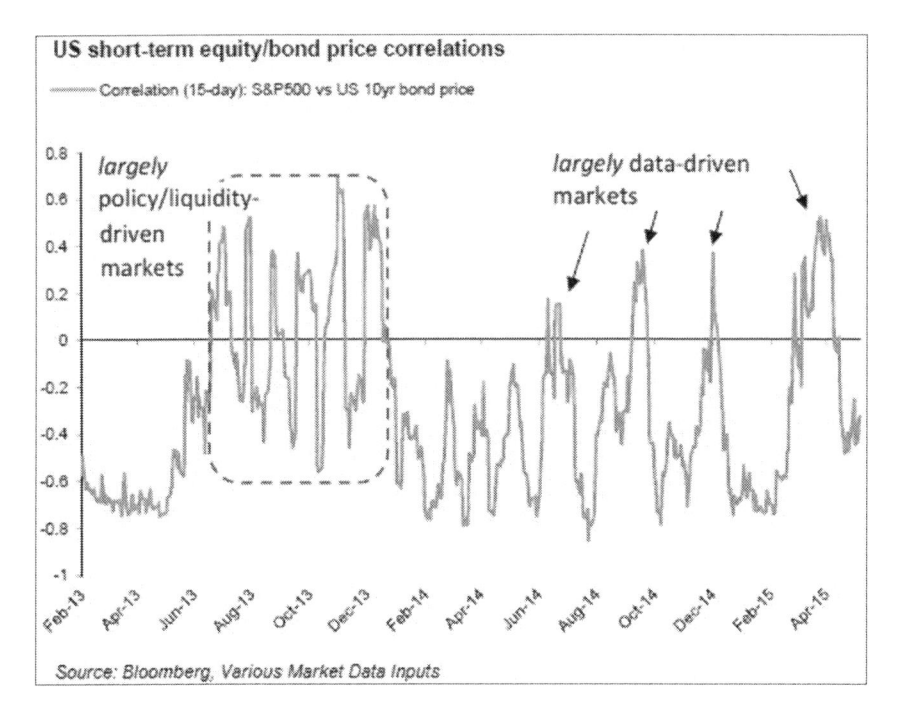

Correlation (15-day): S&P500 vs US 10yr bond price

largely policy/liquidity-driven markets

largely data-driven markets

Source: Bloomberg, Various Market Data Inputs

The equities pullbacks the equities markets have seen aside from those based on pure uncertainty fuelled by momentary bond market disorder, occurred primarily as a function both of the Greece problem (examined in depth below) and on the likelihood at any given point in time of the onset of a US interest rate tightening cycle (usually spurred by some statement either from Chair of the Federal Reserve, Janet Yellen, or by another high-level member of the monetary policy structure).

A notable example of this – that was not also subject to the influence of other major market factors, so it can be regarded as a 'clean' example – was when the Fed initially prompted market speculation that a rate tightening cycle was going to begin imminently in June 2004. This was preceded by two MSCI World pullbacks (and then similarly-sized rebounds) of 5-6% in the few months before the first hike and another -7% pullback shortly after. In the following three years through to October 2007, however, the MSCI World went on to rally some 65% from those troughs, even as the Fed progressively raised interest rates by 425 basis points through to the middle of 2006.

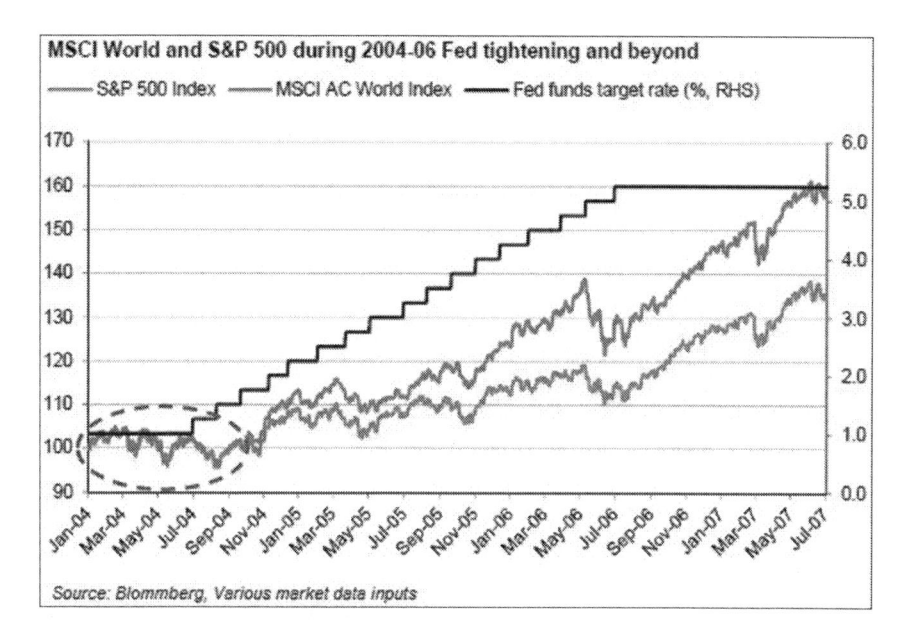

MSCI World and S&P 500 during 2004-06 Fed tightening and beyond
— S&P 500 Index — MSCI AC World Index — Fed funds target rate (%, RHS)

Source: Blommberg, Various market data inputs

Interestingly, though, the absolute level of bond yields also matters for the equity-bond relationship, and certain yield levels are the tipping points at which bond yield rises negatively impact equities prices or bond yield falls positively impact them. As shown below, with US Treasuries it has historically only been when yields exceed roughly 5.0-5.5% that higher yields (i.e. lower bond prices) seem to have a negative impact on equities.

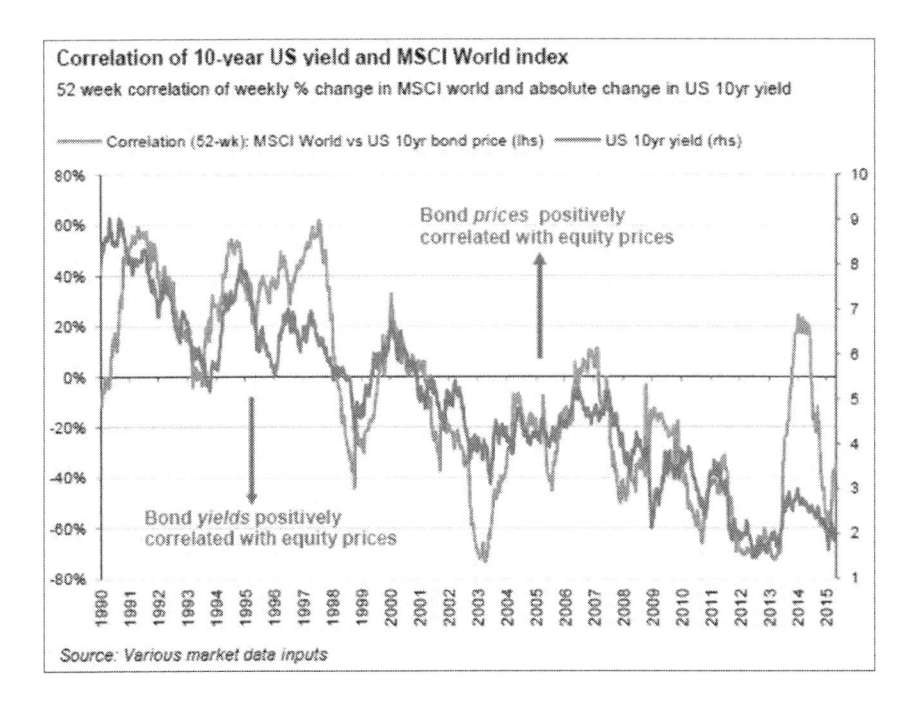

Correlation of 10-year US yield and MSCI World index
52 week correlation of weekly % change in MSCI world and absolute change in US 10yr yield

Source: Various market data inputs

Below that yield range bond prices (rather than yields) have historically been negatively correlated with equity markets, and these reflect strengthening growth prospects and/or reduced deflation risks that should be consistent with equity upside.

Looking at the current position on the US rates tightening expectations curve, then, two scenarios may manifest themselves in trading terms, but each will accord with one or other of the key patterns already described. First, US interest rates continue to rise and trigger an increase in risk premiums across bonds and rates markets globally, which, in turn, pushes up yield curves and forces a de-rating of equities. Second, in the absence of continued higher interest rates, or perhaps because further US rate tightening is once again delayed (as a result of slower growth, a stronger dollar and low inflation), the outcome would be for investors to be pushed further up the risk curve into equities, and valuations could rise further. This second pattern would continue until such point as equity markets eventually became severely overvalued, thereby offering a very poor prospective return.

Equities Trading In A Rising US Interest Rates Scenario

Historically, periods marked by rising US interest rates have generally supported Growth stocks more than Value stocks, not just in the US but globally, and particularly relative to Income-delineated value styles (i.e., Dividend Yield). Indeed, since mid-2014, Growth has been consistently the top-performing equity style, while Value and its subset Dividend Yield have been the weakest, as shown in the chart below.

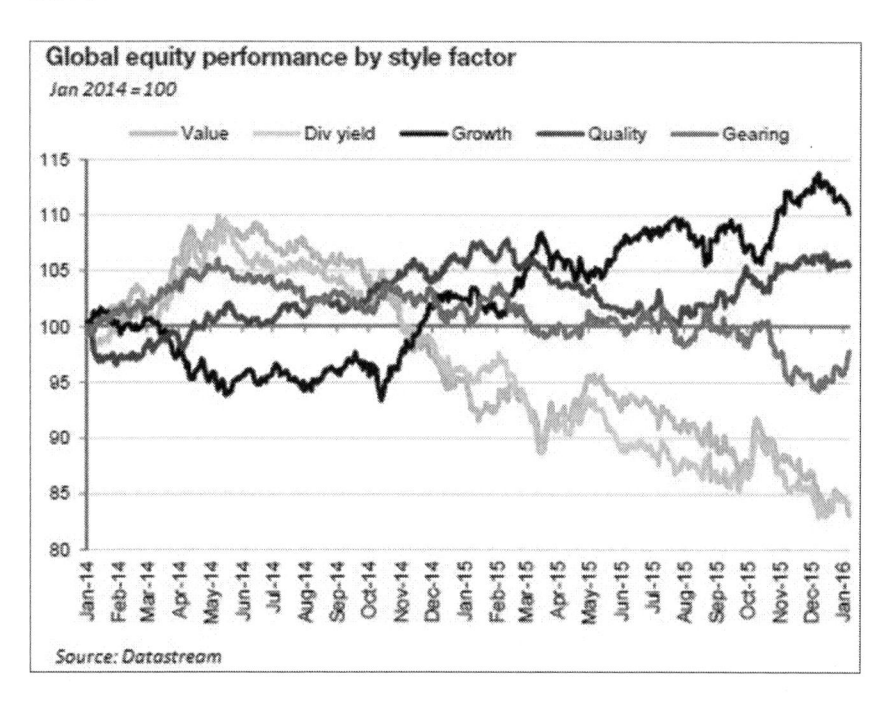

Global equity performance by style factor
Jan 2014 = 100

Source: Datastream

Factoring in the broader economic patterns discussed above (K-Wave, Minsky, Business Cycle), there is reason to believe that the

2016 US interest rate outlook should continue to support a portfolio bias for Growth (i.e., cyclical sectors) over Dividend Yield. Moreover, looking at previous data patterns, it appears that **Yield stocks actually do best when investors are moving into bonds (seeking incremental safety rather than incremental risk) rather than the common view that they do best when investors are initially moving out of bonds and into equities.**

MSCI World High-Yield stock total return and US 10-yr yield

Source: Bloomberg

Moreover, the fact that Growth as a style currently offers a 10% or so valuation discount versus long-term averages suggests that the style remains under-owned by portfolio managers and, given the aforementioned factors, is likely to benefit from rotational buying in the quarters ahead, as rates rise, whereas the highly crowded nature of Dividend Yield plays is highlighted by this type of stocks' elevated valuation premium of more than 25%.

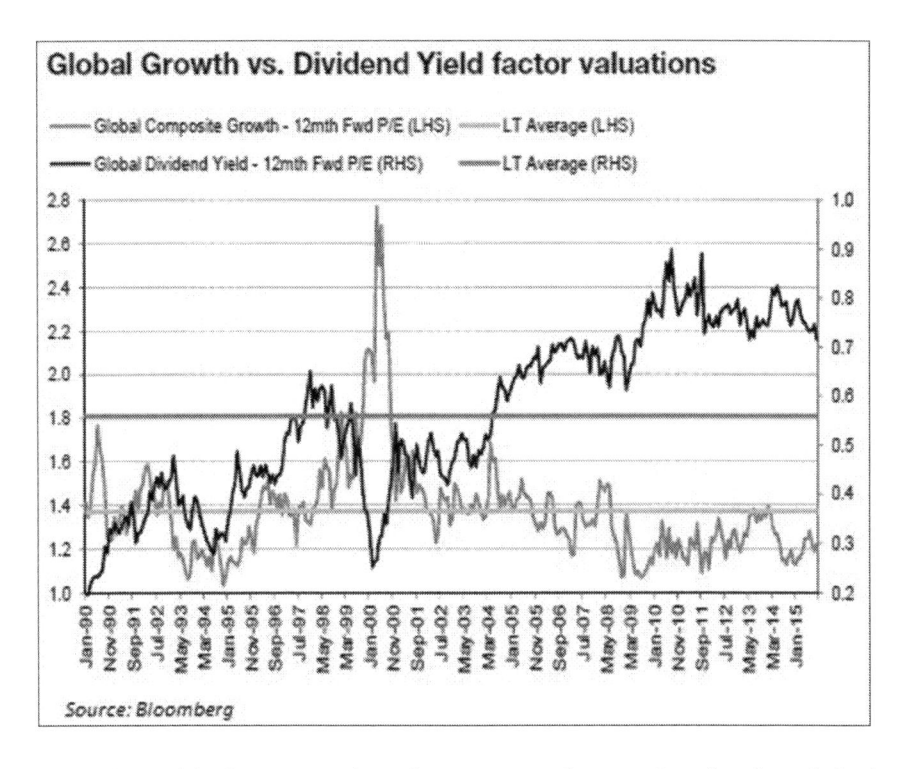

Global Growth vs. Dividend Yield factor valuations

Source: Bloomberg

It is also critical to note that **the current depression in the global hydrocarbons pricing complex (this will be discussed in much greater detail later) is not beneficial to Dividend Yield stocks but is benefitting Growth stocks.** In this context, inflation expectations have historically also usually displayed a strong directional correlation with the relative performance of Growth vs. Income (i.e., Dividend Yield) in the global equities arena. This is a product mainly of the positive relationship between inflation expectations and demand strength (which benefits cyclical stocks) and between inflation expectations and interest rate expectations (which, when rising, undercut the relative performance 'bond proxy' Yield stocks).

However, **despite lower break-even inflation expectations together with declining oil prices since mid-2014, Growth stocks have continued outperforming Income ones (i.e., Dividend Yield), which appears to underline that the market is**

looking more at the demand-positive element in the oil price decline rather than its deflationary element. In this respect, on the one hand, it is true that the oil price decline means that for oil exporters there is a crunch on revenues (which has ramifications discussed later) but, on the other hand, for oil importing nations the reduction in the oil price means first that its costs are reduced (in transport costs and/or manufacturing costs) and that the domestic population has more money in their pockets to spend on products and services. In this latter regard, for example, it is estimated that every USD10 per barrel change in the price of crude oil results in a 25-cent change in the price of a gallon of gasoline and, according to the American Automobile Association in Washington, every cent that the national average price of gasoline falls, more than one billion dollars per year in additional consumer spending is estimated to be freed up.

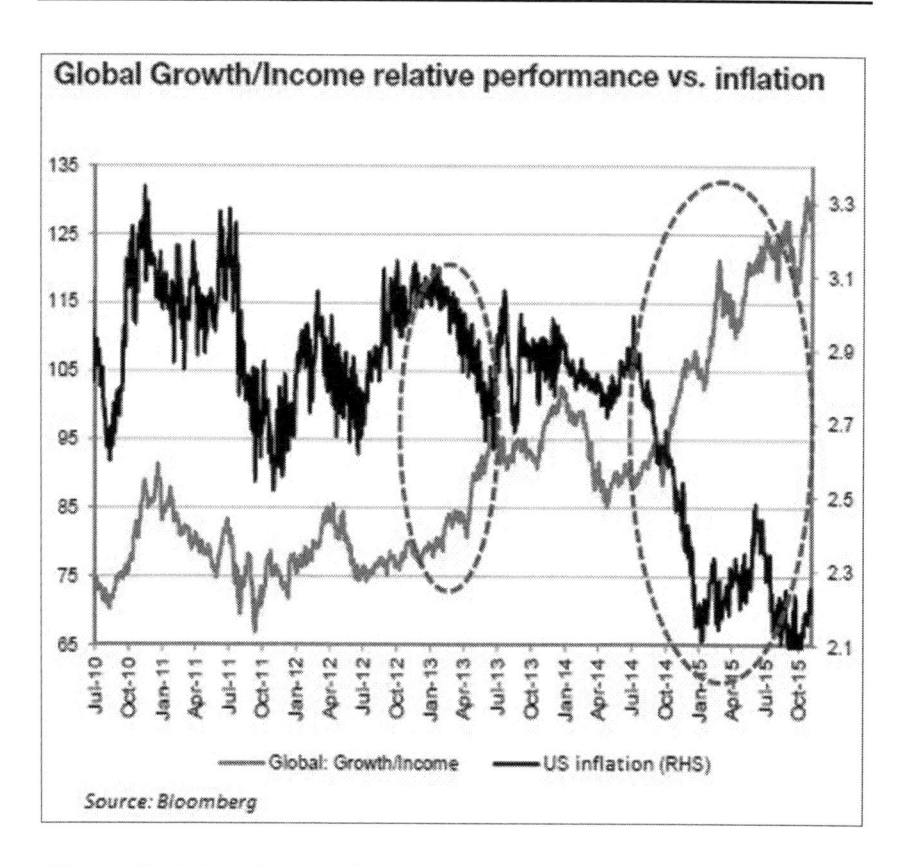

Global Growth/Income relative performance vs. inflation

Source: Bloomberg

Given all of this, for equities, the greatest beneficiaries of such a style bias for Growth over
Yield in the current rising US rates environment would historically appear to be Technology and Industrials, whilst Energy and Utilities are likely to fare particularly poorly. Additionally, whilst it is obvious that many financial stocks will do badly (especially those with connections to high-risk areas, such as the Eurozone and China), property stocks in general virtually always underperform when the US Treasury curve steepens.

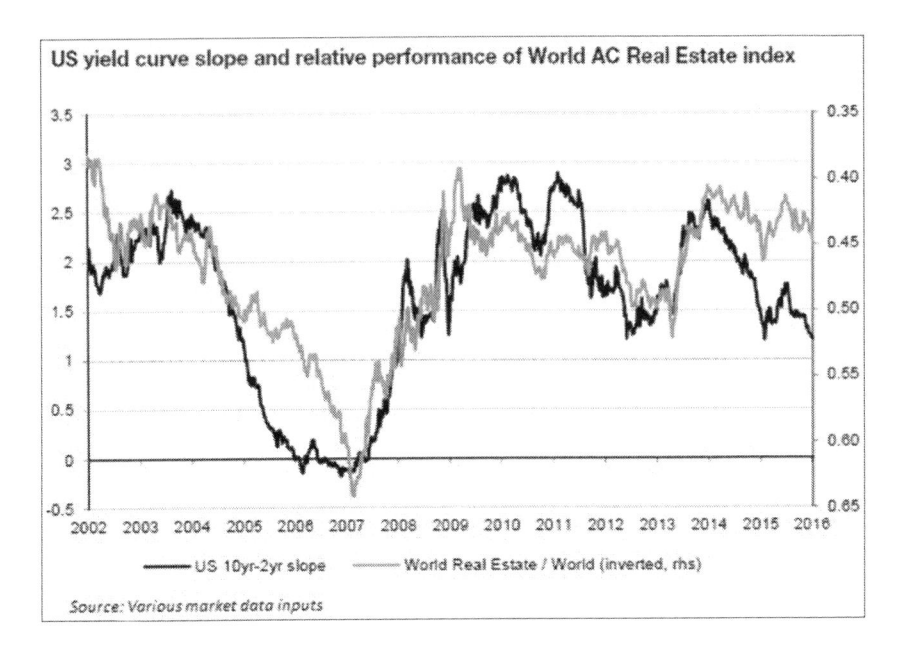

US yield curve slope and relative performance of World AC Real Estate index

US 10yr-2yr slope — World Real Estate / World (inverted, rhs)

Source: Various market data inputs

On a more general front, as highlighted recently by major global ratings agency Moody's, it is apposite to note that December 2015 and January 2016 were the only two months since at least 1982 where the 10-year Treasury yield was up from the same month a year earlier. This was despite a deeper than -15% year-over-year plunge by the base metals price index's moving three-month average (usually, such pronounced decelerations trigger remedial declines by benchmark Treasury yields).

Also, prior to December's Fed rate hike, fed funds had never been raised in the context of both: (i) a deeper than -15% annual plunge by the base metals price index's three-month average; and, (ii) a wider than 650 bp spread for high-yield bonds (recently, the high-yield bond spread was an exceptionally wide 873 bp).

Historical records show that the high-yield bond spread's month-long average has climbed above 800 bp on only four previous occasions: August 2008, July 2002, November 2000 and October 1990. In three of those four incidents, the US was about to enter or already in a recession, with the only exception being

July 2002 (which was the beginning of an economic recovery that only survived for five years).

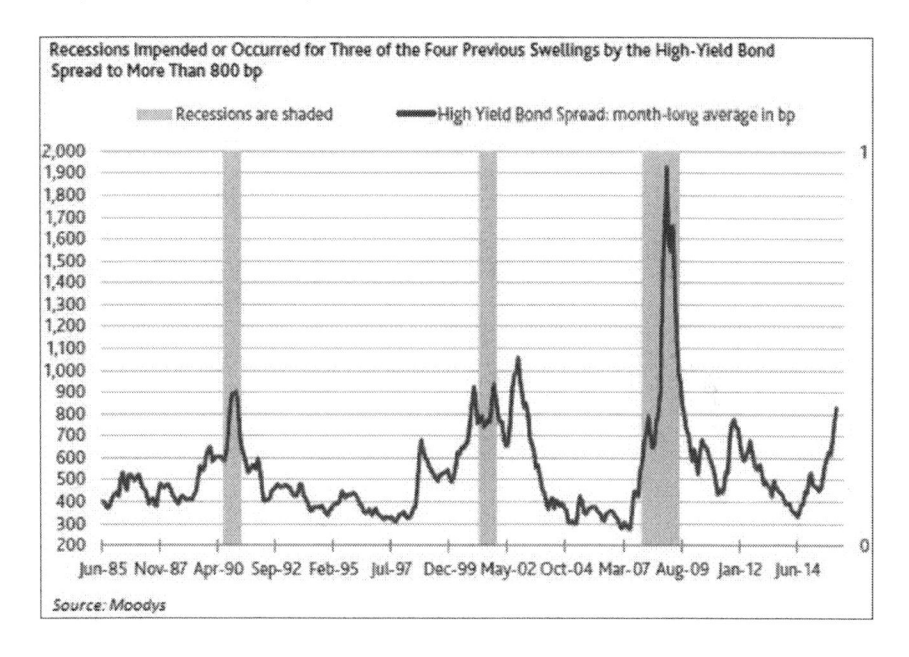

Recessions Impended or Occurred for Three of the Four Previous Swellings by the High-Yield Bond Spread to More Than 800 bp

Recessions are shaded — High Yield Bond Spread: month-long average in bp

Source: Moodys

Oil And Metals In The Correlations Mix

The Current Saudi Oil Price Fix

In October 2014 during private meetings in New York between high-level officials from Saudi Arabia and other senior figures in the global oil industry, the Saudis appeared to reveal that the Kingdom – far from looking to keep prices high (as had been the normal inclination of OPEC for many years, in order to boost the prosperity of OPEC member states) – was willing to tolerate Brent prices between USD80-USD90 per barrel (pb) for a period of 1-2 years. This was to be done through increasing its production from around the 9.5 million barrels per day (mbpd) average of recent years in order to achieve two aims:

1. To destroy, or at least markedly slow progress, in the developing shale energy industry (especially that of the fast-moving US); and,
2. To pressure other OPEC members to contribute to supply discipline in the future as and when it was called for.

This stated price band marked a significant divergence from the acceptable range of prices previously stated by Saudi Oil Minister Ali al-Naimi as being 'USD100, USD110, USD95' and comments later that year that Saudi was not at all concerned even if oil prices fell to USD20pb led to the sustained collapse in world oil prices that we have seen and which is still ongoing.

In the beginning, **there were signs that the strategy was yielding results. By February 2015, for example, the US oil rig count had seen its biggest period-on-period fall since 1991, and** it was estimated that the one third of the 800 oil and gas projects (worth USD500 billion and totalling nearly 60 billion barrels of oil equivalent) scheduled for final investment decisions (FID) regarded as shale-related might not go ahead.

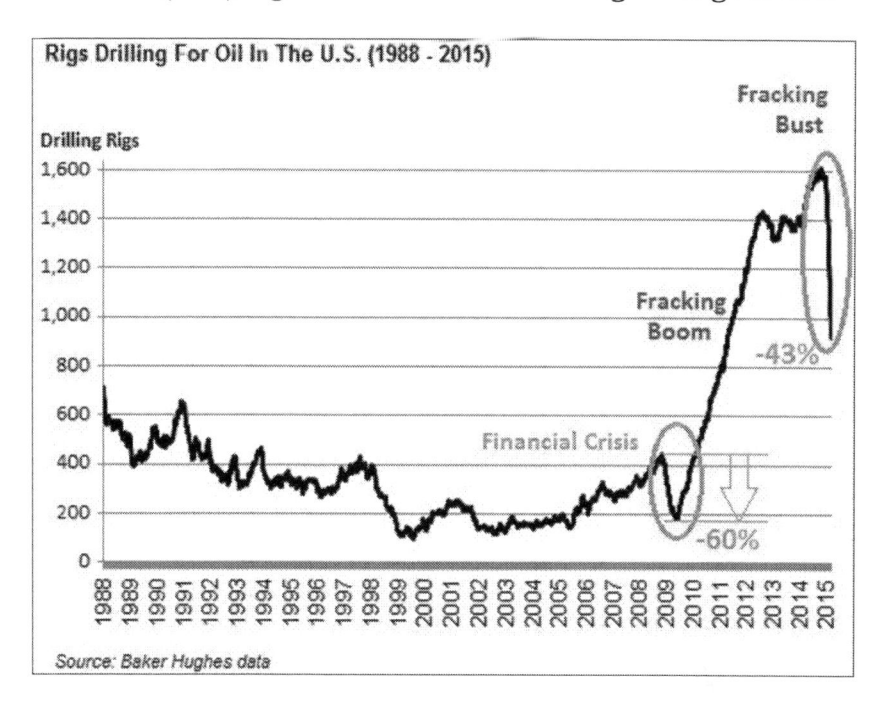

Rigs Drilling For Oil In The U.S. (1988 - 2015)

Source: Baker Hughes data

Among the major shocks were the decision by French energy giant, Total, to postpone the FID on the Joslyn project in Alberta (estimated cost USD11 billion) and BP's putting on hold a decision on its 'Mad Dog Phase 2' deep water project in the Gulf of Mexico after its development costs ballooned to USD20 billion.

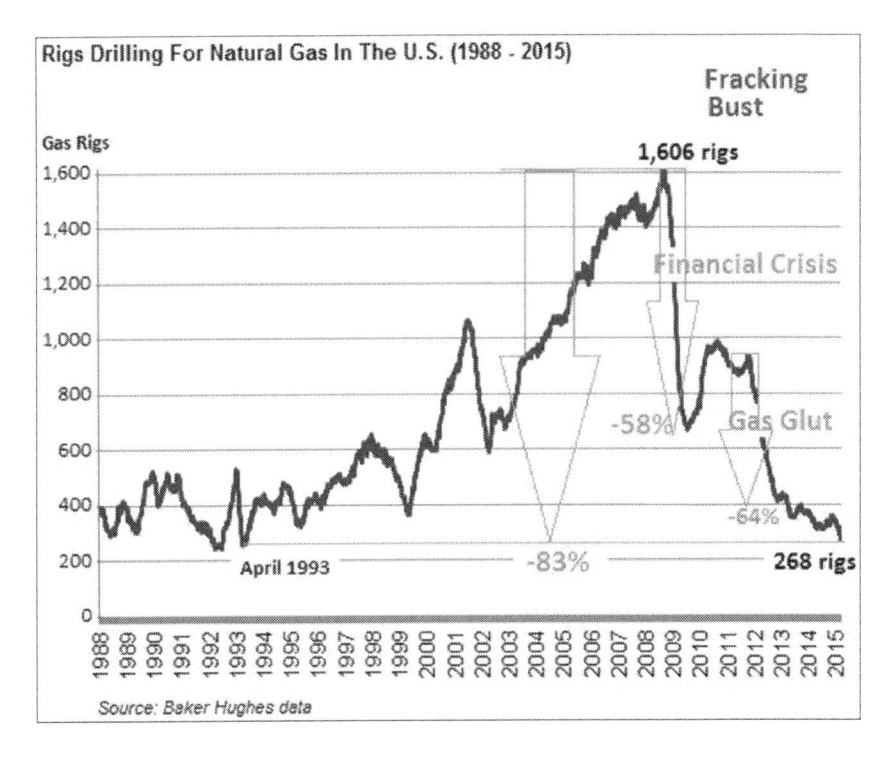

Rigs Drilling For Natural Gas In The U.S. (1988 - 2015)

Fracking Bust
1,606 rigs
Financial Crisis
-58%
Gas Glut
-64%
April 1993
-83%
268 rigs

Source: Baker Hughes data

Over time, although many of the larger, traditional oil companies in the US and elsewhere shelved big investment projects – which take years to realise and equally as long for lower investment to result in the lower supply required for the Saudi strategy to work – the shale industry showed a remarkable, and completely unexpected, resilience in their operations. Although over the course of 2015 production at these typically declined by around 50%, forcing them to cut investment to approximately USD60 billion over the year (compared to the USD100 billion or so spent in 2014), this adjustment was sufficient to keep shale production close to steady for the year after peaking in early 2015.

Allied to this were **remarkable productivity gains, with each rig in the Permian basin, for example – spanning western Texas and south-eastern New Mexico and currently the only major US region with growing production – now producing more than 400 bpd, compared to only 100 bpd in 2012.** Moreover, compared to the steep fall in horizontal rigs (two thirds have been discontinued since November 2014) US shale-oil production only fell modestly, from a peak 5.1 mbpd to around 4.8 mbpd by the end of the first quarter of 2016.

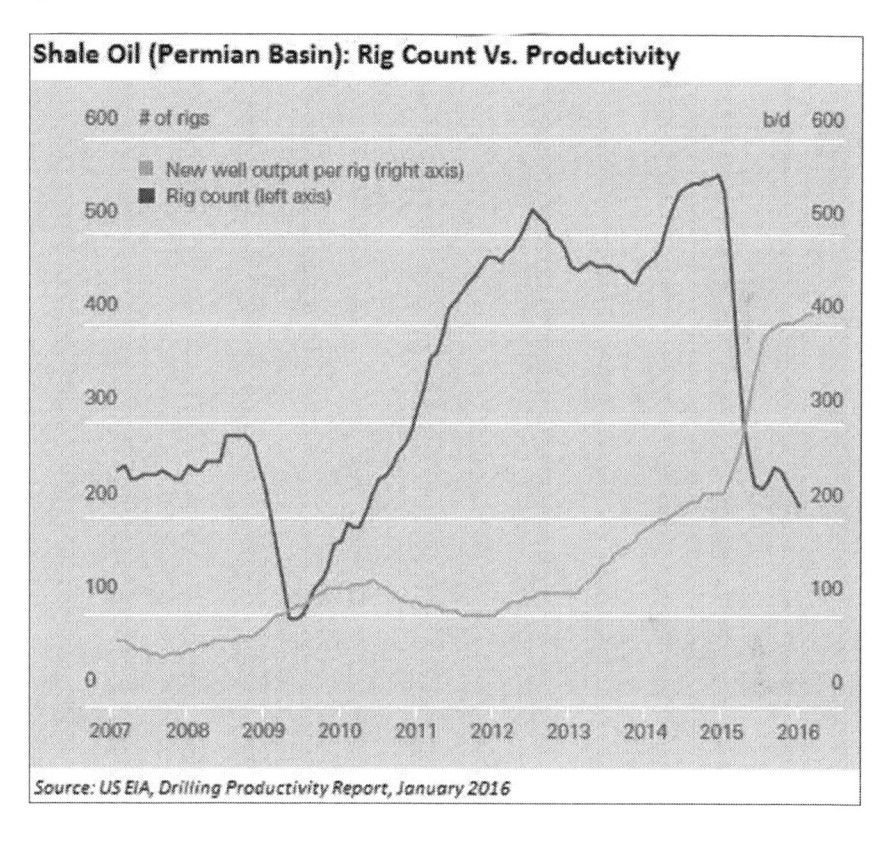

Shale Oil (Permian Basin): Rig Count Vs. Productivity

- New well output per rig (right axis)
- Rig count (left axis)

Source: US EIA, Drilling Productivity Report, January 2016

Prior to the full extent of the gains through cost discipline, improved technology and efficiency by shale producers had begun to come to light, it had been broadly assumed that US shale producers needed an oil price between USD60-90pb to invest in new projects. Now, though, in the core areas of Bakken (in North Dakota), for example, increasing drilling even makes sense at USD50pb, whilst in the best fields of the Permian area break-even costs are now around the USD36pb level, according to industry estimates.

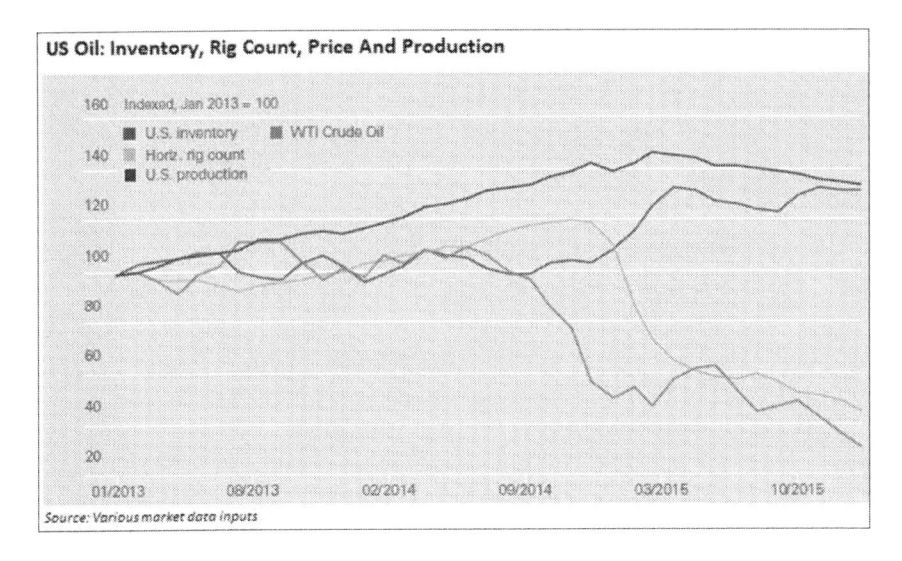

US Oil: Inventory, Rig Count, Price And Production

Indexed, Jan 2013 = 100
- U.S. inventory
- WTI Crude Oil
- Horiz. rig count
- U.S. production

Source: Various market data inputs

Ultimately, as at the end of 2015, total US production of 9.1 mbpd was roughly where it was a year ago when the price war began. In the meantime, according to the International Energy Agency, OPEC member states had collectively lost at least USD450 billion in revenues since Saudi embarked on its shale-stymieing strategy.

The fact that the Saudis then panicked and announced a freeze on production as the price actually started to plummet towards USD20pb has made the situation worse, for four reasons. First, it showed weakness to the financial markets, which always seek to ruthlessly exploit such a trait; second, the 'freeze' was at January 2016 production levels, which were, in fact, still around the highest levels ever and thus was meaningless in absolute terms; third, it was not supported by the newly sanctions-free Iran nor Iraq, two of the world's biggest oil producers; and fourth, the shale producers continued to demonstrate a much greater flexibility in dealing with the lower oil pricing complex than had previously been imagined possible.

Trading Strategies Off
The Current Saudi Fix

Short Oil

Even if the **slew of announcements from the middle of 2013/beginning of 2014 about the much greater scalability of shale resources than had been imagined before had been missed** (in mid-2013, exploration at the edges of the Permian shale and experimentation with new technologies revealed that the aerial acreage of shale was likely double what was initially thought and that much more oil could be squeezed from the shale formations) – shown as Point A and B in the chart below – and the subsequent announcement by Prince Turki Al Faisal, an influential Saudi Arabian royal and businessman, that the Gulf Kingdom planned to dramatically increase its oil production capacity – shown as Point C in the chart below – had also been overlooked, there were plenty of other macro-facts that would have provided good entry points for a short oil position to begin with:

1. As mentioned earlier, there were **private meetings between Saudi officials and other senior figures in the global oil industry in New York in October 2014** (which were publically reported shortly after) in which the Saudis appeared to reveal that the Kingdom – far from looking to keep prices high (as had been the normal inclination of OPEC for many years, as mentioned above, in order to boost the prosperity of OPEC member states) – was willing to **tolerate oil prices as low as USD80-USD90pb for a period of 1-2 years** (through increasing production), shown as Point D in the chart below.
2. Then, in December 2014, Saudi Oil Minister, Ali Al Naimi, openly stated in an interview on CNN that far from contemplating any cuts in production to support the oil price: **"We are going to**

continue to produce what we are producing, we are going to continue to welcome additional production if customers come and ask for it." This is shown as Point E in the chart below.

3. Finally, in the same month **Al Naimi added that Saudi Arabia did not care whether the oil price fell to even as low as USD20pb** (shown as Point F in the chart below). His exact words were: "Whether it [oil] goes down to USD20, USD40, USD50, USD60, it is irrelevant." This was unusually straightforward for a Middle Eastern oil minister and as such should have been acted on immediately.

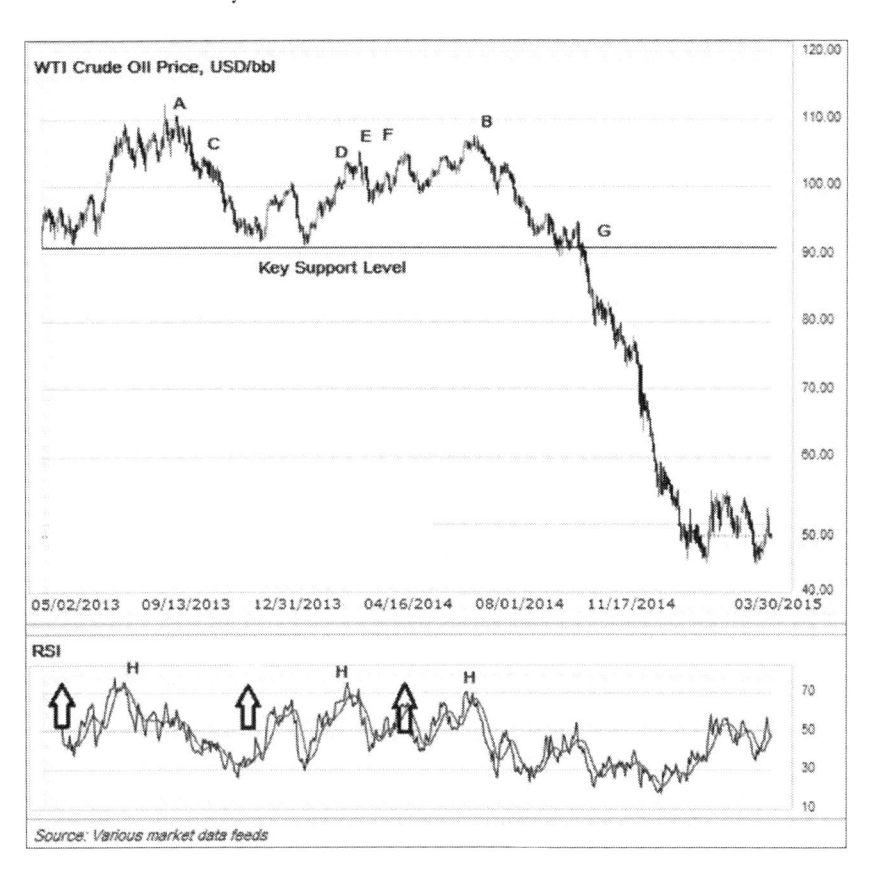

Aside from these huge pointers to going short oil, **technical analysis was also confirming the same position,** breaking through a long-established support level at USD91.50 (shown as Point G in the chart above), and the RSI levels were consistently near overbought levels (marked as Point H in the above chart). For a detailed look at Technical Analysis, please see the dedicated section on the subject later in the book.

As mentioned above, there is no fundamental reason to believe that the oil price is going to turn positive any time soon. Not only was the Saudi-led 'oil output freeze' established at production levels that meant an ongoing global surplus of at least 1.5 mbpd, but it also failed to attract the support of a number of key oil producing countries and – even worse – took no account whatsoever of the effect that the removal of sanctions on Iran implemented around the world on 16 January would have on the global hydrocarbons markets, given its massive oil and gas reserves. Having spent so long under international sanctions, there was absolutely no way that Iran was ever going to agree to be a part of the 'output freeze', particularly as the move was being orchestrated by its historical arch regional enemy, Saudi Arabia, and so it has proven. Even more deleterious for the Saudis, Iran has increasingly come to exercise power over its neighbour, Iraq, which also refuses to toe the line with the Saudis.

Global oil supply, demand and balance

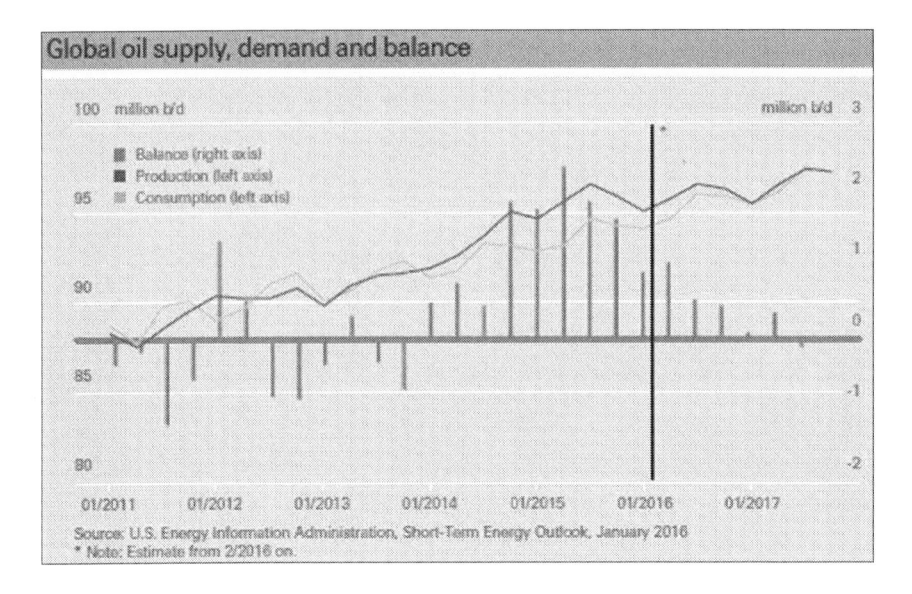

Source: U.S. Energy Information Administration, Short-Term Energy Outlook, January 2016
* Note: Estimate from 2/2016 on.

For its part, **Iran has an estimated 157 billion barrels of proven crude oil reserves, representing nearly 10% of the world's crude oil reserves, and 13% of reserves held by OPEC, making it the world's fourth-largest reserve holder of oil and one of its top 10 oil producers**. The Islamic Republic pledged that almost immediately after sanctions were removed it would increase its output by 0.5 mbpd (from the 2.8 mbpd at that point) and within six months from that point by 1 mbpd, and it is in the process of doing precisely that. It further intends to increase its total crude oil and condensate production to at least 5.7 mbpd by 2020, and there is every reason to believe that it will achieve this as well.

Meanwhile, **Iraq, which is part of a newly forming Shia belt across the central Middle East together with Iran, is home to a very conservatively-estimated 143 billion barrels of proven crude oil reserves – the world's fifth largest** – and, having seen crude oil production grow by 950,000 bpd since 2010, increasing from almost 2.4 million bpd to nearly 3.4 million bpd on average in 2014 and, at points in 2015 over 4 mbpd, is now the second largest crude oil producer in OPEC. It too has **plans for increasing output further: up to 8.4-9 mbpd by the end of 2020** (although the figure was revised down for a while, due to spiking security concerns, to 5.4-6 mbpd).

Short Middle East Hydrocarbons Producers' Stock Markets

Clearly, given the aforementioned catastrophic effect of the Saudi's shale-stymieing strategy on the economies of countries dependent on oil (and/or gas) for a significant proportion of their revenues, **shorting these countries' stock markets – either directly or through an exchange traded fund (ETF) – has been a winning trade through the ongoing oil price downturn.** When thinking about the potential scope for oil-driven local economic damage, the size of the local energy sector – without regard for the destination of that production – is an important metric, and oil accounts for around 50% for some of the Gulf States: **Kuwait, Saudi Arabia and Iraq** (see chart below).

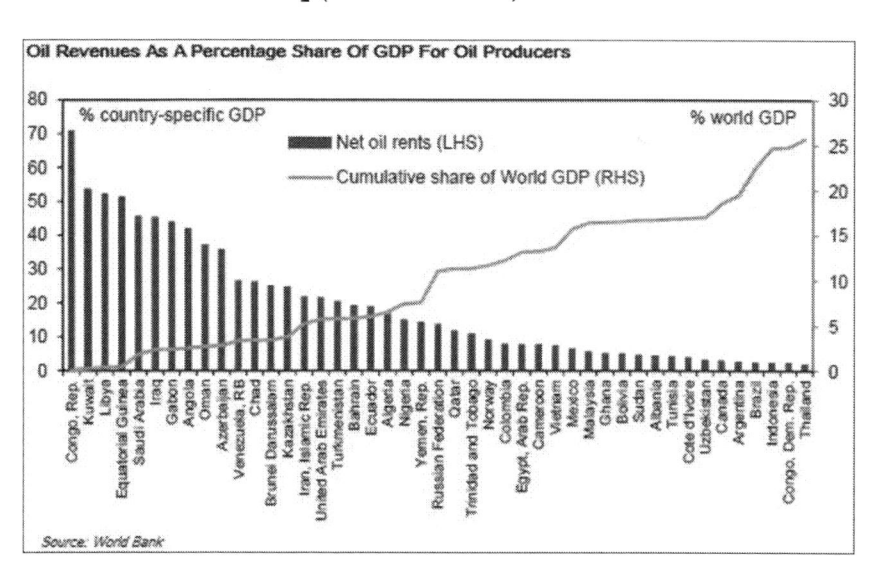

A simple back of the envelope calculation that directly translates a decline in oil prices into a proportional decline in GDP suggests that, **given a 60% decline in oil prices (which is roughly the size of the decline in front-month WTI crude oil over the last 12**

months), nominal GDP in Kuwait and Saudi Arabia, for example, would decline by more than 25%, which is greater than the damage experienced in 2008/09. As an adjunct to this, every USD10/bbl drop in the oil price shaves 3.4% and 4.2% of gross domestic product (GDP) off fiscal and current account balances, respectively, in the Gulf Cooperation Council (GCC) economy as a whole.

Given the view that the oil price will remain subdued (my belief is that it will struggle to break back over the USD50pb WTI level for at least the next 12 months and that the heady days of oil over USD100pb may be a thing of the past), selling any pullbacks on the stock markets of the key Middle Eastern hydrocarbons producers will remain a profitable strategy.

Index	M. Cap (USD Bn)	2015 %	S&P correlation**	ADVT* (USD mn)	P/E TTM	P/B TTM	Div. Yield
S&P Pan Arab LargeMid Cap	107.7	-17.0	0.161	N.A	9.59	1.13	5.86
Saudi Arabia	379.8	-17.1	0.178	1495.30	11.28	1.45	4.97
Qatar	126.4	-15.1	0.105	116.31	12.32	1.53	3.92
Abu Dhabi	116.8	-4.9	0.120	59.62	10.11	1.31	5.69
Kuwait	80.2	-14.1	0.088	39.68	13.33	1.06	3.96
Dubai	79.8	-16.5	0.122	233.49	8.41	1.10	4.83
Egypt	50.6	-24.4	0.070	90.18	9.39	1.26	2.99
Morocco	48.8	-7.2	-0.026	12.12	16.33	2.14	4.32
Jordan	22.1	-0.2	0.017	12.74	14.24	1.28	4.74
Bahrain	17.3	-14.8	0.028	0.74	8.72	0.78	4.38
Oman	15.7	-14.8	0.104	10.77	9.78	1.10	7.20

Source: Reuters * - Average Daily Value Traded for the month, ** - 3-year daily return correlation

In this context, it is – as always with everything being traded – highly advisable to keep an eye on the latest announcements relating to them, as major ones will often afford the opportunity to 'buy the rumour, sell the fact' on these bourses. A good example of this was **the announcement last February by Saudi Arabia that it was to open up its benchmark Tadawul All Share Index (TASI) to**

direct foreign non-Gulf investment participation by 15 June of that year.

With a capitalisation of around USD530 billion at the time – more than the combined capitalisations of the other six major domestic exchanges in the Gulf Cooperation Council (GCC) and only slightly less than Brazil's (USD600 billion) but more than Russia's (USD490 billion) – the mere fact that it was to open to foreigners prompted a brief flurry of buying before it fell back markedly again, allowing investors to add to short positions at better levels.

Adding to the initial buying flurry was the view – quite reasonably – that opening up the TASI to such foreign participation would be a precursor to Saudi Arabia being included into Morgan Stanley Capital International's (MSCI) *Emerging Markets Index* (EMI) within just two years after the adjustment. This would bring with it big block buying from fund managers who are required to mirror the index's composition under the investment mandates of their funds and provide a concomitant lifting of valuations across the board in one fell swoop.

As for how much money might flow in as a result of this was evaluated on the basis that MSCI launched a provisional Saudi index based on the draft rules published the previous year. If this was used as the basis for incorporation into its EMI then Saudi Arabia would have a 1.5-2.0% weighting immediately, on a par with previous investment darling Turkey and larger than perennial global funds' favourites Poland and Chile. With USD1.7 trillion benchmarked against MSCI's EMI according to latest figures, on a straight weightings-alone valuation then such a move would be expected to attract between USD25.5-34.0 billion in new funds in the very short term.

Saudi Arabia TASI Performance

Chart showing TASI performance from 2013 to April 2016, with annotations:
- *"Anticipatory buying ahead of TASI opening up to foreigners ('Buy the rumour')"*
- *"Promises regarding improved transparency and trading environment fail to be implemented ('Sell the fact')"*

Source: Various market data feeds

In reality, though, other considerations are factored in to the overall investment equation of a major global fund manager, particularly operational efficiency, geopolitical risks and a country's macroeconomic picture. In each of these respects major questions remain over the Saudi bourse, and these have been reflected in its trading trajectory since the TASI was opened up. It is also instructive that similar concerns have come into play with the region's other major stock markets, even those – like the UAE and Qatar – that have already been included in the MSCI indices.

Operationally, it is not surprising that given the Kingdom's tightly-regulated political system, the adjustment to such new capital inflows looks like it will be done in a very conservative and incremental way. The Capital Markets Authority stated prior to the TASI liberalisation that, in general terms, each foreign institution would need to have at least USD5 billion of assets under management and investment experience of five years. It added that there would be a 10% cap on combined foreign ownership of the market's value. Additionally, each such Qualified Foreign Investor (QFI) would only be able to hold a maximum of 5% of issued shares in any one listed company; all foreign investors (including resident and non-resident) would have a combined ceiling of 49% ownership of issued shares in any one listed company; and, QFI's together would only be able to own a maximum of 20% of issued shares of any one listed company. Moreover, the Saudi authorities have not said whether there will continue to be a stipulation that investors use the same broker to buy and sell a stock and stipulate same-day settlement, which has made entering and exiting trades very difficult in the past for players in different time zones.

Clearly, therefore, the bullish runs that we have seen in anticipation of market-liberalising moves in the Middle East are more often than not the product of a belief from inexperienced retail investors (a large proportion of the shares traded in these stock markets are from this investment type) who believe that in and of itself, a move such as liberalisation and/or inclusion in key benchmarks, like those of the MSCI, will lead to long-term stock market gains. Indeed, according to Saudi Arabia's Capital Market Authority, as at the end of 2014, there were 4.3 million of these hot money investors in the TASI, accounting for around 35% of total Tadawul share holdings by value, but a near 90% of all volume (compared to 60% of volume in China, 35% in India and less than 2% in the US, according to local bourse figures). **For experienced players, bullish runs at the moment are best regarded as selling opportunities, at least until accompanied by hard and fast rules that point towards greater transparency, ease of trading and improved corporate governance at the key constituent companies of the indices.**

Short Canada

For those investors who, for one reason or another, do not want to trade Middle East assets, **the oil price can also be proxy traded to**

a degree through both the currencies and stock markets of more usually traded sovereigns, as highlighted below. In this context, Canada is extremely interesting in that, like the US, Canada's manufacturing base and consumption has benefited from a lower oil price environment but, unlike the US, its benchmark stock index – the Toronto Stock Exchange (TSX) – has a much greater proportion of its overall composition made up of companies directly or indirectly negatively exposed to low oil prices than their US counterparts. So, the TSX has theoretically been more prone to a downside move than the DJIA.

This disconnect between two key elements of a country's economic profile as exhibited in its principal stock market – and as has happened elsewhere in connection with the oil price, which is for some countries both a key cost in manufacturing but also a key part of income – offers clear hedging and arbitrage possibilities.

To see this more clearly, it is necessary to superimpose the cumulative returns profile of the TSX and of Brent crude, as below.

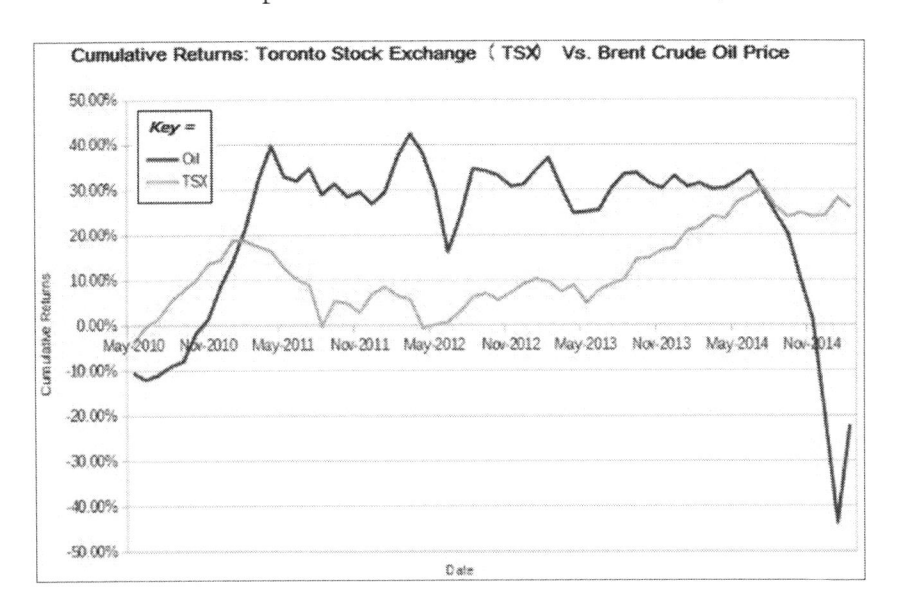

As can be seen above, for much of the past five years or so the TSX and Brent crude returns have been very closely correlated in trend terms. At the beginning of the Saudis' negative comments over the oil price direction, the TSX's and Brent crude's cumulative returns directions markedly diverged, with the TSX buoyed up (relative to the Brent price) by the factors mentioned above and by other non-energy sectors performing well.

Given that the TSX index and oil prices had not diverged to such a degree in a very long time, but that the TSX has a very heavy weighting of energy stocks, historical correlations suggested that this relatively recent divergence would narrow over time, and this is precisely what has happened, as shown below.

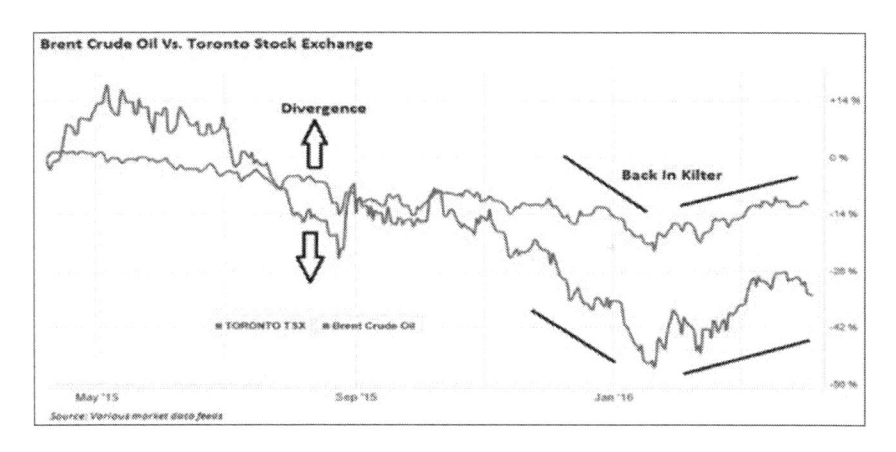

For the longer-term trade, then, any discrepancy in trend should continue to be rectified in one of two ways: either oil prices rise with a concomitant increase in returns to match the TSX's or oil prices remain low and the TSX falls accordingly to reflect this.

This is an illustrative example of the way in which such divergences between energy-heavy stock markets (see above) and the oil price can be utilised to generate alpha returns with very little inherent risk having to be dealt with through further risk management strategies. **This can also be found in other similarly**

constructed markets, although rarely to such a degree, including most notably perhaps Australia, Mexico, Norway, Venezuela and Russia. Unsurprisingly, given the equities flows involved, the Canadian dollar has been broadly pressured during the ongoing oil price depression (see chart below).

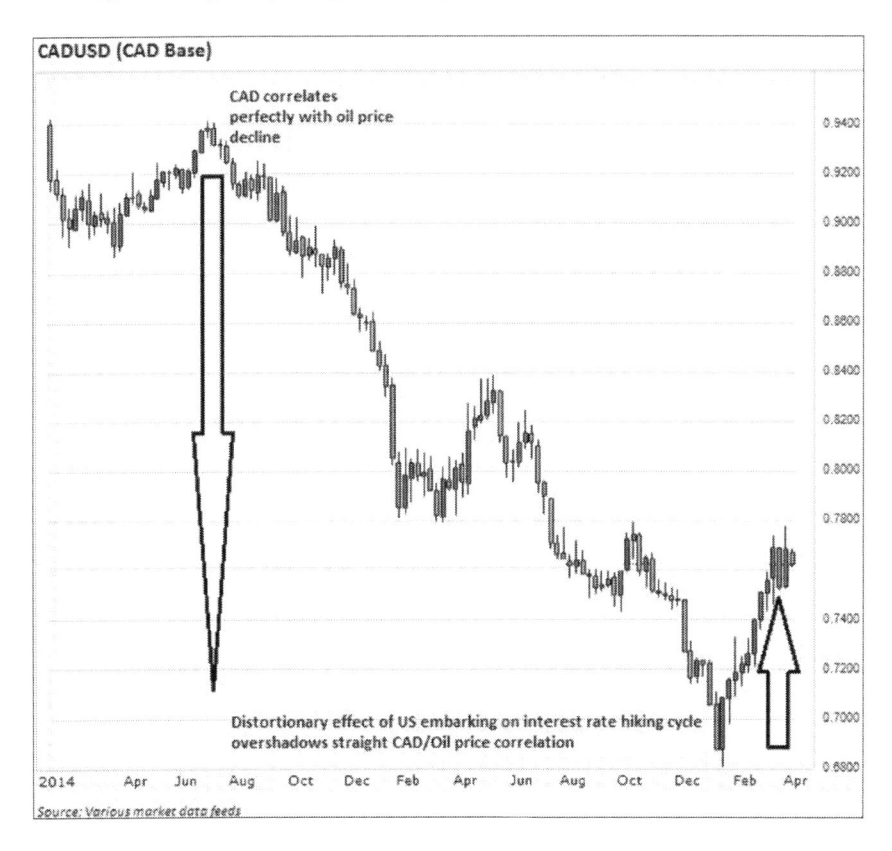

CADUSD (CAD Base)

CAD correlates perfectly with oil price decline

Distortionary effect of US embarking on interest rate hiking cycle overshadows straight CAD/Oil price correlation

Source: Various market data feeds

The same can be said for the currencies of those countries just mentioned, whilst the effect on the currencies of most major Middle Eastern oil producers has been militated against by the fact that they have pegs to the US dollar. **Nonetheless, spectacular gains could be made by trading against the possibility of these pegs enduring, albeit in a slightly more tangential fashion than usual.**

In this context, the **first quarter of 2016 was marked by consistent pressure on forward Saudi riyal prices all the way out to one year duration on the curve,** indicating speculation over whether the riyal's 3.75 effective currency peg to the US dollar, which has existed since 1986 and has been regarded as a cornerstone of the country's economic stability, will survive intact. Interestingly, with the Saudi Arabian Monetary Authority (SAMA) having been active in attempting to shore up the value of the riyal across all dates, short and long, since the beginning of this year, **hedge funds in particular have been looking to effectively short the riyal – and by implication bet against the survival of the peg at 3.75 – by buying interest rate swaps (IRS).** At the end of March 2016, in fact, Saudi IRS' hit multi-year highs, with the idea being that as SAMA eventually runs too low on USD reserves to prop up the riyal (selling the USD to buy the Saudi currency) then it will have to embark on interest rate hikes to bolster the currency instead. In this vein, two-year Saudi IRS climbed by around 100 basis points (bps) from the end of September 2015 to the end of March 2016, to over 2% by the end of the first quarter 2016 – their highest since January 2009 – a massive number, given that the Saudi central bank has raised official interest rates by only 25 bps over the same period.

This trading direction has been exacerbated by negative ratings moves on Saudi Arabia, including the downgrade in March by S&P of its long-term foreign currency debt rating. The problem with the downgrade was not just that it occurred very quickly in ratings agency terms after the previous downgrade in October, nor even the new rating itself (A-), but rather that it was an unusual double-digit cut (from A+), as opposed to the single digit moves that ratings agencies usually use. The fact that Moody's had a materially higher credit rating for Saudi than does S&P – three notches more, in fact, at Aa3 (and Fitch Ratings' was four notches higher, at AA) is completely irrelevant from the international investor perspective, as they take the lowest rating into account and not the highest.

The ratings curve, as mentioned earlier, is essentially a risk curve for global investors and the speed at which a country's rating changes is seen as a function of how volatile the risk situation in it currently is, so a double-digit cut implies that the risk inherent in Saudi – and therefore in investments into it – is extremely high. Moreover, **at A minus, Saudi is now at the lowest rung of upper medium grade investment status, with one further move down putting it into lower medium grade territory, with the next category being non-investment grade, which would be catastrophic from the perspective of 'real money funds', many of which would not be allowed under their investment mandate to invest in a product with such a rating.**

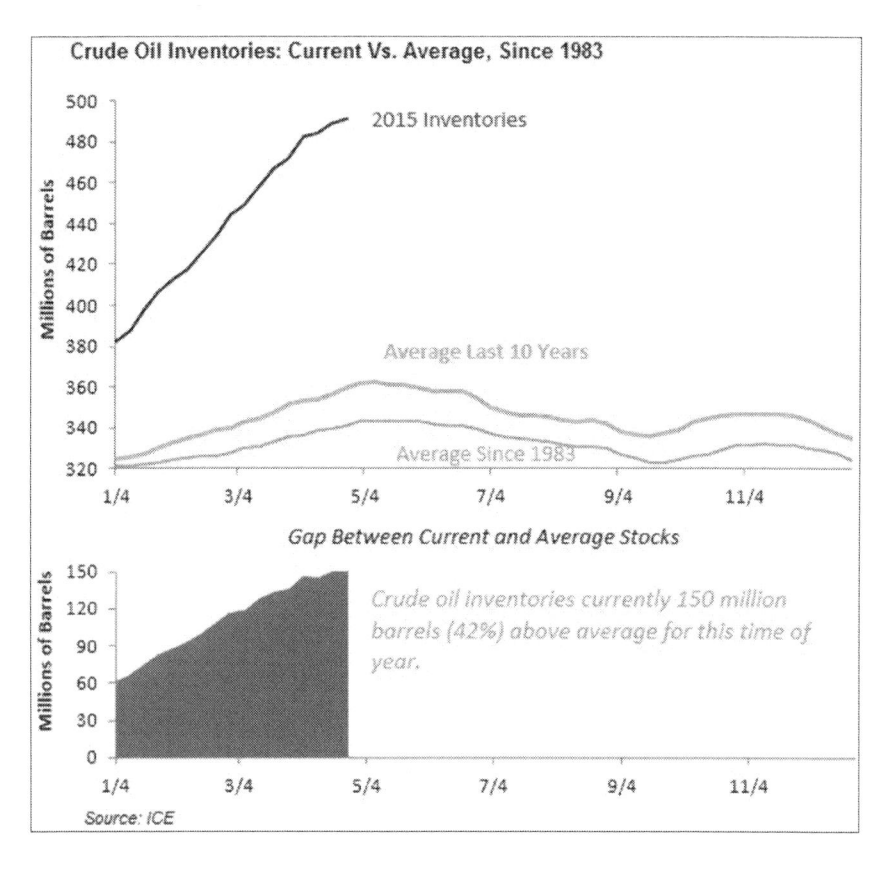

Long USD

Another currency trading correlation to note is between the oil price and the US dollar, as oil is priced in the US currency. **Twenty years ago,** it seemed that there were fairly clear principles for investors to follow with regard to the link between the oil and USD prices: **the higher the crude oil price, the higher the USD (the rationale being that as oil prices rose then the demand for dollars to buy it would increase and thus the USD would strengthen) and vice-versa.**

Over the past 10 years or so, this relationship has completely broken down, as **rising oil prices have coincided with a broadly weaker dollar. This has been explained by the idea that rising oil prices lead to deterioration in the US trade deficit (oil and oil products historically represented around 50% of the entire US trade deficit) and thus a negative outlook for the USD and corollary selling of it. The reverse, of course, is equally true, in that a downward trending oil price has coincided with a rising USD.** Although some of this is due to a cessation in the vast number of dollars being released into the US economy (in the three QE programs) and a consequent rebalancing of supply and demand rules in favour of the historical norm, it is also due to the fact that a lower oil price has historically been a huge spur to growth in the US, as it both increases consumer spending and also lowers manufacturing costs (thus, in turn, making exports more competitive in the global market).

As mentioned earlier, but worth reiterating, **it is estimated that every USD10/bbl change in the price of crude oil results in a 25-cent change in the price of a gallon of gasoline, and the American Automobile Association in Washington has stated that for every penny that the national average price of gasoline falls, more than one billion dollars per year in additional consumer spending is estimated to be freed up.**

As it now stands, this historical relationship has been somewhat distorted by the US embarking on an interest rate hiking cycle (this virtually always results in its earlier phases in a weaker USD, as explained in depth a little later). Nonetheless, stripping out this factor, which will be taken out of the equation as the interest rate hiking cycle develops, **the flipside to the straight short oil trade, as the correlations showed, is a long USD trade. The cleanest way to trade this is going long the USD Index** – established in 1973 (based at 100) as a measure of strength of the US currency against the currencies of six major other currencies: the euro, the Japanese yen, the Canadian dollar, the British pound, the Swedish krona and the Swiss franc. **Obviously, added profits can also be made by buying USD against currencies of countries that are highly dependent on oil for their trade revenues, such as those mentioned earlier (Canada, for example, and Mexico offer the easiest trading opportunities in this regard).**

USD Index chart (2013–2016)

Annotations on chart:
- Recent historical correlation held good, with USD rising as Oil fell
- Distortionary effect of the anticipation of US interest rate hiking cycle beginning, and then the first rise in rates prompted a pullback

Source: Various market data feeds

Short Emerging Markets FX

Whilst, by definition, many currencies in the world depreciated as the USD began its major rise ahead of the first US interest rate hike in 2015 ('buy the rumour'), expectations of interest rates rises in the US (and the end of QE in the country) also meant a shift in general away from 'riskier' investments, both by asset class and by country. This was then reversed markedly once the US had actually hiked interest rates, as the US lost ground ('sell the fact') and riskier investments benefitted to a degree. **Since then, as highlighted at the beginning of this book, there has been an ebb and flow of investment into and out of 'safer' and 'riskier' assets, depending on which investment factor has been prevalent at any one time in the markets, and the speed and degree of swing of these**

moves has been unprecedented in market history. Even during the Great Financial Crisis there were extended periods where investment broadly favoured safer or riskier assets. In general terms, the risk curve moves from least risky asset class to most risky asset class as follows: cash (in a solid currency), bonds (in a solid country), equities (in a solid country), FX (riskier than the previous three categories but extremely liquid) and commodities (riskier than the first three categories and relatively extremely illiquid). It also moves from least risky country type to most risky country type in the following fashion: developed market, emerging market, frontier market.

Prior to the US' interest rate hike in 2015, there had been a clear weakening of emerging market currencies in general and those of hydrocarbons producers and major exporters of other commodities in particular. This had a reinforcing effect on this investment paradigm, as it was seen as reducing the costs to the US's manufacturing base, because the price of raw materials falls, making exports more competitive and boosting demand at home. From the viewpoint of boosting consumer demand, quite aside from cheaper goods being available in shops (electronics that utilise commodities from emerging markets, for instance), demand for the biggest product that most people will buy in their lives – housing – is also inclined to be boosted, as steel and copper costs fall relative to the US dollar. For example, in an average US house enough copper is used to fill an Olympic-sized swimming pool.

As it now stands, though, **the relationship between commodities and EMFX is more nuanced, with a feedback loop that plays back into where in the global economic cycle differing market payers believe we are.** Notably in this regard, while the supply story in commodities (most visibly evident in the oil market) has received significant attention over the last year and a half or so, it does not fully explain the entire investment picture. Specifically, the extended fall in commodities prices that the markets have seen might usually have been expected to have fed through into a re-acceleration in global economic activity by this point; that is, the 'recovery phase' mentioned earlier in this book in the section looking at *Economic Patterns*.

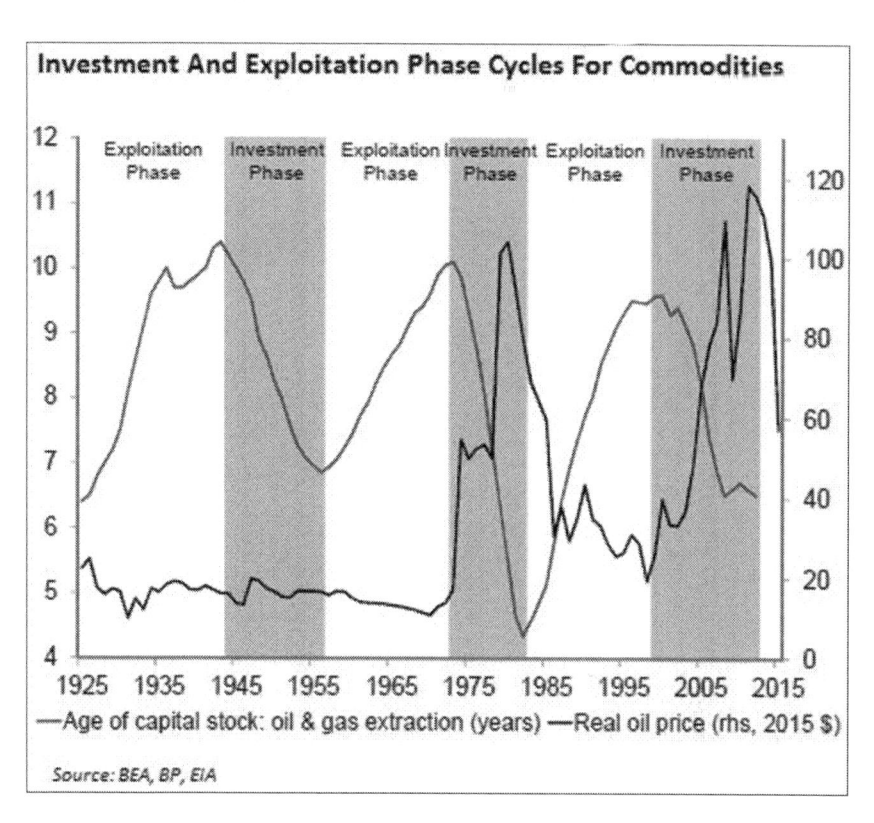

Investment And Exploitation Phase Cycles For Commodities

— Age of capital stock: oil & gas extraction (years) — Real oil price (rhs, 2015 $)

Source: BEA, BP, EIA

In fact, though, this broad-based global economic recovery has proven to be much more elusive than initially expected, and demand weakness has been compounding the negative returns associated with the ongoing supply shift, militating into a situation that might better be characterised as being in a much earlier stage of economic re-development than thought; in many key economies, in fact, the 'contraction phase'.

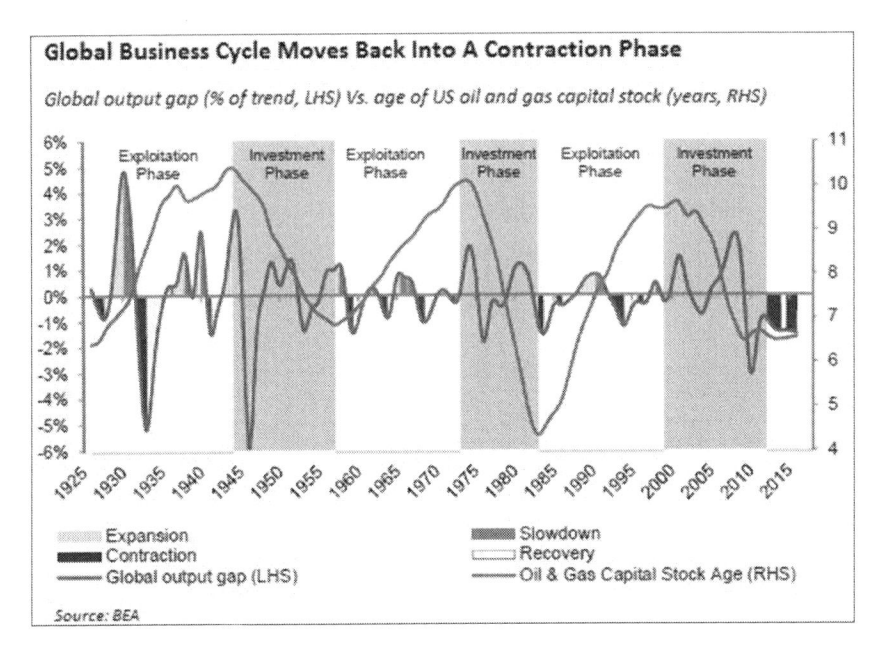

Global Business Cycle Moves Back Into A Contraction Phase

Global output gap (% of trend, LHS) Vs. age of US oil and gas capital stock (years, RHS)

[Chart showing global output gap and oil & gas capital stock age from 1925 to 2015, with alternating Exploitation and Investment Phases marked. Legend: Expansion, Contraction, Global output gap (LHS), Slowdown, Recovery, Oil & Gas Capital Stock Age (RHS). Source: BEA]

A key factor in this stalling of recovery has stemmed from emerging markets, with growth weakness having been driven by the nature of the private credit involved (see later focus on China) and sovereign debt and terms of trade shocks depressing activity. This could be regarded as the third phase of the Global Financial Crisis, with the first being the crisis in developed markets and the second being the sovereign crisis in Europe. In China – the major source of metals and oil demand growth for the last decade – economic expansion is not just slowing, but is also rebalancing towards being consumption-led (through the development of a larger middle class) and away from fixed investment-led (through government-supported infrastructure projects). Attesting to this, for example, has been the global copper market, which, although seeing limited change in supply during 2015, saw an extraordinary slowdown in demand, resulting in around a 30% decline in price over the year.

Three Phases Of The Global Financial Crisis

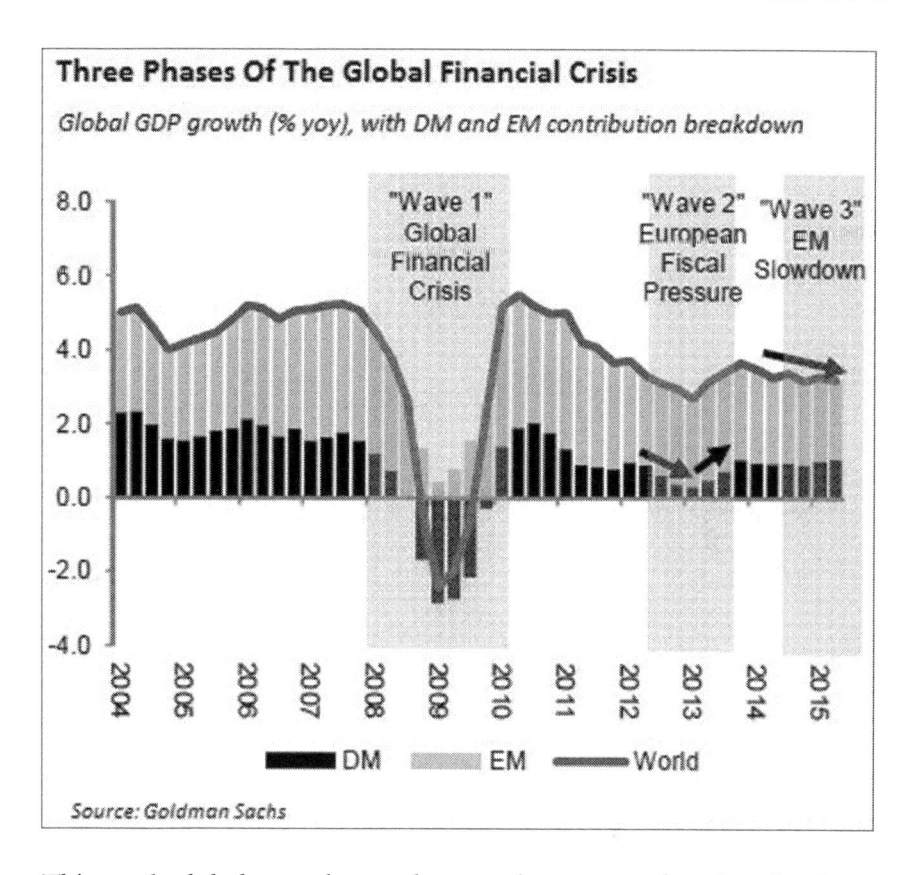

Global GDP growth (% yoy), with DM and EM contribution breakdown

"Wave 1" Global Financial Crisis — "Wave 2" European Fiscal Pressure — "Wave 3" EM Slowdown

Source: Goldman Sachs

This weak global growth – and worsening terms of trade – has been feeding back into commodity price falls through significant EMFX depreciation, including amongst commodity producers. Specifically, as the local currency costs of production have fallen, commodity cost curves have been pushed lower and flatter (in USD terms) and this, in turn, has been exacerbating oversupply and making new equilibrium price levels a moving target, to the downside.

Weak EM Demand Feedback Loop Into Global Commodity Supply Through The FX Channel

- Shale Revolution
- More US Economic Growth
- Lower US Energy Prices
- More Commodity Supply
- US (positive) income effect channels
- More US Economic Growth
- EMFX (weakness) channel
- US monetary policy channel
- Less Emerging Markets Demand
- Less Accommodative US Monetary Policy

Source: Goldman Sachs

Short European And US Banks With Significant Energy Exposure

With no sign that the ongoing slump in the oil price will reverse any time soon – even the historically bullish OPEC said recently that crude would not return to USD100pb until 2040 at the earliest – the prospect of tougher government stress tests and market-targeting of weak equity links in the shale energy investment universe means that **global banks are looking more carefully than ever at their shale industry debt exposure. This, in turn, will continue to push shale firms' high-yield debt spreads higher, pushing up financing costs and so increasing their lending banks' debt exposure to the sector, at least until an equilibrium is reached, which it has not been as yet.**

Fears of energy-sector bankruptcies have long weighed on the **US banking sector**, to begin with, as it almost single-handedly financed expansion of the shale industry over the past decade, both through direct loans and through the structuring of high-yield bond issues, of which, as underwriters, the banks themselves often ended up holding a large part. Indeed, **according to industry figures, some USD360 billion worth of high yield bonds have been issued by US energy companies since 2003, most of it from shale oil and gas producers.** Although the redemption curve is not an urgent issue in the next three years, with only USD35.5 billion due until 2019, after that the maturity profile worsens dramatically, soaring over USD30 billion per year in 2020 and 2021 and then to over USD40 billion in 2022.

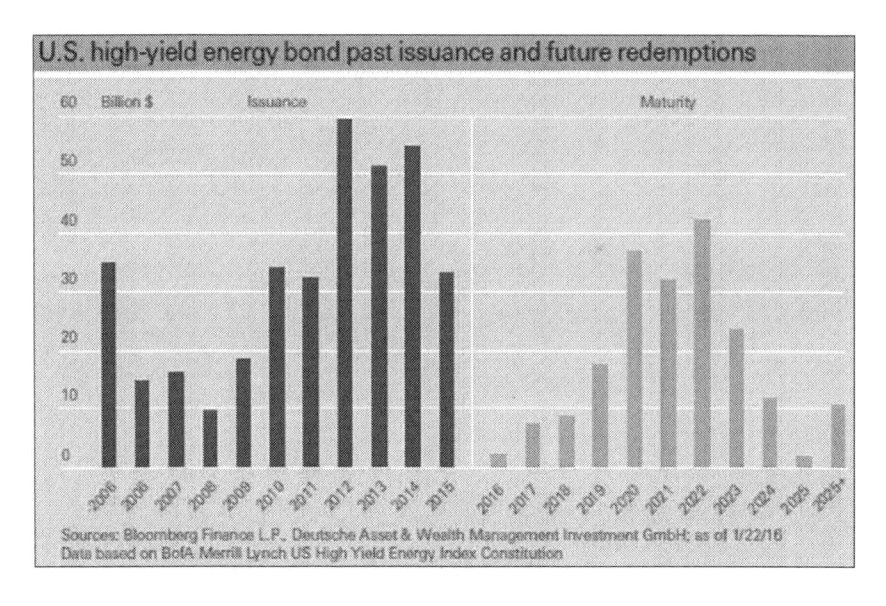

U.S. high-yield energy bond past issuance and future redemptions

Sources: Bloomberg Finance L.P., Deutsche Asset & Wealth Management Investment GmbH; as of 1/22/16
Data based on BofA Merrill Lynch US High Yield Energy Index Constitution

With a growing consensus that oil prices will remain lower for longer and spreads higher, this means more companies will be at risk of defaulting during the next few years and, additionally, more companies in the same sector defaulting at roughly the same time may result in forced sales. Already, in fact, such bankruptcies in the second half of 2015 rose to 28, compared to 13 in the first half. Among high-yield issuers in the US, riskier credits have an increasingly difficult time raising money in the bond market, and the decrease in liquidity combined with the low oil price has increased the expectations of defaults in the market. An additional negative factor for the sector's banks is the low recovery rate. According to industry data, the market may currently be pricing in an implied five-year cumulative default rate of almost 50% for US high-yield bonds as a whole, assuming a 40% recovery rate.

The reason why all of this is much worse news now than, say, the banks' holdings of mortgage-backed securities before they blew up and prompted the Global Financial Crisis in 2007/08, is that precisely because of that laxity by the US regulators, oversight has been tightened markedly and 2016's 'Comprehensive Capital Analysis and Review' (CCAR) and 'Dodd-Frank Act' stress test exercises (that monitor capital adequacy) will be a lot tougher than previously. The 33 bank holding companies (with USD50 billion or more in total consolidated assets) will face testing scenarios in which the price of oil would weigh much more heavily than ever before, with oil prices now already around 55% below the level when the Fed set last year's stress test scenarios in October 2014. This will test those banks for both the direct effects of oil price falls on their oil or commodity trading business (as they did last year) but importantly as well the indirect effects of lending to energy companies, lending in areas of the country that are more dependent on energy companies and energy-related revenues (which they have never done before).

Of these top 33 banks, Wells Fargo & Co, the world's largest bank by market value, said early in 2016 that bad energy loans climbed 49% in the last three months of 2015, whilst JP Morgan Chase stated that its reserves for impaired energy loans would increase by about USD500 million in the first quarter and it would have to add an additional USD1.5 billion to the set-aside if oil prices held at around USD25pb for about 18 months. **Even more specific to the energy firms were comments made in February 2016 by the head of JP**

Morgan's commercial bank, Doug Petno, in New York, that such companies could see a further 15-20% cut in their credit lines, adding that, although banks had previously been flexible enough to be more lenient with their energy clients, all that is now changing. According to Petno, JP Morgan for one was not waiting for April, when banks traditionally reassess the value of oil reserves underpinning energy loans (the 'redetermination process') to reassess its exposure.

It is true to say that the most distressed clients know when they are going to be pinched and are taking the steps to deal with it, with most of these clients working with their banks way in advance of redeterminations, so compelling mergers and acquisitions, asset sales and discussions with private equity. **However, there would be a meaningful number of these players who have no options, and it is likely that the range of bankruptcies in oil and gas have only just begun.**

For some of the smaller regional banks in the US, the situation is more advanced, with major global credit ratings agency Moody's having placed four of them – BOK Financial Corporation, Cullen/Frost Bankers, Hancock Holding Company and Texas Capital Bancshares – on review for a downgrade of their long-term ratings and standalone baseline credit assessments (BCA) at the end of the first quarter of 2016. Moody's explained that these banks held significantly higher direct energy-related loan concentrations than the median for US regional banks, 40-110% of tangible common equity, compared to the 10-15% median for roughly 60 rated US regional banks. Consequently, the agency believes that it is reasonable to assume increased problem loans in the energy sector as a result of weakening liquidity as energy borrowers experience reduced cash flow, pressure from bank-loan covenants and a withdrawal of bank and capital market liquidity.

The same regulatory concerns were brought into focus by the markets on the European banking system in the first quarter of 2016, as traders awaited the results' breakdown from the 2016 European

Banking Authority's banking sector stress test for institutions in the Eurozone. **Traders always look for weak links and push those until they break, which is precisely what happened with European banking stocks seen as having considerable exposure – across their global network – either to the shale industry segment or to the oil and gas segment in general.** Such trading dynamics reached their zenith – so far – in February 2016 when the Stoxx Europe 600 Banks index was pushed to a 25% loss over the first eight weeks of the year, with Credit Suisse down by 40% over the period and Deutsche Bank by just over 30%.

Although some banking analysts – albeit, at European banks – said at the time that only around 20% of the European banking sector's loans to energy companies are high-yield and projected losses of around EUR6 billion out of combined EUR400 billion in outstanding energy company debt held by Eurozone banks, the fact remains that – in Europe – it is anybody's guess, due to the opacity of the reporting. In this context, **European banks do not publish deep-down data on the extent of their exposure to the energy sector, so in reality nobody has a clue who holds what exposure. Therefore, the market view is to go after the big names – like Credit Suisse or Deutsche – in the belief that a weak target will be hit sooner or later.**

Indeed, figures released in the first quarter of 2016 by US bank, Bank of America Merrill Lynch, stated that European banks could book USD27 billion in loan losses from energy firms, or 6% of the industry's entire pre-tax profits over three years. The increased link being made by traders between European banks and the oil price in general is highlighted by the huge spike in the correlation between the aggregate price of European bank shares and the price of oil. On a scale of 0 to 10 (where 0 is no correlation and 10 is total correlation), the correlation in the first quarter of 2016 was nearly 0.5, according to UBS analysis of industry data, compared to 0 just over a year before.

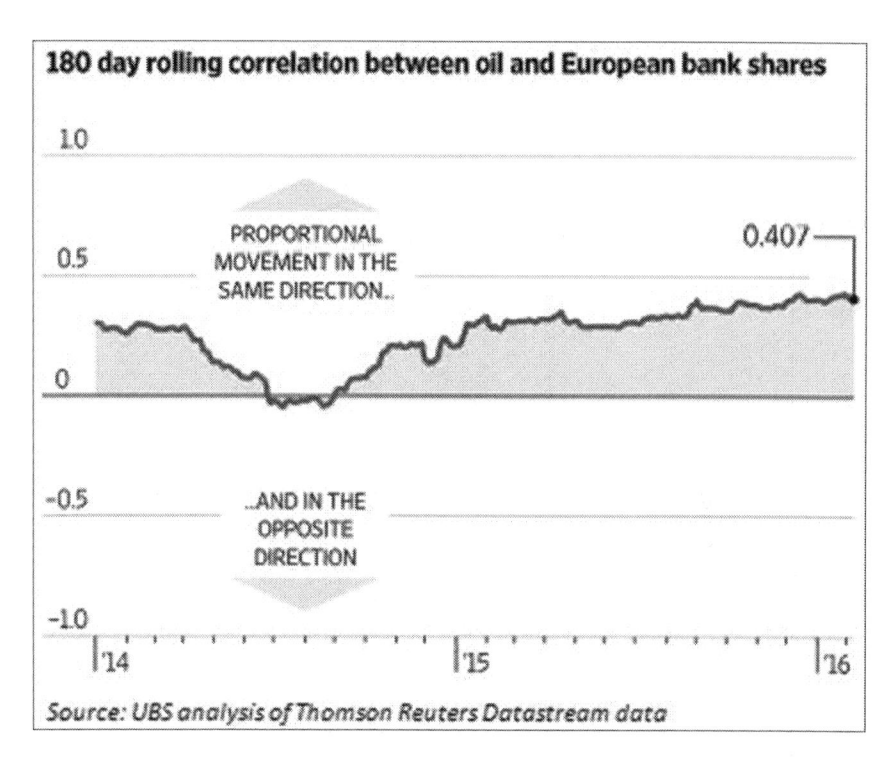

180 day rolling correlation between oil and European bank shares

- 1.0
- 0.5 — PROPORTIONAL MOVEMENT IN THE SAME DIRECTION...
- 0
- -0.5 — ...AND IN THE OPPOSITE DIRECTION
- -1.0

0.407

'14   '15   '16

Source: UBS analysis of Thomson Reuters Datastream data

The extra bonus of shorting certain European banks is that because of their capital structures, their share price could collapse as and when they breach the new capital adequacy rules, which have been markedly tightened up under the new Basel III international regulatory framework for banks. **In this context, in order to bolster its Basel III-mandated Tier 1 capital, Deutsche Bank was 'persuaded' into raising nearly EUR20 billion in 2010 and 2014, most of it by selling shares, but also by issuing the equivalent of EUR4.6 billion in 'contingent convertible (CoCo) bonds', which convert automatically into the bank's shares if its capital drops below certain thresholds**, so – in theory – saving the Eurozone taxpayer the cost of having to bail it out. This structure is like waving a red flag at a bull for traders; they receive a 6% yield at least just for holding the bonds, and they then sell the shares down to a level where the bonds-equity conversion takes place, they already have the yield from the bonds, plus the short profit from selling the shares, and then the free long at low levels from the new stock they are given, so it is in this respect a no-lose trade.

Long Gold

Historically, gold has been the usual beneficiary of heightened risk across the globe, on the basis that, unlike currencies, more cannot simply be produced at the drop of a central bank's printing presses (as in QE). So, for example, the correlations for gold were fairly simple: if the USD looked weak then gold would be strong, and this generally still holds true.

Gold had been regarded as the archetypal **'safe-haven' commodities asset in times of political uncertainty** (troubles in the Middle East, for example, sparking buying not just in that area but around the globe) **and economic uncertainty** (ongoing anaemic growth in some key global economies) in the same way that the Swiss franc is seen as such in currency terms. **Additionally, it has been seen as a hedge against inflation concerns** that have risen sharply on the basis of the QE policies adopted by the Fed, the BOJ, the ECB – the long-term refinancing operations (LTRO) was QE by another name – and until recently the BOE as well.

Recently, as well, gold is seen as a good buy in the unusual interest rates scenario that we are seeing playing out around the world (negative rates, that is, as mentioned at length earlier). One factor in this context is that, although the uncertainty and distress associated with negative rates would tend to increase interest in gold anyway, the more pronounced shift of monetary policy in this direction by central banks is encouraging even greater flows into bullion.

In particular, **there is no sense yet that negative rates could not be cut even further, so the opportunity cost of holding gold (which has no yield attached to it) is reduced.** To this depression of the global yield curve has been added a flattening as well, with risk-off plays, to the degree that the difference between the 2 and 10-

year US Treasury yields stood at less than 100bp by the end of the first quarter of 2016. A flattening yield curve often presages an economic slowdown, which may trigger policy responses that generally support gold; indeed, the last time the differential was that low was in January 2008, in the early stages of the Global Financial Crisis, which, in turn, produced one of the biggest bull runs in gold for many years.

The Ghosts In The Machine

There are a number of major factors that individually could continue to twist financial markets into trading patterns that swing exceptionally quickly into wildly contradictory modes, if they are not thoroughly understood in terms of accurate historical precedent, correlations and geopolitical dynamics. These 'ghosts in the machine' are questions of growth in the US, Eurozone, China and Japan, with corollary concerns over the global hydrocarbons market and the risk/reward balance in emerging and frontier markets, in addition to fears over global security pressure points. **At any one moment, one or more of these take precedence in dealing terms over the others, but the order can change in a split second, so thoroughly understanding these 'ghost' factors is vital to ensuring correct portfolio positioning in order to skew the risk/reward balance in a trader's favour, and this is what this section is about.**

Oil

Global energy concerns, both feeding from the price of oil and from geopolitical factors relating to the commodity, will continue to play a huge part in the overall trading dynamics of all asset markets for the foreseeable future. This book has already gone into great depth looking at this problem (and opportunity) from a number of key angles, but the primary takeaway from all of the facts, figures and announcements relating to this sector is that **the Saudi shale-stymieing strategy is not working, that it is threatening to irreparably damage the economies both of Saudi Arabia and all other hydrocarbons-centric countries, that it is unlikely to work** ever, and that, in this context, virtually every announcement that Saudi makes is damaging to the oil price, to all related assets and the global economic growth profile taken as a whole.

A telling example of the way in which global traders regard Saudi Arabia came with the reaction to the announcement in the first half of 2016 that the Kingdom was to attempt to address budgetary pressures (inflicted on itself, of course) by beginning a 'megafund' that would eventually substitute for oil revenues in its revenues mix.

'Moronic', 'barely even half-baked' and 'the sort of thing that you'd expect from a 15 year old doing a basic course in economics' were comments from senior oil traders at serious trading banks to whom I spoke following the announcement, principally on the basis that there was quite obviously a lot less than met the eye to the idea outlined by Saudi Arabia's Deputy Crown Prince Mohammed bin Salman. As far as market players were concerned, in fact, even what was visible was profoundly flawed, reinforcing the market view that **the Saudi heir apparent has no meaningful idea of how to extricate his country from the hole it has dug for itself since it embarked on its strategy to stymie the growth of the nascent shale oil industry two years ago.**

Looking at the latest idea first, the headline news that Saudi Arabia was to create a sovereign wealth fund (SWF) with enormous global market purchasing power – at least USD2 trillion was the figure mentioned by Salman – was, in itself, at the most basic level, extremely misleading. In fact, what was envisioned was that the existing Public Investment Fund (PIF) would have the proceeds of the planned initial public offering of Aramco put into it – itself a hugely dubious prospect – and that the remaining shares in Aramco would also be transferred into the PIF. **However, the net result was likely to be negligible for Saudi Arabia as a whole, as the vast bulk of the fund would, in fact, just be an ownership interest in Aramco and other domestic firms which the Saudis already own. In practical terms, then, it would be just a shift on balance sheets, rather than any new assets or investable funds.**

As for the portion of the fund that did constitute liquid money, available for investment around the globe, in a similar manner to the neighbouring Qatar Investment Authority SWF, it was highly unlikely to amount to anything approaching a significant amount for a top-flight global SWF. **Initially the idea mooted was that all of Aramco was to be floated, then just its downstream operations, and then the indications were that it would just be a relatively small part of its downstream operations, amounting to no more than five percent of the firm at most. Even this, though, is not assured of success.** On the one hand, the usual buyers of such an offering – the SWFs of neighbouring countries – are going to be reluctant to participate in helping Saudi out, given what the Kingdom's shale strategy has done to their economies (at least USD300 billion in lost government revenues for GCC countries in the past two years, according to the IMF), not to mention that they would regard any possible investment monies in Aramco as being better invested by themselves in Western enterprises and/or market assets. On the other hand, Western investors would demand an international level of transparency in Aramco's accounts and operations as a pre-requisite for any investment, which Saudi will never provide.

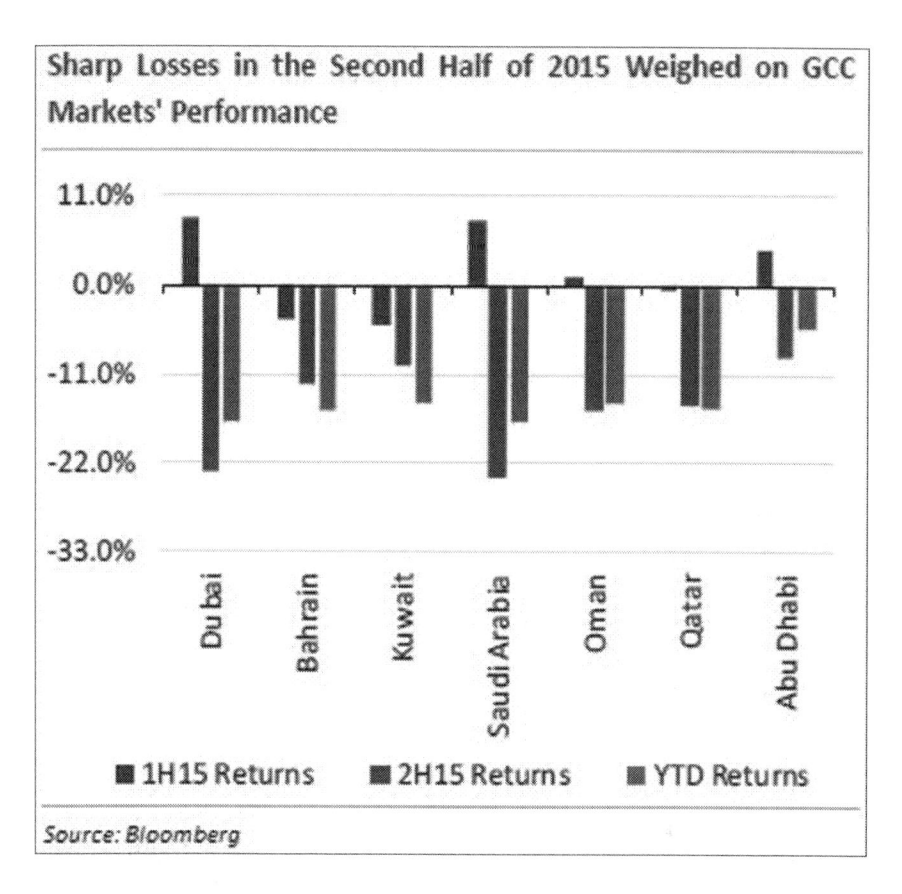

Sharp Losses in the Second Half of 2015 Weighed on GCC Markets' Performance

[Bar chart showing 1H15 Returns, 2H15 Returns, and YTD Returns for Dubai, Bahrain, Kuwait, Saudi Arabia, Oman, Qatar, and Abu Dhabi, with y-axis ranging from -33.0% to 11.0%]

Source: *Bloomberg*

Feeding into this negative investment scenario is the way in which the Tadawul All Share Index (TASI) has performed and operated since it was opened up to direct foreign non-Gulf investment participation in June 2015. Over and above the fact that it was the second worst performer of all MidEast stock markets in 2015 (after Egypt's Hermes Index), the worst in 2016 and has seen its market capitalisation fall from around USD530 billion in June 2015 to about USD377 billion by the end of the first quarter of 2016, the assurances of the Exchange's chief executive officer, Adel al-Ghamdi, in Riyadh, that the market would move quickly towards Western levels of compliance and ease of trading have proved hollow thus far.

Severe limitations on Qualified Foreign Investors (QFIs) still remain in place (including the ownership cap of 10% of a firm by value, which raises serious questions about forced liquidations of existing holdings at that 10% mark when the value of the market falls), concerns over minority shareholders persist and, on even the most basic level, only around 45% of company announcements in the Saudi market are in English as well as Arabic. **Meaningful announcements, either of the accounting or operational variety, in whatever language, are also few and far between.** A very large proportion of the emails sent out every day from the TASI say that X or Y company has failed to provide any accounts for the month or the quarter, even some of the bigger names.

This lack of a coherent strategy to build out its benchmark stock exchange as promised only confirms the financial markets' general view that Saudi Arabia's overall vision is profoundly confused. **The way the market sees it is that Saudi started out with the absolute objective to push the oil price down to whatever level was necessary to destroy as much of the shale industry as possible – Saudi Oil Minister, Ali Al-Naimi, in December 2014 said whether it goes down to twenty dollars is irrelevant – but, having ruined the finances of its neighbours and its own to a degree, it suddenly turns around and announces an output freeze, with the aim of boosting the oil price, even though the shale industry is still going strong.**

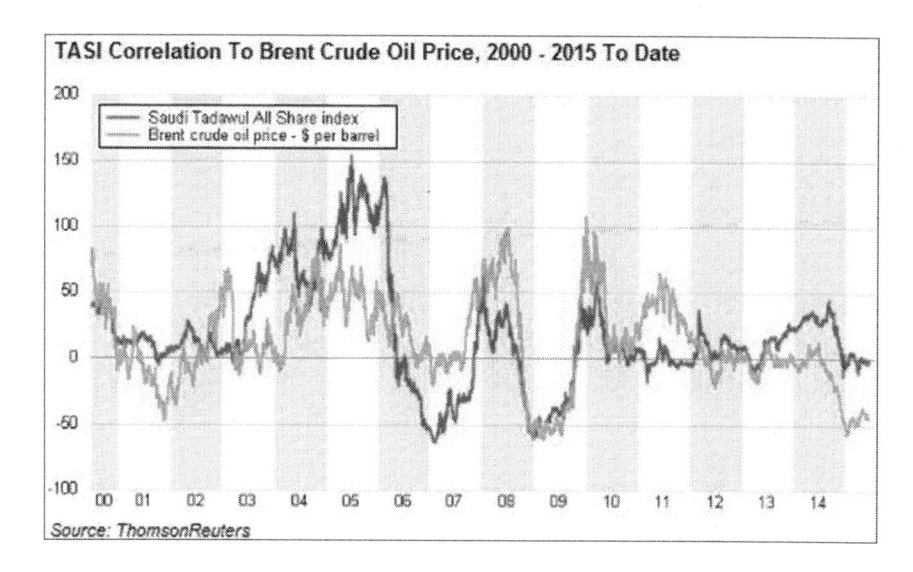

TASI Correlation To Brent Crude Oil Price, 2000 - 2015 To Date

Source: ThomsonReuters

If that did not look incompetent enough to dealers, who essentially make their living sussing out and exploiting stupidity, even the tactic was ill-judged, in that it involved freezing output at record high levels and did not take into account that some of the biggest producers, like Iran and Iraq, would obviously not take part. The Saudis shot themselves in the foot from every direction, and now the markets think that it does not know what it is doing at all. Attesting to Saudi Arabia's increasing lack of investability is the dramatic decline in both capital flows and foreign direct investment (FDI) into the Kingdom, much more than has been seen in neighbouring Middle East hydrocarbons producers over the ongoing oil price downturn.

In this respect, net capital flows to the Kingdom averaged just under USD8 billion from 1961 (when records began) to the beginning of 2015, but went into negative territory in the first quarter of 2015 (negative USD14.787 billion in that quarter alone), where they have remained ever since, whilst FDI has similarly plummeted from an average of just over USD5.1 billion from 2006 until the beginning of 2015, to a record low of just under USD2 billion in the first quarter of that year, around which level it remains.

Finally, having inveigled a number of its neighbouring hydrocarbons-producing neighbours into an oil output freeze, even after its over-production strategy had caused such profound economic damage to them, Saudi Arabia then (in April 2016) decided to abandon its own notion of extending the freeze once more. **'Betting on the stupidity and lack of market savvy of Saudi is a one hundred per cent winning trade, whichever method you use to do it'**, was the judgment of perhaps the most successful oil trader still active.

At some point, oil will see its fortunes turn around in a significant way, as the global supply and demand mix rebalances, and when this has clearly manifested itself into an upwards oil price trend then obviously the positions to be taken would be the opposite of those outlined above.

China

Changing Growth Model

At the centre of the new trading environment mentioned at the beginning of this book is the changing nature of China's economy in the global growth mix. Even when the rest of the world, and particularly the major growth markets of the West, were reeling from the Global Financial Crisis, China was still posting near double-digit GDP growth. **In fact, the annual economic growth rate in China averaged 9.85% from 1989 until the beginning of 2016, reaching an all-time high of 15.40% in the first quarter of 1993.**

For the vast majority of this period, China's growth was powered through the manufacturing industry, which leveraged low-cost labour into low-cost products that were sold in enormous quantities around the world. In the process, China became the largest importer of many commodities, almost single-handedly creating the 'commodities super-cycle' over that period. When the Global Financial Crisis hit, any slack in the pace of China's economic growth was compensated for by enormous government-sponsored infrastructure projects (at the height of these programmes, China was building the equivalent of a city a week).

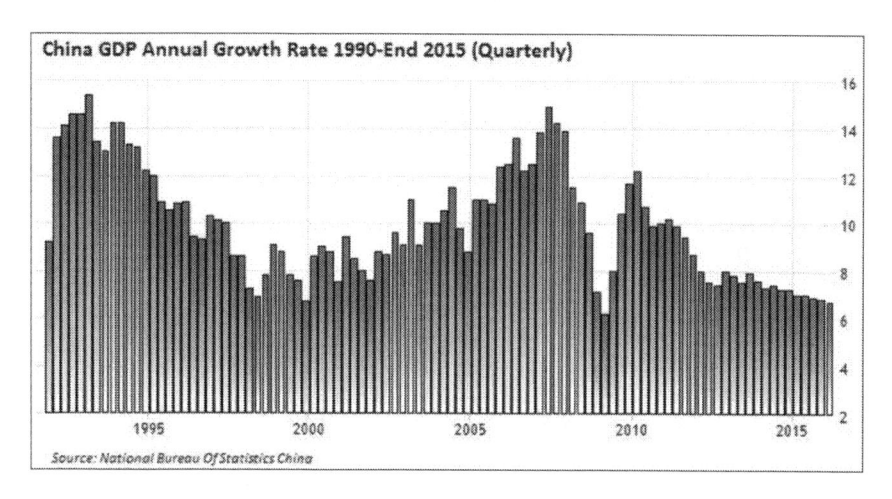

China GDP Annual Growth Rate 1990-End 2015 (Quarterly)

Source: National Bureau Of Statistics China

Recently, **China has sought to shift the driver of growth more towards increasing consumer-led spending and away from manufacturing,** as part of a broader socio-economic policy of building out the middle class in the country, which is seen as a more stable and sustainable growth driver than manufacturing. This consumer-led growth, though, as economic models around the world show, will never engender the quantum of growth that the markets became accustomed to from China in the past.

The effect on the oil market – as mentioned, an ongoing key driver adding to the global economic uncertainty – has also been profound, as China has accounted for an average of 35% of global oil demand growth since 2000. In this context, as China's National People's Congress (NPC) concluded at the end of March 2016, there was little cause for optimism for beleaguered oil-producing states. **The NPC's economic growth forecast for 2016 was 6.5-7%, the first time the government has acknowledged a goal below 7% in** two decades, following the nation's slowest economic uptick in 25 years in 2015, with 6.9% growth. Even this forecast, though, looks unduly bullish, according to many seasoned China analysts, with some positing a maximum economic growth over 2016 of 5.8%. The notion, then, that Chinese demand may offset ongoing supply surpluses, not just in oil but in other commodities markets, looks ill-founded, which itself could continue to feed into a negative asset valuation loop that may result in oil prices being depressed for many years to come.

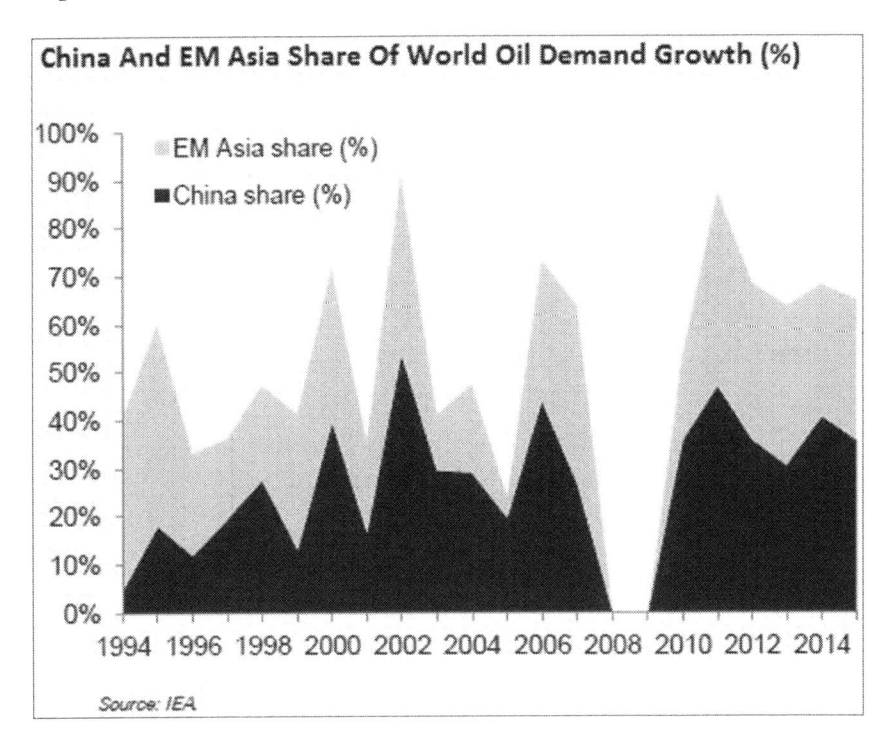

China And EM Asia Share Of World Oil Demand Growth (%)

Source: IEA

Factoring into the predicted massive fall in China's oil imports, aside from the broad-based shift away from energy-intensive manufacturing, is an expected change in the transportation sector. In particular, **oil demand growth from the passenger vehicle sector – which has made up 66% of Chinese total oil demand growth since 2010 –** is forecast to slow in the medium term and then

begin to decline by 2024, and this casts doubt over the capacity for continued long-term oil demand growth at current trend rates in China and, by extension, the world. This is even without factoring in strong assumptions over the possible growth in electric vehicle market share in China, which, if also taken into account, would in and of itself reduce Chinese oil demand by 1 million barrels per day by 2035.

Not only are there likely to be fewer passenger vehicles around but they may also travel less distance, so decreasing fuel consumption further. According to an extensive study on vehicle-use intensity in China by Tsinghua University, historical annual distance travelled per passenger vehicle in China has been high relative to developed countries by virtue of a high proportion of taxis. In comparison to the average taxi which travelled 99,200 km in 2009, the average private light-duty vehicle travelled only 16,900 km. Factoring in the relationship between total annual vehicle kilometres travelled to economic growth, it is predicted that the annual kilometres travelled per vehicle will fall from an estimated 24,000 km in 2000 to 13,000 km in 2030 and then to 12,950 km in 2035.

This view is predicated on the expectation that China will more closely follow the example of Europe and Japan rather than the United States, owing to high population densities in Chinese cities and progress towards an extensive rail network. **The key conclusion is that Chinese oil demand growth, the largest single contributor to world oil demand growth, may begin to flatten more quickly than some long-term projections indicate and, all else remaining equal, this could result in world oil demand growth falling from its 2000-2016 trend of 1.1 million bpd year-on-year to only 800,000 bpd by 2024.**

Significant Danger Of A Major Banking Crisis

This said, it is entirely possible not only that China's economic growth will drop by even more than many analysts forecast but also that **it may be subject to a systemic banking crisis of a similar scale to the US sub-prime mortgage-inspired credit squeeze that sparked the global financial crisis in 2007/08.** Despite some limited pullbacks recently, property prices in China remain fundamentally disconnected to the basic dynamics of supply and demand, with the Chinese Academy of Social Sciences, in Beijing, estimating (based on electricity meter readings) that there are currently still around 65 million empty apartments and houses in urban areas. This number is just over five times that of the 12 million or so at the height of the US sub-prime mortgage bubble. Indeed, according to various industry figures, there is currently an excess of around 3.3 billion square metres (sq.m) of floor space in the country, but another 200 million sq.m is being constructed each year. As an adjunct to this, according to relatively recent estimates by the European Chamber of Commerce in China, the country has used just 65% of the cement it has produced in the past five years and just 70% of the steel, after exports, but is still producing more of each.

This housing bubble has resulted in the corollary effect of making the balance sheets of China's financial institutions ever more stretched, creating a banking bubble to add to the mix. Back in 2010, Fitch credit ratings agency was the first of the global ratings agencies to highlight that, despite the apparent deceleration in bank lending over the course of 2010 shown up in official data, the reality was that lending has not slowed nearly as much as the official data suggested. This was due to the increasing amount of credit being shifted off Chinese banks' balance sheets via informal securitisation for sale to investors: that is, **the re-packaging of loans into credit-backed wealth management products (CWMPs), the data on which has always been highly limited.**

Loan Repackaging Time Bomb

Prior to 2010: Typical Loan Repackaging Transaction

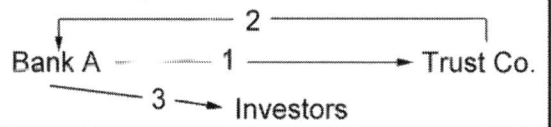

```
         ┌─────────── 2 ───────────┐
         ↓                         │
   Bank A ────── 1 ──────────→ Trust Co.
         ╲
          3 ──→ Investors
```

Post-2010: A Second Bank Becomes Involved in the Deal

Type 1 - Banks Sell Each Others' Products

```
   Bank A ── 1 ──→ Trust Co. ── 2 ──→ Bank B
                        ╲              ╱
                      Investors ←── 3
```

MATCHED BY

```
   Bank A ←── 2 ── Trust Co. ←── 1 ── Bank B
         ╲
          3 ──→ Investors
```

Type 2 - Bank B Assists Bank A in Selling the Loan, Enabling Bank A to Distribute the Product

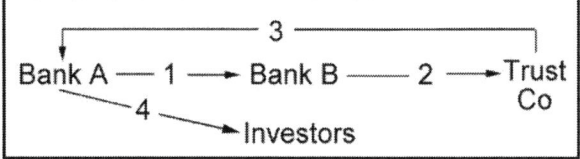

```
         ┌─────────── 3 ───────────┐
         ↓                         │
   Bank A ── 1 ──→ Bank B ── 2 ──→ Trust Co
         ╲
          4 ──→ Investors
```

> **Post-2010: Trust Company Plays A More Active Role**
>
> *Type 1 - Trust Company Sells the Product*
>
> Bank A —1→ Trust Co. —2→ Bank B
>
> *Type 2 - Trust Company Originates the Loan*
>
> 1. Trust Company signs a loan agreement with a borrower
>
> 2. Trust company creates a trust product that it or a bank pre-sells to investors (sometimes the bank is the investor, and the purchase is booked in its investment securities portfolio)
>
> 3. Monies raised in pre-sale are passed on to the borrower
>
> Source: Fitch

Despite the government banning in July 2010 all such informal securitisation deals between trust companies and banks, Fitch observed a noticeable worsening of Chinese banks' already poor disclosure of this activity. Some banks very actively engaged in transactions in 2009 then showed up in 2010 data as minimally involved, yet the bank's own salespeople – responding to Fitch's enquiries – stated that business remained as strong as ever. Meanwhile, private placements of products to institutional investors were becoming more commonplace, most of which were never disclosed to any entity but the Central Bank of the Republic of China.

Indeed, Fitch estimated at the time that as much as 40% of these deals went uncaptured in H110 alone, compared to less than 10% prior to the end of 2009. So, the agency concluded, as these obligations were not included anywhere in financial statements (and hence represented a hidden call on liquidity), although it was theoretically possible that China's larger, liquid banks, might be able to manage these obligations, smaller banks could encounter strains.

Independent of Fitch's analysis at that time, a number of other serious organisations stated that the level of Chinese financial sector bad loans would equal 98% of total bank equity if Local Investment Companies-owned non-cashflow producing assets were recognised as non-performing. They also dismissed the notion that the Chinese government had ample resources to bail out its banks, positing that **the ratio of China government debt to GDP was actually at minimum around 107% (five times higher than official published numbers) and, without conservative assumptions, as high as 200% at that time.**

Nothing has changed at all in the way Chinese banks have been hiding their bad loans in general, including the enormous unprofitable credit lines extended to the property sector, a fact which has recently been picked up on by domestic investors in the China stock markets. This is why we have seen sudden collapses in them over the past few months, with crushing effects on global equities markets, and we can expect more of the same in the coming months and years. This has been exacerbated in the stock markets – shown with huge single-day falls that led to collapses in markets around the globe – by the type of investor that is prevalent in China's stock markets. **That is retail investors, both large and small, who are notoriously skittish. This category includes national and local government officials who 'diverted' some of the massive central government funding intended to be used on infrastructure projects during the Global Financial Crisis into their own pockets and invested it in the stock markets, as**

reflected in these markets' enormous unmitigated rise before the reality check manifested itself.

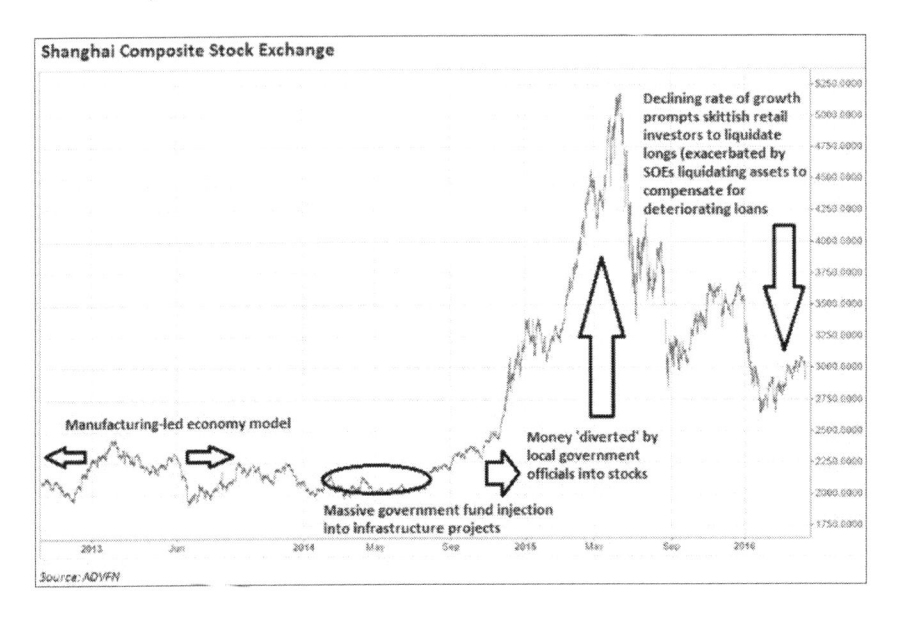

Shanghai Composite Stock Exchange chart showing: Manufacturing-led economy model; Massive government fund injection into infrastructure projects; Money 'diverted' by local government officials into stocks; Declining rate of growth prompts skittish retail investors to liquidate longs (exacerbated by SOEs liquidating assets to compensate for deteriorating loans). Source: ADVFN

This dynamic has permeated across both type of shares (A and B) in both of China's mainland stock exchanges, in Shanghai and Shenzhen, and indeed in the stock markets of Hong Kong and Taiwan (although this latter one to a lesser extent). The key distinction remains that A-shares are denominated in renminbi and B-shares in foreign currency (US dollars in Shanghai and Hong Kong dollars in Shenzhen) but the participatory demarcation has changed. That is, for a long time, the other main difference between the two, from a regulatory standpoint, was that the A-share market was closed to foreign investors while the B-share market was open only to foreigners. However in 2001, the Chinese authorities tried to boost the B-share market by opening it to individual Chinese investors and in 2003 a scheme was introduced whereby select foreign institutions were allowed to buy A-shares. Some companies have their stocks listed on both boards, but their B-shares trade at a large discount to their A-shares, which tend to see much larger trading volumes.

Japan

Shinzo Abe's Big Plan

It might be difficult for those under 50 years of age to imagine, **but before China was a major driver of global economic growth, Japan was.** Its growth model was essentially the same as that previously evident in China as well, founded on the idea of manufacturing relatively low cost products for export to the developed economies (mainly in the West). Its unique selling proposition was not very low labour costs, though, rather it was the ability to produce technology products more quickly and efficiently than anywhere else. **For many years, it was hoped that it would again emerge as a major driver of global economic growth, but this did not prove to be the case. These hopes were fanned again when Shinzo Abe became prime minister in December 2012,** but the results have been mixed.

Japan's Trade Balance Since 1950 (JPY trn)

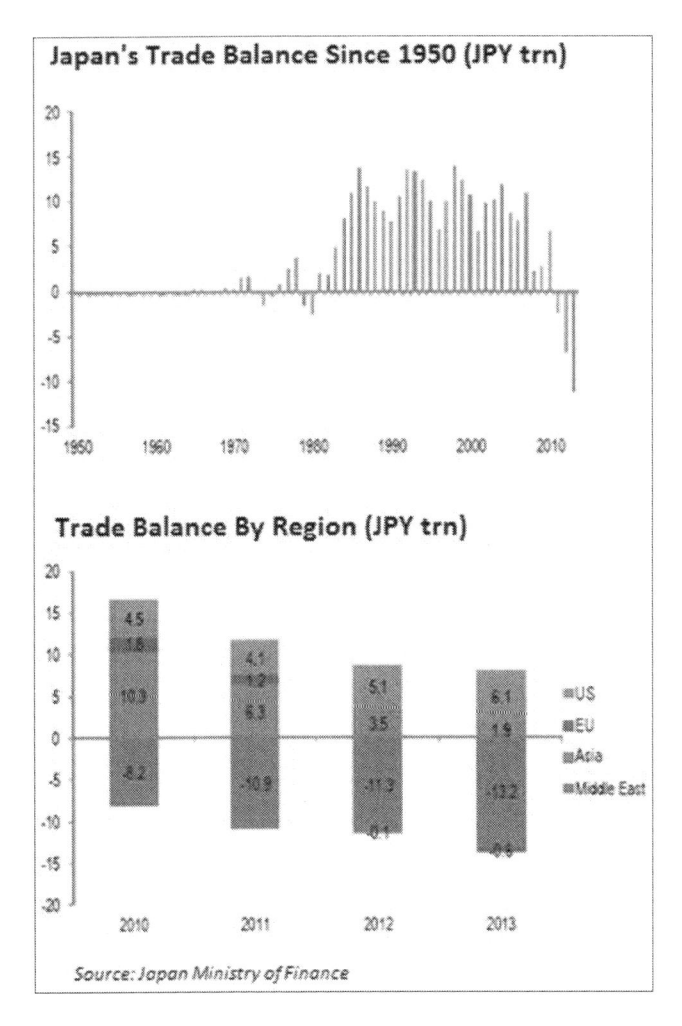

Trade Balance By Region (JPY trn)

Source: Japan Ministry of Finance

Abe put centre-stage the concept of undertaking more fiscal stimulus and 'unlimited' monetary easing (QE of varying sorts), pledging to achieve nominal economic growth of 3% (there had been no nominal GDP growth for 15 years at that point) and a specific 2% growth-oriented inflation target for the Bank of Japan. All of this was to be implemented over and above the stimulus measures taken by the previous government that were still in operation, in which the BOJ increased its asset-purchase program by JPY11 trillion (USD38 billion) to JPY55 trillion (a separate credit loan program was held at the JPY25 trillion level).

Japan Change In GDP (%) At Time Abe Took Over As PM

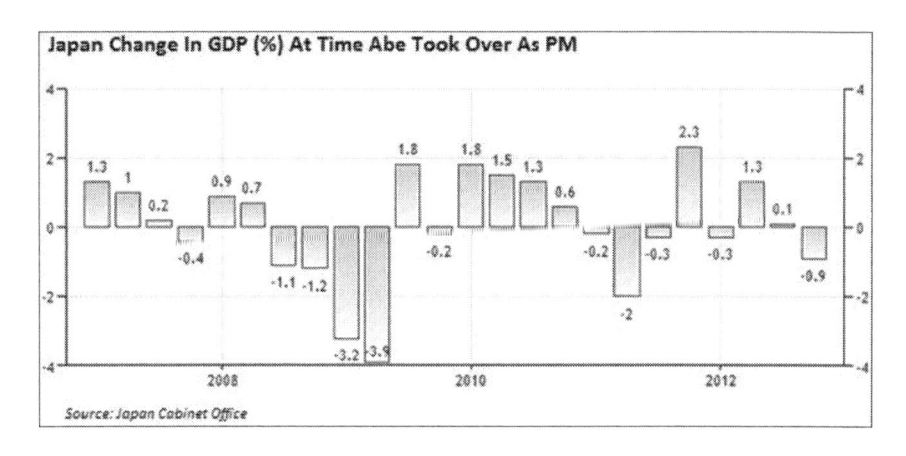

Source: Japan Cabinet Office

Under the direction of new PM Shinzo Abe, the BOJ expanded its asset-purchase program initially to JPY76 trillion (USD905 billion) from JPY66 trillion, whilst maintaining its credit lending program unchanged at JPY25 trillion. This followed earlier figures showing that Japan's exports fell for a sixth month in November 2012 and the trade deficit ballooned, underlining the necessity for something to change policy-wise on the back of Shinzo Abe's LDP victory in the Diet elections. The hard figures were that exports declined by 4.1% y/y and the trade deficit for the first 11 months of this year swelled to JPY6.28 trillion, more than double the record deficit in 1980.

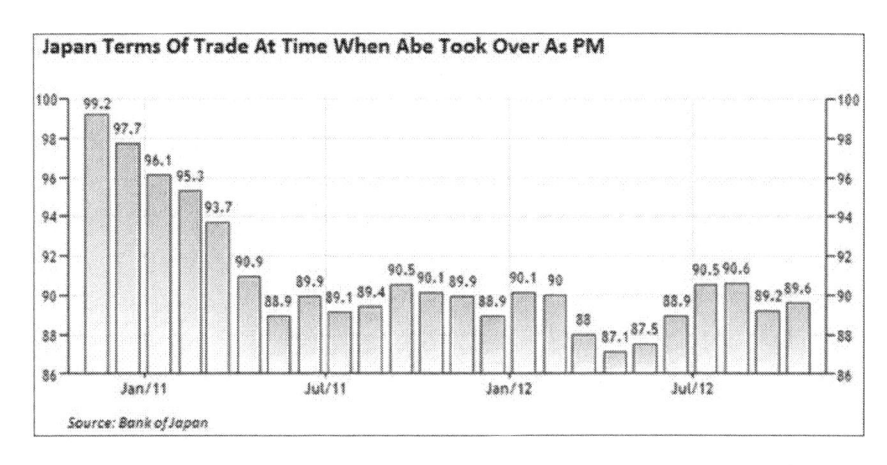

Japan Terms Of Trade At Time When Abe Took Over As PM

Source: Bank of Japan

This monetary easing should have resulted in a number of economic and corollary market effects. First, and the key point, is that it should have **weakened the yen** (as just the expectation of its coming into effect weakened the currency from around USDJPY78.00 to USD85.00 in just a few weeks after Abe took over as PM). Indeed, USDJPY did continue to weaken considerably for a relatively long time thereafter. The LDP also implemented a 'currency warfare fund' to weaken the yen further with massive buying of foreign bond purchases, copying Switzerland's long-enduring success in capping the value of the Swiss franc.

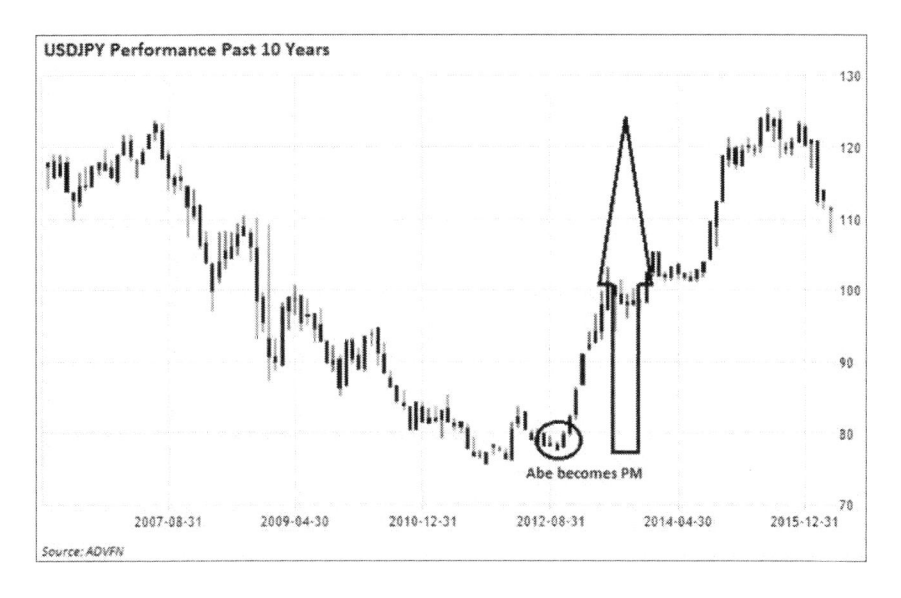

USDJPY Performance Past 10 Years

Abe becomes PM

Source: ADVFN

Theoretically this plan would make exports cheaper relative to Japan's competitors, so boosting economic growth, increasing employment and leading to domestic consumer-led growth kicking in together with export-led growth as well. **This would also boost the stock market, which it did,** as would the lower interest rates available in the domestic money markets (money switches out of bank deposit-related investment to higher yielding investments like stocks when interest rates go down).

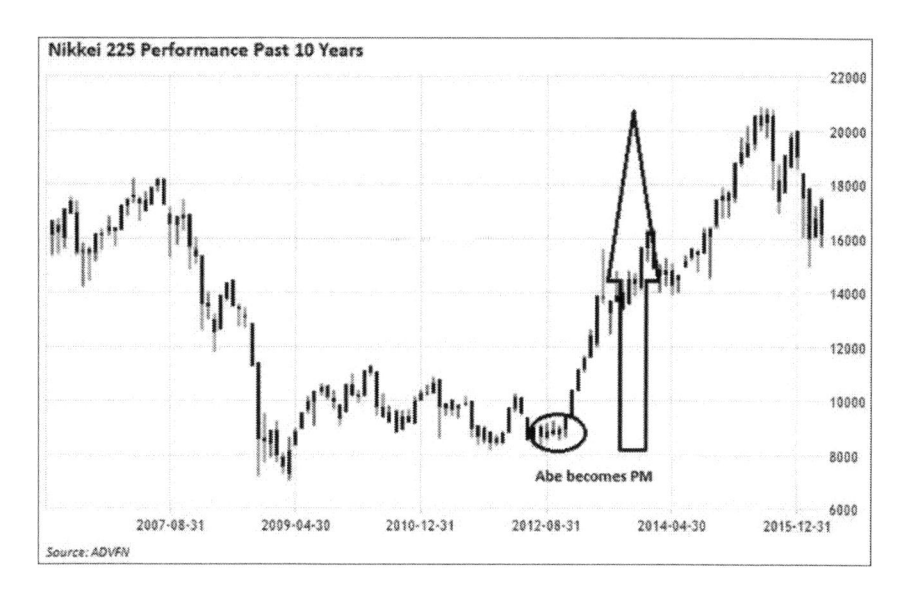

There were potential downsides for Japan in pursuing such ultra-loose monetary policy, of course. Although Japan was trapped in chronic deflation, it was a stable equilibrium, with the real value of savings rising (due to low inflation). In this respect, **a return to higher inflation could have set off a spike in debt costs and a flight from Japanese government bonds (JGBs).** Indeed, an evident risk was that any meaningful sell-off in the JGBs could trigger a serious problem in Japan's banking system, as the holdings of JGBs by Japanese banks account for 900% of their Tier I capital.

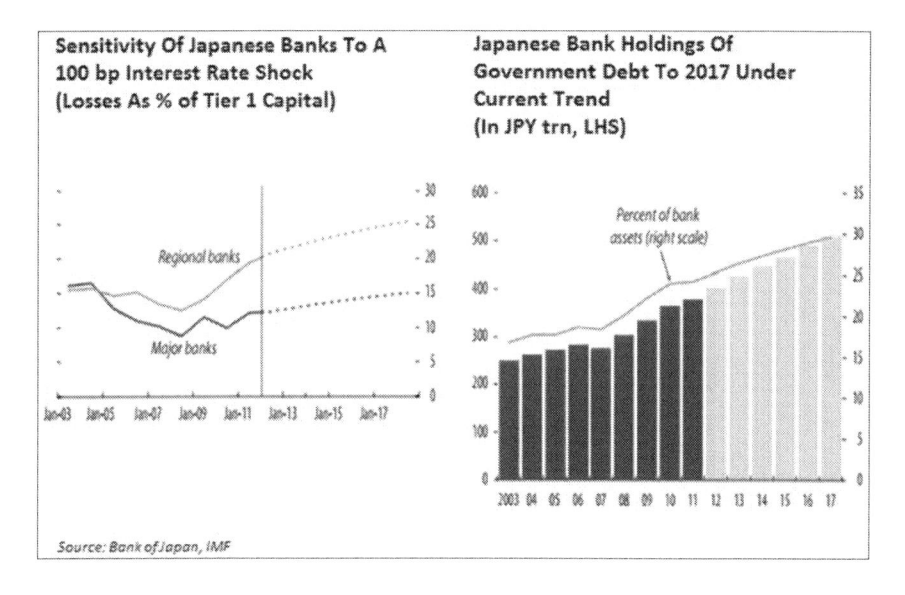

Sensitivity Of Japanese Banks To A 100 bp Interest Rate Shock (Losses As % of Tier 1 Capital)

Japanese Bank Holdings Of Government Debt To 2017 Under Current Trend (In JPY trn, LHS)

Source: Bank of Japan, IMF

In fact, this high level of debt holding by Japan's banks, according to the IMF around the time Abe took over as PM, were as characteristic of Japan as they were of euro area sovereigns under serious market pressure at that time (and now, partly for exactly the same reason). Moreover, the IMF added, the concentration of bond risk within the banking system was expected to increase over the medium term, particularly for smaller, regional banks, which, in fact, it has.

'Abenomics' Hits Predictable Problems, Especially Yen 'Safe-Haven' Status

As highlighted above, there were always inherent problems in a number of aspects of Abe's big economics plan ('Abenomics' as it was termed). Very early on, markets started to doubt how enduringly effective these policies might be, based as they were on the continued depreciation of the yen and in tandem massive QE, as both of these factors eventually would be priced in. **As 2015 wore on, several external factors made matters worse for Japan. First, weaker US data (especially in manufacturing) has caused markets to question the strength of the US economic recovery and** consequently the pace and scale US interest rate hiking cycle, resulting in the **JPY gaining ground against a weaker than expected USD**. Second, as mentioned, the downside risk to China's economy has increased and **uncertainty in China's policy response has added to global risk aversion, and the yen has been seen as a relative safe-haven in this context.**

Given the weakness of its economy in recent years, **this safe-haven status is a mystery to some, but this is explained by the fact that – despite all of its shortcomings – it does meet the key criteria of such a currency:** that is, Japan has low interest rates, a strong net foreign asset position and deep and liquid financial markets. This has militated into the yen being a reliable safe-haven for many years. Since 2008, the yen has appreciated steadily against the US dollar in effective terms in the aftermath of various shocks.

First, the Global Financial Crisis was associated with a large real exchange rate appreciation by over 20%. Second, in May 2010, higher market distress about peripheral European sovereigns led to a large jump in the VIX, followed by a 10% yen appreciation against the euro within a matter of weeks. Third, following the Great East Japan Earthquake, the yen appreciated further on account of expectations about sizeable repatriation of foreign assets by insurance companies, which in fact subsequently did not occur. Fourth, on 25 February 2013, uncertainty surrounding the outcome of the Italian elections led to an intra-day appreciation of the yen against the euro of 5.25% and about 4% against the dollar.

These examples illustrate that appreciation of the yen during episodes of increased global risk aversion is recurrent. Indeed, **since the mid-1990s, there have been 12 episodes where the yen has appreciated in nominal effective terms by 6% or more within one quarter and these often coincided with events outside Japan. In practical terms, the yen appreciates against the US dollar when US stock prices decrease and US bond prices and FX volatility increase. The yen and Swiss franc are, in fact, the** only two currencies that on average appreciate against the US dollar during risk-off episodes.

Compounding this basic problem derived for the trading dynamics of the yen, Japan has also not reacted appropriately to the aforementioned global shocks. Japan's monetary policy became more aggressive in January 2016 when the Bank of Japan introduced a **negative interest rate policy** (NIRP) in addition to its asset purchase programme. As the JPY strengthened post the introduction of NIRP, some regard Japan's move to NIRP as a failure. It could be, of course, that the BOJ has not cut enough, but this looks highly doubtful, and any realistic-sized further cuts will make minimal difference to Japan's overall economic picture. An **unequivocal error was in the decision to hike VAT** (from 8% to 10% scheduled for April 2017, but already pricing in). The hike is expected to subtract about JPY4.4 trillion from household consumption or 0.9% of GDP; much larger than the impact of NIRP, which released about JPY60 billion.

Eurozone

Similarly running out of policy options and also stymied by a relatively safe-haven currency, is the Eurozone. Worse than China and Japan, though, it has the additional huge political and economic burden of mass immigration into the area and the constant threat that a number of its weaker members will again undermine confidence in the area, eventually fatally.

Fundamental Flaws

There are **two basic flaws both in the European Union (EU) in general and in the Eurozone even more particularly. These will lead either to its complete dissolution or its major restructuring over time.** The first of these is that the **EU was borne of fear and**

greed: fear by France of what an increasingly powerful Germany might do in Europe again; and greed by Germany to have a captive market for its goods and services that were broadly superior to those of any other country in the EU. The second of these was, and is, **that the vast majority of the EU's inhabitants do not perceive themselves in terms relating to their being 'European' or even Northern European or Southern European, but rather in practical nationalistic terms as being German, French, Italian, Spanish, Greek and so on, and they always will.** They might think of themselves in the second instance as being European, but this is an ideological luxury and, in crunch times, every single national identity plays the first and foremost role in all decisions relating both to the individual and the member state involved.

These crunch times have been coming thicker and faster than ever before in the past few years, with the zone seemingly lurching from one near-fatal catastrophe to the next. The reason for this, of course, is down to the second flaw of the system: **it is impossible to cobble together a disparate group of states with different economic drivers running in different ways at differing speeds and expect them all to meet broad economic criteria that were designed by the economically stronger member states.** So, what has had to occur to allow for this, in practice, is that the stronger states (generally the heavy manufacturing dominated economies of northern Europe, which also, as a corollary of this, dominate in heavy hitting financial services sectors) have been faced with the decision to either bail out the weaker members states (generally, the southern European countries) or leave them to either go bankrupt (and invalidate their Eurozone membership) or voluntarily pull out of the zone (in order not to have to repay their debts), both of which would break-up the Eurozone as a viable structure.

This dynamic was worsened by two factors. First, the German central bank (Bundesbank) was the key architect of the zone's unified euro currency, the value of which was pitched at a level way below the Deutschmark at the time it was

introduced in 1999, which gave – and has continued to give – the Germans a massive advantage in its exports pricing, compared to where it would have been had it continued to be priced in Deutschmarks. It also gave the Germans a captive market for its products, with the types of trading architecture that pervades the Eurozone.

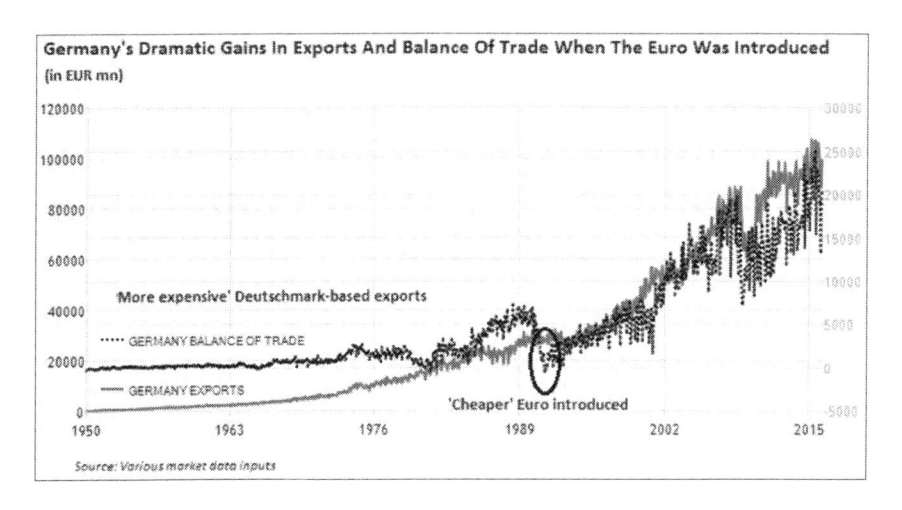

Germany's Dramatic Gains In Exports And Balance Of Trade When The Euro Was Introduced (in EUR mn)

'More expensive' Deutschmark-based exports
····· GERMANY BALANCE OF TRADE
——— GERMANY EXPORTS
'Cheaper' Euro introduced

Source: Various market data inputs

The second factor that has worsened the entire dynamic was the blind rush to get in as many other countries on Continental Europe into both the European Union and then the Eurozone as possible, despite their actually being – in stark economic terms – completely unfit to be members, not meeting many of the basic economic qualification criteria (without lying about them). For its part, at the time when countries such as Greece, Portugal, Spain, Italy and selected East European states were aggregated, Germany was keen to overlook such economic shortcomings, as it meant new customers for its more competitively priced exports, and France was always keen to expand the Union and the Eurozone on the hopeful basis that the more members there were the less dominant one nation – that is, Germany – might become over time. All of these assumptions have been proven completely wrong, as has now become clear.

Deteriorating Backdrop

Aside from the basic existential threats just outlined, the specific factors that are worsening the outlook for the EU and the Eurozone are too multitudinous to go into in all their appalling details now, but some stick out as being likely to move from the transitory to the permanent and to become themselves an existential threat to the EU and the Eurozone.

Migration is a key factor that, although bad now, is likely to become one such factor that not only has significant implications for the economic outlook in both the short and longer term, but it also challenges the fragile political equilibrium both within and between European countries that underpins the process of European integration and the integrity of the euro area, as outlined in the fundamental flaws analysis. Economically, of course, the cost, which has fallen largely on Germany thus far, of housing, clothing, feeding, educating and keeping healthy the more than a million refugees that entered the EU in 2015 is enormous and enough to cripple already weak economies in the area if unchecked. **Even in Germany, the capacity to absorb an additional inflow of another one million refugees this year (although there may be many more than this) is very small:** aside from the obvious political difficulties, the fiscal costs of accommodating such a number would push Germany back into fiscal deficit in 2017; a politically sensitive issue at a politically sensitive time, with federal elections due in December 2017. **The capacity to absorb a large number of additional refugees elsewhere in Europe is even more questionable.**

Politically, aside from the German election question, one of the core notions at the very heart of the EU has been destroyed, with many countries closing borders to migrants, even those who have been granted asylum by other member countries. As this notion has been broken so there has been a rise in the radical edges of politics in many of the member states, either to the extreme right (anti-immigration being a central tenet, but also against EU oversight) or to the extreme left (anti-EU mandated austerity).

In Greece, for example, which has been close to destroying the existing Eurozone structure for many years now, numerous challenges remain for the government. At the most basic – but politically contentious level – pension reform needs to be tackled before its official creditors will deem it compliant with the new adjustment programme, disburse further financial support and entertain some form of debt relief. However, the fragile majorities that the country's governments tend to command means that any of them will struggle to pass the far-reaching reforms that many elsewhere in Europe want to see. **A failure to move forward with reform could tip the fragile political balance both in Greece and between Greece and its creditors into renewed chaos. The large number of Middle Eastern refugees entering the EU via Greece further complicates the picture.**

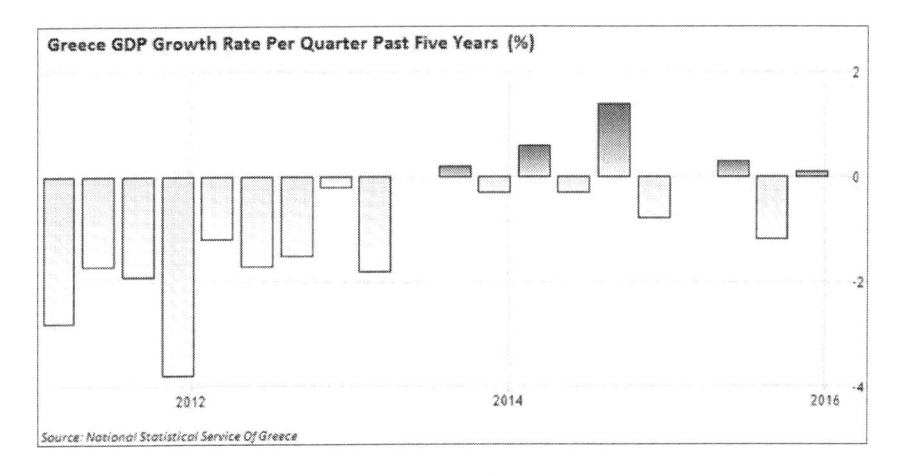

Greece GDP Growth Rate Per Quarter Past Five Years (%)

Source: National Statistical Service Of Greece

Similar political and economic chaos looks likely to continue in Spain, with the political stalemate that emerged from the recent national elections looking likely to endure for some considerable time. The issue of whether to permit a referendum on Catalan independence further complicates matters for the formation of any new coalition governments. The implied political uncertainty will weigh on business and consumer confidence, and ultimately on the economic outlook, so exacerbating an unemployment level that is causing grassroots discontent.

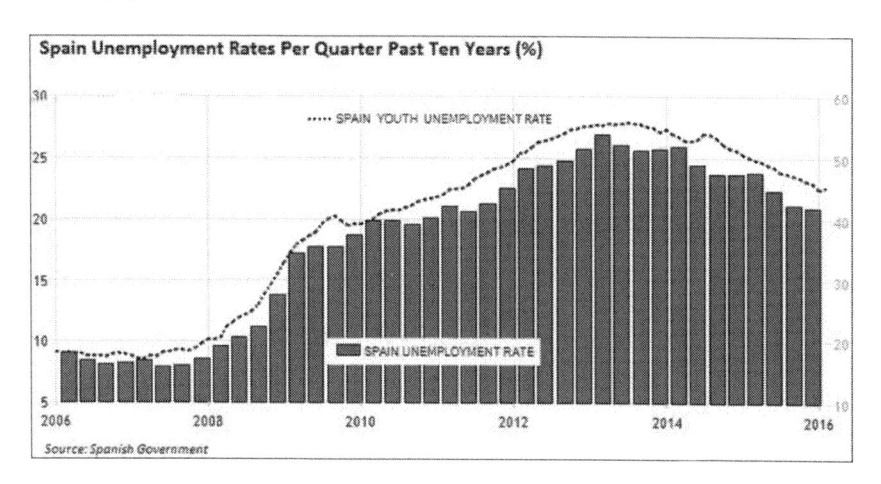

Spain Unemployment Rates Per Quarter Past Ten Years (%)
Source: Spanish Government

The move to extreme politics as well is evident in France and may yet gather even further impetus following the recent first round of regional elections showing the far-right Front National (FN) gain 28% of the nationwide vote, primarily on growing disquiet among the public over the level of immigration. **While the FN failed to gain power in any region in the second round, the continued strength of its support ahead of the Presidential election due in May 2017 will continue to undermine the practical power of any of the mainstream parties, and consequently the ability to combat the fact that France is technically bankrupt, like Spain, Italy and Greece.**

Having said this, despite going into near-freefall in December 2015, **the euro has its perennial buyers, a key proportion of which are central banks who use any major weakness in the currency to bolster their FX reserves.** In this context the euro is, of course, part of the Special Drawing Rights – SDR – global reserve currency, along with the US dollar, British pound, Japanese yen and Chinese renminbi, and one of its major weighted constituents: USD 41.73%, EUR 30.93%, RMB 10.92%, JPY 8.33% and GBR 8.09%.

This was **compounded during the US QE programmes as when the Fed began to print an unprecedented amount of USD, many FX reserve manager roles shifted towards a more active role where investment and diversification become pivotal.** For a select few reserve managers tied via their passive receipts to the USD – and thus Fed policy – this new strategy led to ongoing 'USD-recycling', or rebalancing, into a broader portfolio of currencies. **So strong was this USD-recycling effect that it came to dominate FX markets for long periods in recent years, helping to explain otherwise inexplicable EUR resilience, especially against the USD.**

In this context, although the IMF publishes its central bank FX reserve manager allocations (the 'Commitment of Foreign Exchange Reserves') each quarter, these are reported on a voluntary basis, with three of the world's largest FX reserve managers (China, Russia and Saudi Arabia) choosing not to participate. As a result, the IMF reports that only 54.1% of total reserves are accounted for, leaving a gaping hole. Initially, to estimate a more accurate amount of true EUR FX reserve holdings during this USD-recycling period, various banks took the weights from IMF-reporting managers (the largest being Norway, Japan, euro Area, Switzerland and Singapore) and overlaid these on the unallocated reserve component.

Using this approach exposed the fact that an extra USD1.25 trillion in EUR reserve holdings is estimated to be in the system during the big US QE period, bringing total central bank EUR reserve holdings to USD2.75 trillion; close to double the IMF-reported USD1.5 trillion figure. Beyond this simple approach, and assuming that an additional 20% of passively received USD receipts (such as those from Norway's energy sector) were diversified into EUR each quarter, it is estimated that 'hidden' EUR reserve holdings rose to USD1.7 trillion, taking the total amount of EUR held by central bank reserve managers to USD3.12 trillion providing a significant source of artificial support for the currency as this process continued. **This all feeds into the euro's status as being a safe-**

haven currency, although not to the degree of either the CHF or the JPY.

This said, whilst it has been possible for the euro to maintain its value up to now, the fact is that the European Central Bank is facing unprecedented problems in the Eurozone: increasing migration, rising political discontent, enduring low growth and ongoing high unemployment in southern members states. It is also short on options in all of these areas, with QE simply allowing the Eurozone to just about hold on and negative rates having been taken as a sign of weakness by the markets. **As a result of all of these factors, dealers are itching to attack the next weak link in the Eurozone chain, in the – perfectly justified – hope that the entire Eurozone will crumble (not from any ideological standpoint, but simply because there is a lot of money to be made when major financial structures are broken up.**

The US

The performance of US assets since the Fed raised rates for the first time since the Global Financial Crisis has led to large losses for many market players, however apparently experienced and skilful, but **an examination of historical trends relating to US rates rises and corollary US assets' trading patterns would have not only avoided these losses but would have led to big profits instead.**

The chart below shows **the path of the USD over the 100 trading days following the first rate increase in each of the Fed's tightening cycles over the past 30 years. On each occasion, the USD fell even though there were additional rate increases during the period.** This attests to the fact that markets always pre-empt a major macroeconomic and/or announcement move by pricing in the expected effect on an asset. The common market phrase of 'buy the rumour, sell the fact' is not quite accurate in this context: it is actually 'do whatever the expected effect is on the rumour and then do the opposite on the fact'.

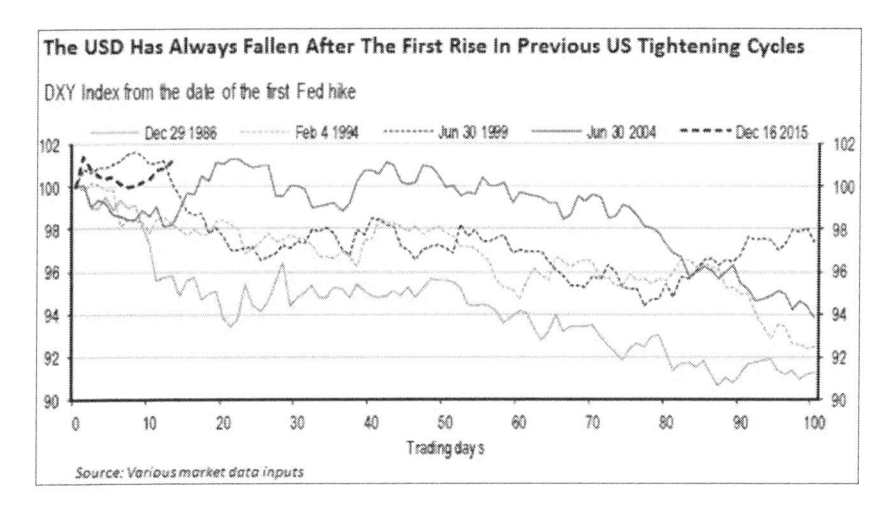

The USD Has Always Fallen After The First Rise In Previous US Tightening Cycles
DXY Index from the date of the first Fed hike

Source: Various market data inputs

So, in the case of the Fed hike, and bearing in mind that money moves to where it is best rewarded for the concomitant risks involved, a US rate hike would be expected to lift the value of the US dollar, of course, but this happened before the hike. **When the hike was announced, the market looked for further reasons to buy the US dollar, as the hike itself had already been priced in.** However, such further reason – principally, the pace of further rate hikes – was not forthcoming, rather Fed Chair Janet Yellen made it clear that all would depend on key macroeconomic figures hitting their marks. Hence, when such figures are good, the US dollar rallies and when they are not it falls.

Indeed, there is **a fragility evident in a number of these key figures that has raised the distinct possibility in the minds of serious traders that they do not just alter expectations of the pace of hikes but actually open the door to the possibility of the tightening cycle ending early, or even being reversed.** Key to these figures are that the US economy continues to grow sufficiently quickly to generate enough internal inflation to offset the disinflation it imports by virtue of a stronger USD, and the big data releases relating to this idea have often been less than convincing.

The potential for even further dramatic reversal in the US dollar's fortunes is even greater as Fed funds futures are already fully priced for further hikes during 2016. Consequently, unless the Fed embarks on a round of rate hikes unprecedented in its history, then there are no good reasons for buying the USD.

Looking at the last nearly 50 years of USD trading patterns and breaking it down into smaller chunks than the 'big picture' chart earlier, it can clearly be seen that apart from two major rallies – the first in the early 1980s when the dollar nearly doubled in value and the second in the mid-1990s when it rose by nearly 50% – the average USD rally has been around the 20% mark and has lasted just under one year. The USD bull run that manifested itself up to the huge reversal just before Christmas 2015 had already exceeded this historic average: since the low in April 2011, the rise had already been just less than 40%, a massive rise in historical terms, much greater than the average seen since the early 1970s.

Emerging And Frontier Markets

Prior to the release of the September US non-farm payrolls on 2 October 2015, emerging markets FX (EMFX) was set for its worst yearly performance against the USD since 2008. Indeed, the scale of the preceding decline had prompted many to compare the situation to that seen in previous EM crises such as the 1994 'Tequila crisis' and the 1997 Asian financial crisis. The bounce-back that occurred after the payrolls can be attributed to a number of factors, all of which remain vital to the fortunes of emerging markets assets. These are: the balance between interest rates across the curve and inflation in the US, the market perception of the new growth paradigm in China and the low level of inflation globally. This latter factor has meant lower core bond yields for longer, which caps debt servicing costs and foreign capital reversals for EM economies. Additionally, EM central banks in this environment do not need to tighten monetary conditions via rate hikes and FX reserve depletion, as they did in the 1990s, but rather can loosen policy as and when necessary to support growth. This section looks at the key drivers for an effective emerging market and the risk/reward factors therein, with a tangential look at frontier market drivers and opportunities.

Basic Convergence Premise

In broad terms, all emerging markets can be regarded as the ultimate convergence trade, as most palpably evidenced perhaps in the way that the valuations of eastern European countries' assets in line for EU-accession gradually began to align (equities up, bond yields down, currencies strengthening) with those of EU countries the nearer to accession they drew. How far off an EM is from having converged into being a DM, of course, can be seen from its credit rating, most palpably, aside from other tangential factors, the parameters of which are outlined in the first section of this book.

Consequently, **all EM trades can be regarded as 'risk-on', whatever the asset class involved. However, within this all-encompassing description, there has been a re-emergence of those EMs that can be regarded as further along the development path than all of the others and thus investable in a more risk-off environment**, as shown in the chart below.

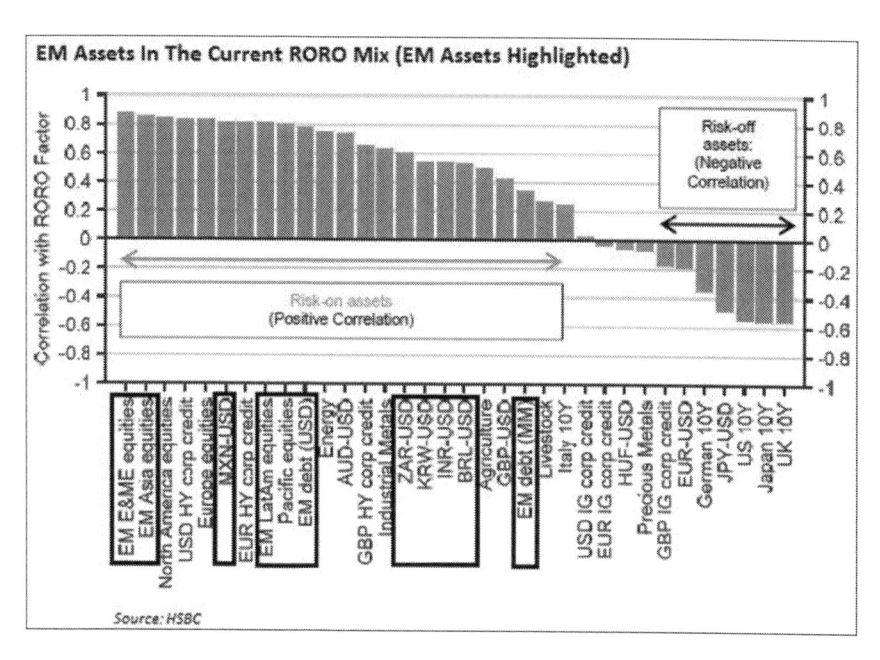

![EM Assets In The Current RORO Mix (EM Assets Highlighted) chart, Source: HSBC]

Prior to 2008, this more investable group was probably best symbolised by the **BRIC** countries, comprised of Brazil, Russia, India and China, which led the way on EM valuations by dint principally of their projected growth paths. These were followed by the **Next-11** (Mexico, Indonesia, South Korea, Turkey, Bangladesh, Egypt, Nigeria, Pakistan, the Philippines, Vietnam and Iran), of which the first four of the grouping had consistently outperformed the remainder, earning the sobriquet of the **'MIST'** countries along the way.

In pure currency trading terms, investment in selected emerging markets can accrue the benefits both of carry compensation in the short-term and of growth prospects supporting real exchange rate appreciation over the longer term. The carry trade element of this is predicated, of course, upon the interplay of two key factors: wide (but stable) interest rate differentials (between the currency being sold to fund a higher-yielding currency) and low currency volatility on the first leg of the trade.

Before the 2008 Crisis, the rolling correlation between returns from a traditional carry basket and returns from the S&P500 fluctuated around zero in developed markets and positive for emerging markets currencies. In the most recent major 'risk-on' environment, though, it is interesting to note that the same rolling correlation for both developed and emerging markets moved into positive territory.

Consequently, it might be said that at that point either the emerging markets' currency carry trade risk has converged to that of the developed markets or, more accurately, that this risk for developed markets' currencies has moved up the risk curve towards a level more associated with an EM currency equivalent. Indeed, holding a carry basket at that point was almost the equivalent of holding a pre-crisis carry basket together with some S&P futures. In this situation, then, attention tends to focus on the underlying fundamentals of EM countries now and on their projections going forward. In fact, as the relative risk perception between DM countries and EM ones began to narrow from around the 1980s investment flows into emerging markets increased from USD25 billion in 1980 to USD1.2 trillion in 2013, and over the past 10 years alone these flows averaged 5-6% of GDP of the recipient countries, up from around 2% in the '80s and 4% in the '90s, before EM weakness as a product of the fallout from the lower growth in China permeated into the EM asset class as a whole.

Even as it stands, though, any gaps in the developed markets' landscape is likely to be filled increasingly over time by the assets of those emerging economies that meet **the basic criteria of an investment destination:**

1. A sustainable fiscal policy
2. A sound balance of payments profile
3. A solid financial and political system

The **additional benefits of EM investment destinations is that more often than not they benefit both from momentum trading and carry trading strategies, given their relatively high interest rates in a broadly zero (or negative) interest rate policy developed markets world.** In this context, it is highly likely that incrementally value-added returns will be accrued from investment in the BRICs, MIST and N-11 countries over time simply as they converge towards developed markets status.

Euro-Convergence Template

Looking at the EU (and, by extension, Eurozone) convergence history is useful in that it provides a real life template of how convergence trading – from EM to DM status – actually occurs. In this respect, all of the countries that used to be part of the Soviet bloc but gained independence as the USSR disbanded saw their currencies gradually strengthen as the time of their accession to the euro grew closer. These were specifically entitled **'euro convergence trades'** and every one of them was an absolute winner.

For example, despite the appalling economic and then social consequences that have befallen Greece since its adoption of the euro in 2001, from the currency trading perspective it was a 'no-brainer' up to its accession. **Prior to joining the euro, there were, roughly, around 250 Greek drachma (GRD) to the US dollar. After it joined the euro project all drachma were replaced by euros, meaning that the rate had gone from 250 to under 1 within a year: a spectacularly profitable trade if the drachma specifically had been sold or drachma-based assets in general. Exactly the same can be seen in the stock markets of those countries that were looking to join the EU.** For example, Hungary's BUX stock exchange progress can be regarded for a long time as a simple convergence trade: first, away from the USSR and towards the West; secondly, from the West towards the EU; and thirdly, from the EU to the euro, as seen below:

Hungary BUX Convergence Trading (15 Years, Monthly)

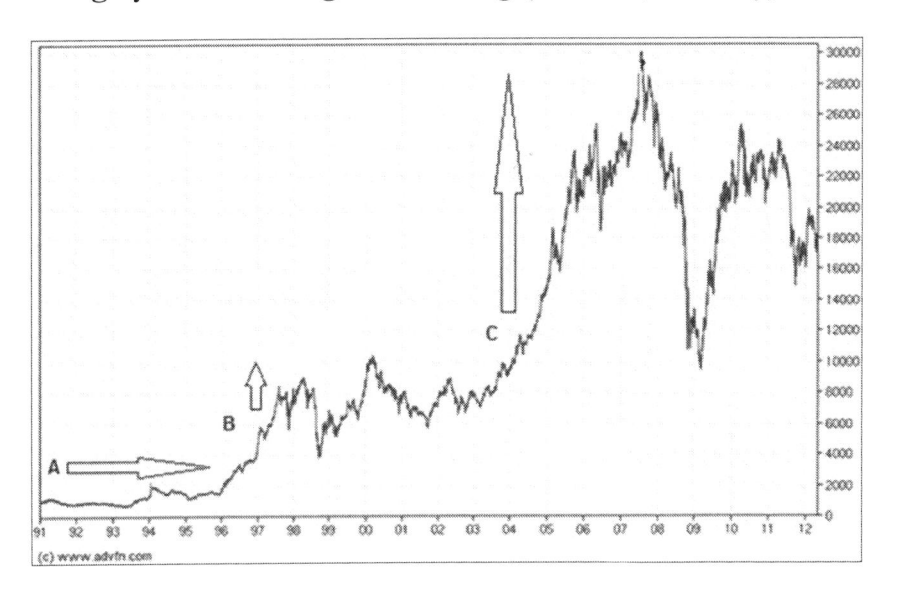

[Key:
A = After the fall of the USSR in 1991, Hungary flatlines for a while before traders start to view it as gradually becoming an EU-grade state
B = Traders are regarding Hungary as an EU state more firmly by the month, as it approaches its official EU accession date of 1 May 2004

C = Traders are now looking for Hungary to replace the forint (HUF) with the euro at some point in the relatively near future]

Convergence-Driven Top-Down Trading

In stock market terms, this approach is **'Top-Down Trading' but with a convergence twist (a positive paradigm shift).** This approach involves looking at the big picture, beginning with the area in which a country is located, then the economic and political dimensions of that country including where it is in the business cycle, then the various sectors of the economy and then the specific details pertaining to a target company including management and key investment numbers and ratios.

A number of the greatest stock investors in history have used this style of trading to outperform all others in the market, but George Soros and his partner Jim Rogers in their early days at Soros Fund Management are as good an example as any. Basically, when they first began, whilst George worked through the minutiae in the numbers on his computer, Jim would tour the world on his motorbike (recalled in his excellent book *'Investment Biker'*) attempting to spot small changes at ground level in countries that were possibly on the cusp of major changes, through seeing tiny changes in general economic behaviour.

Country	IMF	FTSE	MSCI	S&P	Dow Jones
Argentina	✓				
Brazil	✓	✓	✓	✓	✓
Bulgaria	✓				
Chile	✓	✓	✓	✓	✓
People's Republic of China	✓	✓	✓	✓	✓
Colombia	✓	✓	✓	✓	✓
Czech Republic		✓	✓	✓	✓
Egypt		✓	✓	✓	✓
Estonia	✓				
Greece			✓	✓	✓
Hungary	✓	✓	✓	✓	✓
India	✓	✓	✓	✓	✓
Indonesia	✓	✓	✓	✓	✓
Latvia	✓				
Lithuania	✓				
Malaysia	✓	✓	✓	✓	✓
Mexico	✓	✓	✓	✓	✓
Morocco		✓		✓	✓
Pakistan	✓	✓			
Peru	✓	✓	✓	✓	✓
Philippines	✓	✓	✓	✓	✓
Poland	✓	✓	✓	✓	✓
Qatar			✓		✓
Romania	✓				
Russia	✓	✓	✓	✓	✓
South Africa	✓	✓	✓	✓	✓
South Korea			✓		
Taiwan		✓	✓	✓	✓
Thailand	✓	✓	✓	✓	✓
Turkey	✓	✓	✓	✓	✓
Ukraine	✓				
United Arab Emirates		✓	✓		✓
Venezuela	✓				

Source: Various

Typically this might involve Jim stopping off at a cafe in Hungary in the early 1990s and noticing that the locals were suddenly happy to spend a dollar (equivalent) on a cappuccino. In Jim's mind this indicated the following rationale: people have more money to spend on small luxuries following Hungary's departure from the umbrella of the USSR in 1989 – therefore, people are earning more money as a whole – therefore, people are being paid more – therefore, companies are making more money – therefore, their earnings per share ratios will increase – therefore, current stock values will look cheap – therefore, domestic companies will attract more foreign investment – therefore, their corporate transparency will increase – therefore, their share price will continue to go up – therefore, more companies will float on the domestic stock exchange – therefore, more money will enter into the economy – and so on and so forth.

As one can see from the chart above, buying into a nation's changing broad economic architecture – in this case moving from the confines of the Soviet-style system to that of free enterprise and the increased consumerism that this entailed – yielded exceptional results for Soros and Rogers. This example can often be seen in areas that are undergoing such a shift in behavioural paradigm, as the same investment curve can be seen across the board, for example, in every country that broke away from the former Soviet Union. In this respect, this investment story can be seen as the reverse of negative contagion.

In the case of the former Soviet Union itself exactly the same theory applied as well, although with a delayed effect to those of its former satellite states, as a break with centralised state control occurred only later on, under the presidency of Boris Yeltsin which began in December 1991. Indeed, in the 'CE3 countries', the Polish stock market rose 150% in US dollar terms between 2000 and the end of 2005, Hungary by 179% and the Czech Republic by 338% (by contrast, the FTSE Eurofirst 300 index fell 5% in US dollar terms over the same time period).

Czech Republic and Poland Stock Exchanges (1999-2005)

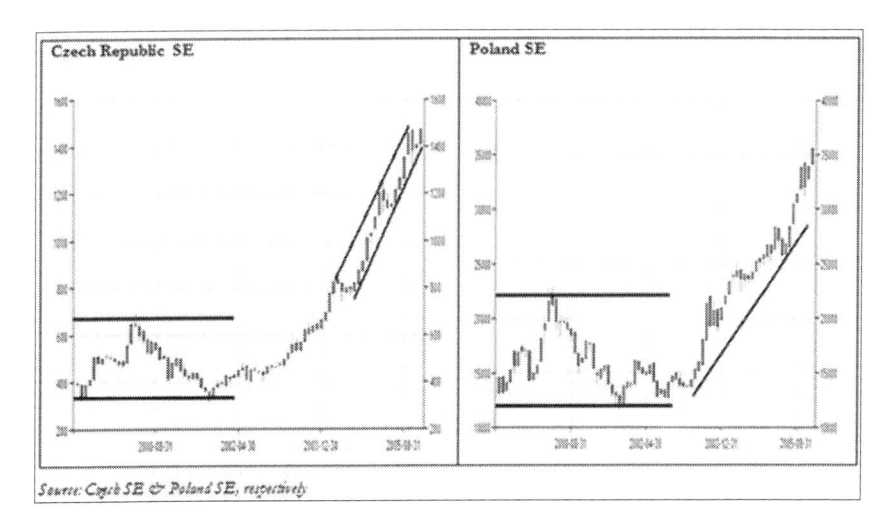

The returns were even greater for the further outliers of eastern Europe, with Ukraine up 833% in US dollar terms over 2000-05, Romania up 757%, Slovakia up 607% and Estonia up 522%.

Ukraine and Romania Stock Exchanges (1999-2005)

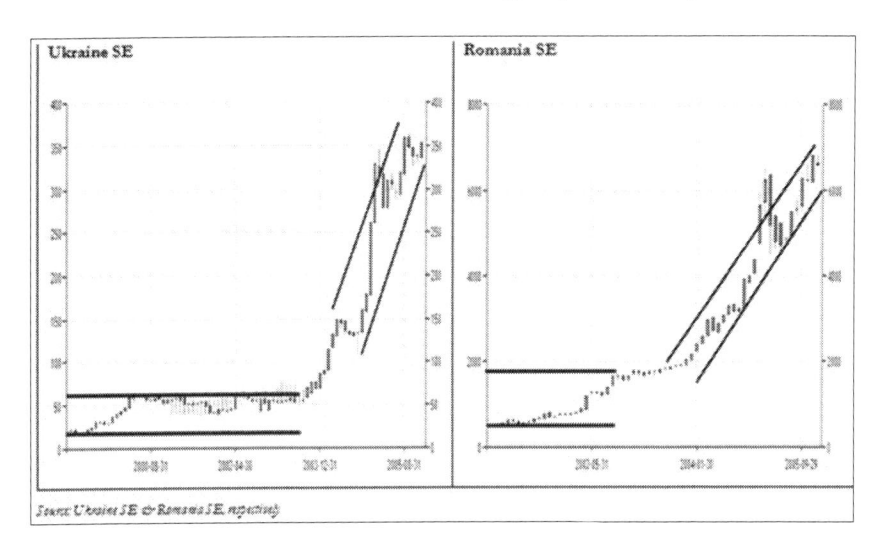

For those top-down investors who had learned the lesson from what happened to stocks (which are, after all, simply investment in companies, which are in turn an investment on the most basic level in a country's prosperity) in the former satellite nations of the USSR then the opportunity for the next phase of investment was obvious.

Russian Stock Exchange (RTS) After Yeltsin Took Power

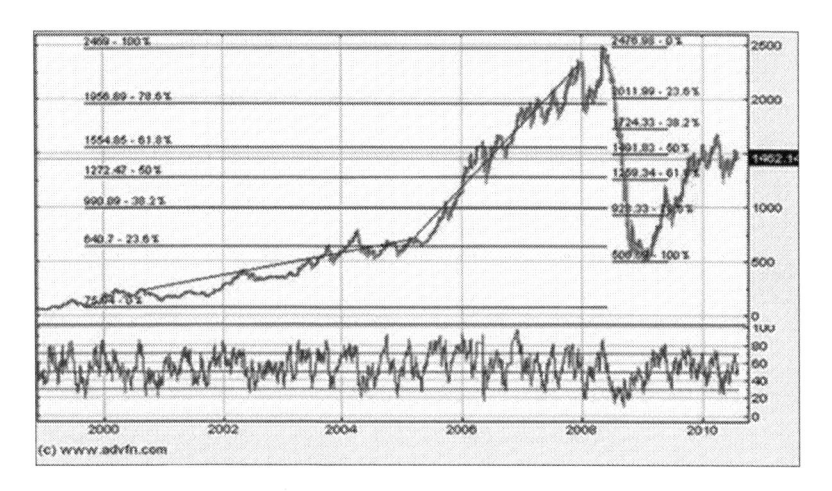

And this type of approach – of convergence from a 'less developed' (emerging) market to a more developed one – is duplicated time and again across all markets and asset classes, and therein lie the real nuggets of value.

Further Convergence Criteria For EM Assets

In addition to the aforementioned basic investment criteria for countries to be considered top-flight candidates for the transition from EM to DM status, **in order to achieve a genuine leap into the big league of truly international currencies, EM currencies need:**

1. **To have increasingly evident economic clout**
2. **To be used as an international reserve asset**
3. **To be utilised as a tool in invoicing and the settlement of international transactions**
4. **To be regarded as objects of speculative desire in FX volume trading (and therefore to possess FX regimes favourable to such free capital flows)**

On Point 1, in terms of **economic growth and corollary trade flows alone**, to begin with, **EM currencies should theoretically come to dominate the global FX landscape within a very short period.** By 2030, for example, the USD-valued economy of China will have overtaken that of the US for the number one spot, according to various major finance houses, whose views are in line with those of the IMF.

By 2050, and maybe before, the Asian Tiger will have almost double the GDP of the States (in theory), with India ranked third, Brazil fourth, Mexico fifth, Russia sixth, Indonesia seventh; South Korea and Turkey will be thirteenth and fourteenth respectively. Indeed, already emerging market countries account for nearly half of global output, up from just over a quarter in 1971.

For Point 2, **size is not everything, it is what you do with it that counts;** more specifically, if you cannot trade it, it is not moving anywhere. **In some EM currency cases, stringent capital controls and fixed or highly managed FX regimes have led to a marked disconnect between trade flows and currency usage.**

In the case of the **long-vaunted BRICs** (Brazil, Russia, India, China), for example, although India and South Korea **notionally have free-floating exchange rates, in practice they are carefully managed by their central banks.** In **Russia's case**, from 2000 to its financial crisis in 2008 a currency board system prevailed, with the rouble pegged to a basket (55% USD and the remainder EUR), with all changes in liquidity coming from the Central Bank of Russia's (CBR) sales and purchases of foreign currency.

Additionally, during the height of the Ukraine crisis, the central bank policy allowed the currency a great degree of flexibility to float within a corridor against its target dollar-euro basket, and the central bank stated that it would set the amount of market interventions it took to shift the trading band on a daily basis, giving officials more flexibility in determining how many dollars it sold at a given price level before weakening the rouble's trading band. This was a major advantage for the rouble.

In **the case of China itself, the opportunity for any speculative gains remained highly limited for a very long period:** the central bank only widened the trading band for the RMB to 1% either side of a central rate of USDRMB6.8300 in April 2012, from the previous 0.5% variance, and then widened it out to a 2% variance in March 2014. **This situation continues to change, though.**

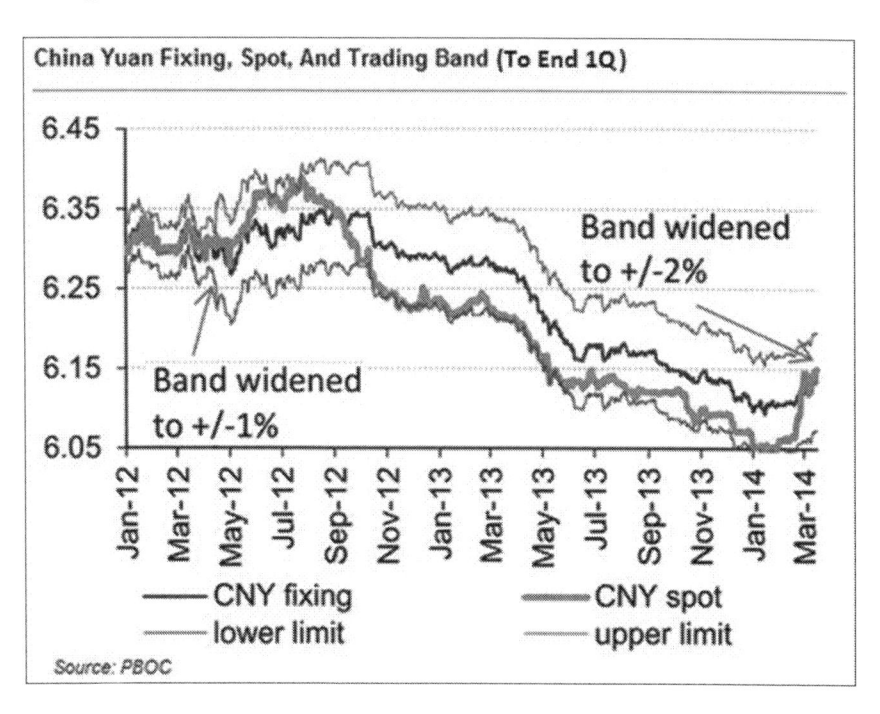

China Yuan Fixing, Spot, And Trading Band (To End 1Q)

[Chart showing CNY fixing, CNY spot, lower limit, and upper limit from Jan-12 to Mar-14, with annotations "Band widened to +/-1%" and "Band widened to +/-2%"]

Source: PBOC

Regarding Point 3, usage in international settlements and transactions, in 2010 Russia's then first deputy prime minister, Igor Shuvalov, said that a currency union between Russia, Belarus and Kazakhstan might be formed as a 'logical extension' to the introduction of the customs union between the three nations that came into effect on 1 January of that year. With an aggregated population of around 180 million people and accounting for about 83% of the GDP of the former USSR, the final hurdle for these three countries' planned formation of a single economic market by the end of 2012 would certainly be freedom of capital movement and the use of a common currency. This idea was augmented by that of then Finance Minister, Alexei Kudrin, that the country was examining ways to sell its oil in roubles and that agreements in principle were struck in 2009 to allow trade between Russia, Belarus and China to be conducted in roubles and Chinese renminbi.

In China as well, **renminbi trade settlement took off after a small pilot RMB trade settlement scheme was introduced in July 2009, to the extent that total trade settled in RMB had increased four-fold by the end of 2011 to reach RMB2.1 trillion (USD330 billion), about 9% of China's total trade in that year**. 2012 saw cross-border RMB trade settlement total RMB 2.94 trillion, about 12% of China's total trade.

Moreover, as early as November 2009 China had established RMB650 billion in currency swaps to help importers in Argentina, Belarus, Hong Kong, Indonesia, Malaysia and South Korea, avoid having to pay in US dollars for Chinese goods (these **bilateral currency swaps now total around RMB2 trillion**), whilst recently it allowed all firms in the country to pay for imports and exports in RMB.

Whilst the RMB was convertible under the current account for 15 years, recent steps have been taken to make it more convertible through the gradual liberalisation of the capital account, and **these moves to permit greater investment into real estate, stocks and bonds are set to gather in pace.** Building out the capital markets' temporal curve is also a prerequisite for RMB convertibility, and the keys to this will be more government and corporate bond issues across a range of maturities. Quite aside from anything else, this type of financing, rather than simply state-directed funding via the troubled state owned enterprise (SOE) vehicles, will produce the type of sustained and healthy high-quality efficient growth that the Chinese government now wants to replace the previous 'throw cash at everything' type of growth that traditionally creates asset price bubbles.

Key Opportunity And Risk Factors For EM Assets Now

The US

One of the two major concerns that caused the big sell-off in EM assets in 2015, as mentioned at the beginning of this section, was the fear that the US would raise rates before solid economic growth had established itself (prior to the NFP figures in October, in fact, there were signs that growth was slacking). By the end of Q1 of 2016, though, the expected pace of hikes from the Fed had been pushed back significantly, so concerns about the cost of capital rising sharply and hurting EMFX have become less acute. Moreover, even if the Fed does hike sooner and steeper than is currently expected then it would at least appear to be doing so in a more positive economic environment as US data has started to turn upwards relative to expectations.

US Data More Positive Than Expected

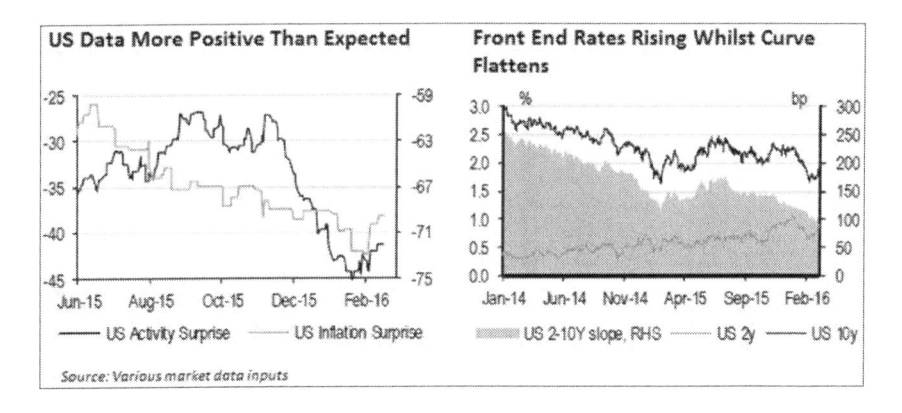

Front End Rates Rising Whilst Curve Flattens

Source: Various market data inputs

Crucially as well this improved growth is so far occurring without pushing inflation markedly higher, indeed it is low by any markers, implying that front end rates may keep rising as data supports near-term rate hikes, but back end rates may remain low due to few longer run inflation concerns. Therefore, EM assets can benefit from low long-term funding costs whilst also gaining from the support to global growth being given by the US economy.

China

Given the significant share that China's exports play in the trade mix of Asian and other EM economies as a whole, slowing growth in the country has been an ongoing concern for the region's markets. Having said that, although the years of double-digit economic growth look permanently over for China, there seems more acceptance in the markets that a China growing anywhere near the 6.5-7.0% outlined at the 2016 National People's Congress – as well as expectations of further easing, both fiscal and monetary – is a perfectly healthy outlook and does not constitute the 'hard landing' feared.

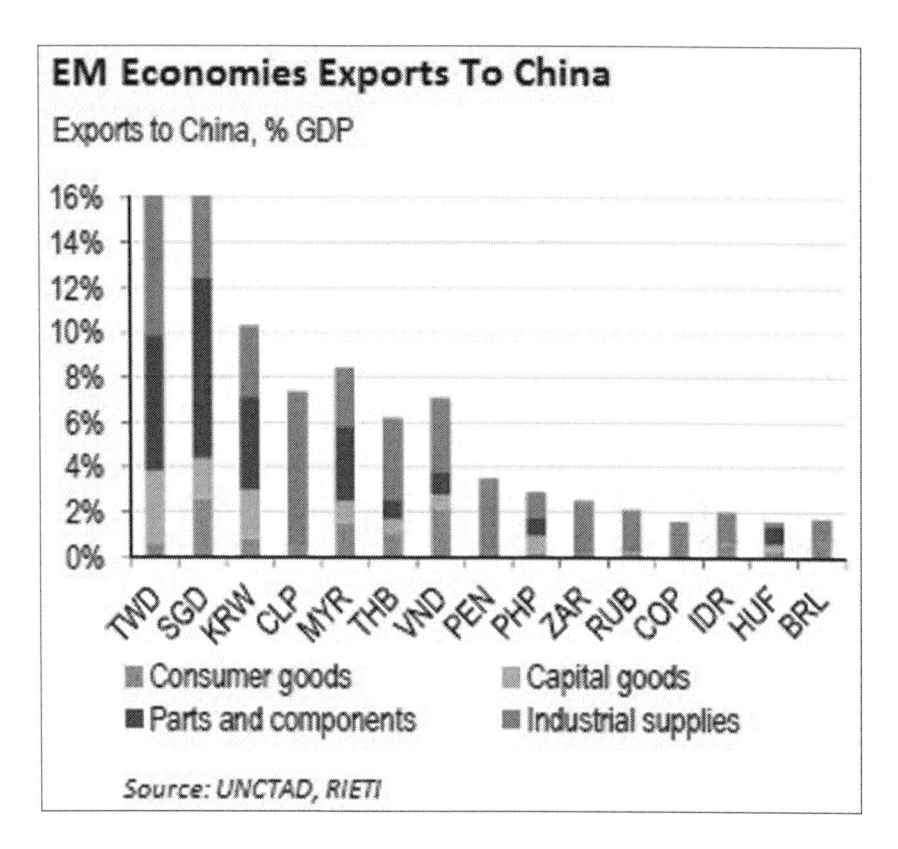

EM Economies Exports To China
Exports to China, % GDP

[Bar chart showing exports to China as % of GDP for: TWD, SGD, KRW, CLP, MYR, THB, VND, PEN, PHP, ZAR, RUB, COP, IDR, HUF, BRL, broken down by Consumer goods, Capital goods, Parts and components, and Industrial supplies]

Source: UNCTAD, RIETI

The renminbi currency has also been more stable into Q2, after an initial two week sharp depreciation at the beginning of 2016, and the narrowing of the spread between the offshore CNH and the onshore CNY FX rates suggests that speculative depreciation pressures on the RMB have waned for the time being. Although this may well come back into play, there is increasing evidence that it will not be taken necessarily as a sign of a much deeper and broader malaise, in and of itself. In any event, **there are signs that there is increasing differentiation between the fate of the renminbi and that of other Asian and EM currencies, as shown in the chart below.**

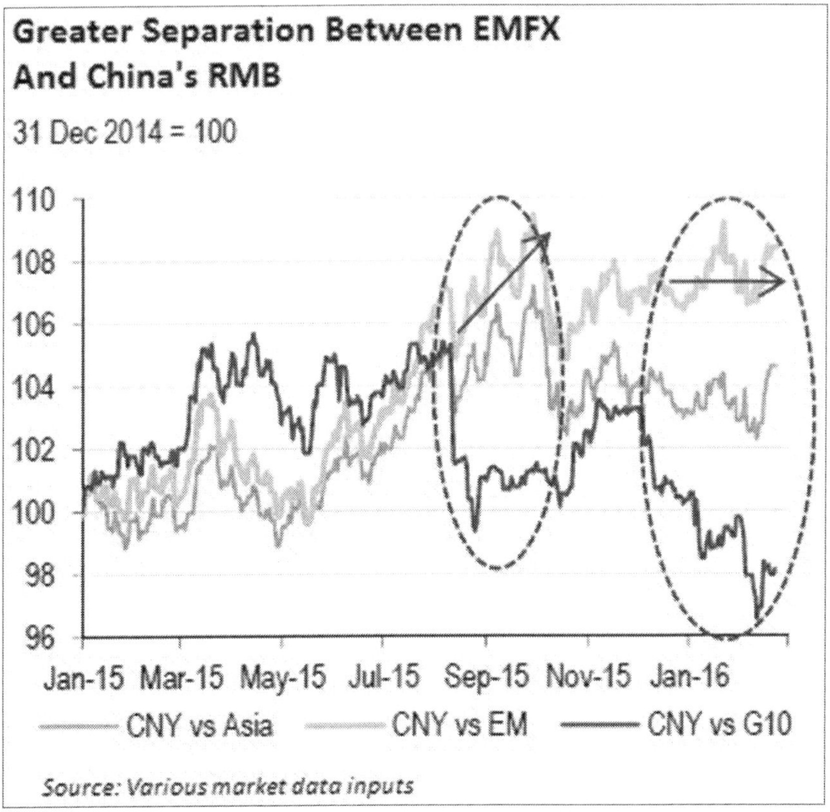
Greater Separation Between EMFX
And China's RMB
31 Dec 2014 = 100
110
108
106
104
102
100
98
96
Jan-15 Mar-15 May-15 Jul-15 Sep-15 Nov-15 Jan-16
CNY vs Asia
CNY vs EM
CNY vs G10
Source: Various market data inputs

Frontier To Emerging Market Can Offer Alpha Returns

Emerging To Developed Market Progress Is Rarer Than Thought

Having said all of this, the assumption that is still prevalent amongst global investors of all degrees of talent and experience – that an emerging market equity indices value will eventually converge into those of developed market ones – has not in fact been borne out historically, although from the pragmatic trading standpoint it is important to know the fact that the investment community largely believes the idea. **It is worth noting that it remains the case that just five of the 38 countries with stock markets in 1900 have moved from emerging to developed market status to date.** Of the rest, 17 were and are developed, 14 were and are classified as middle-income emerging and those with developed markets in 1900 still dominate the equity landscape, comprising 84% of the MSCI All World Index.

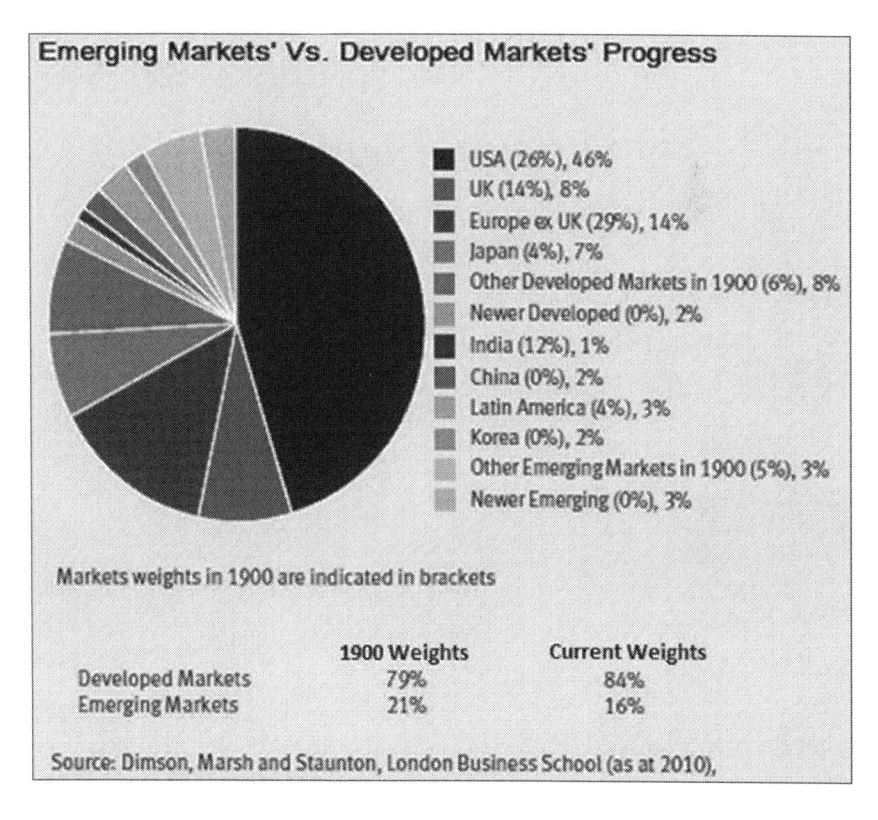

Emerging Markets' Vs. Developed Markets' Progress

- USA (26%), 46%
- UK (14%), 8%
- Europe ex UK (29%), 14%
- Japan (4%), 7%
- Other Developed Markets in 1900 (6%), 8%
- Newer Developed (0%), 2%
- India (12%), 1%
- China (0%), 2%
- Latin America (4%), 3%
- Korea (0%), 2%
- Other Emerging Markets in 1900 (5%), 3%
- Newer Emerging (0%), 3%

Markets weights in 1900 are indicated in brackets

	1900 Weights	Current Weights
Developed Markets	79%	84%
Emerging Markets	21%	16%

Source: Dimson, Marsh and Staunton, London Business School (as at 2010).

Moreover, academic research into the 'middle income trap', which assesses the likelihood of an economy progressing to DM status, suggests that the distribution of income also matters. **In this respect, the studies suggest that the more equal the distribution is (that is, the lower the GINI coefficient), the more likely a country is to move up from one level to another.** Other factors that influence development outcomes include the soundness of a country's institutions, progress on structural reforms and sustaining superior growth rates over the decades it would take for income levels to converge with those of developed markets. In this context, in aggregate, **the emerging markets did particularly well during the boom years of 2003-2007, rising from 20% to 34% of global GDP and from 4% to 10% of global equity markets but subsequently, after an initial bounce in 2009, there has been little progress overall.**

Emerging Markets' Progress

GNI per Capita (USD)		GINI coefficient		Sovereign Credit Rating	
Singapore	High Income	Hungary	Less than 40	Hong Kong	Investment Grade
Ireland		South Korea		Ireland	
Hong Kong		Greece		Israel	
Israel		Ireland		Singapore	
Greece		Poland		South Korea	
South Korea		India		Poland	
Hungary		Indonesia		Brazil	
Poland		Israel		China	
Russia	Upper Middle Income	Turkey	Greater than 40	India	
Brazil		Russia		Malaysia	
Turkey		Malaysia		Mexico	
Mexico		Singapore		Russia	
Malaysia		China		South Africa	
South Africa		Mexico		Greece	
China		Brazil		Hungary	Junk
Indonesia	Lower Middle Income	Hong Kong		Indonesia	
India		South Africa		Turkey	

Source: World Bank, CIA World Factbook, Standard & Poor's

For a country to continue to enjoy enduring appeal to international investors – which creates a push effect on it achieving DM status over time (historically, markets tend to underperform the EM benchmark in the 12 months after an upgrade, for the reason mentioned earlier) – there needs to be a sea-change in the type of stocks available in which to invest. In this respect, entities that tend to list first and dominate domestic emerging market indices include former state-owned enterprises, resource companies and financials, which might not represent the more dynamic elements of the economy.

Nonetheless, as mentioned often before, **the truth does not actually matter that much in investment terms: it's the perception of reality that counts.**

Spotting Paradigmatic Shifts In Frontier Markets Is The Real Key To Big Profits

There are two types of frontier markets. First are those that are to all intents and purposes emerging markets anyhow, but require minor tweaks to regulation, transparency and systems in order to be awarded official inclusion in one of the key emerging markets indices that are used as a benchmark for global investment by many fund managers, especially real money funds (pension and insurance funds, for example). Second are those that – for one reason or another – are about to see a fundamentally positive shift in their economy that will transform it completely into a much bigger proposition. Making any meaningful short-term returns on the first group is predicated on getting in very early ahead of the date announced for formal inclusion into one of these major EM benchmark indices, as after it has actually been included there is normally a long sell-off over time. **For the second group of countries, either the Soros/Rogers approach is required, as outlined earlier, or there needs to be a major leap of faith (based on sound logic) that something of seismic significance is about to happen to a country.**

In recent months, Saudi Arabia is a prime example of the first category, and this is analysed in depth earlier in the book, whilst Iran is a prime example of the latter. With its enormous oil and gas reserves (see earlier), Iran was long a giant of the global hydrocarbons industry, but one which had been put to sleep effectively by various sanctions that stretched back to 1979 when they were first imposed by the US following the seizing of US hostages in the US Embassy in Tehran. If a trader had been looking at all markets, as all traders should, as this series of books has always stressed, then he would have noticed from 2015 that moves were afoot to roll these sanctions back.

As the holder of the world's fourth-largest proven crude oil reserves and its second-largest natural gas reserves, the promise of hydrocarbons' riches had long been tantalisingly close to being realised by Iran, with only ongoing sanctions standing in the way. Having said that, as the original expiration date (20 July 2015) for the United Nations' P5+1 limitation to an average of 1 million barrels per day (bpd) of Iran's exports drew near, speculation rose that such sanctions may be relaxed further by various countries, if not dropped entirely, before the newly extended 1 million bpd limit expired six months later.

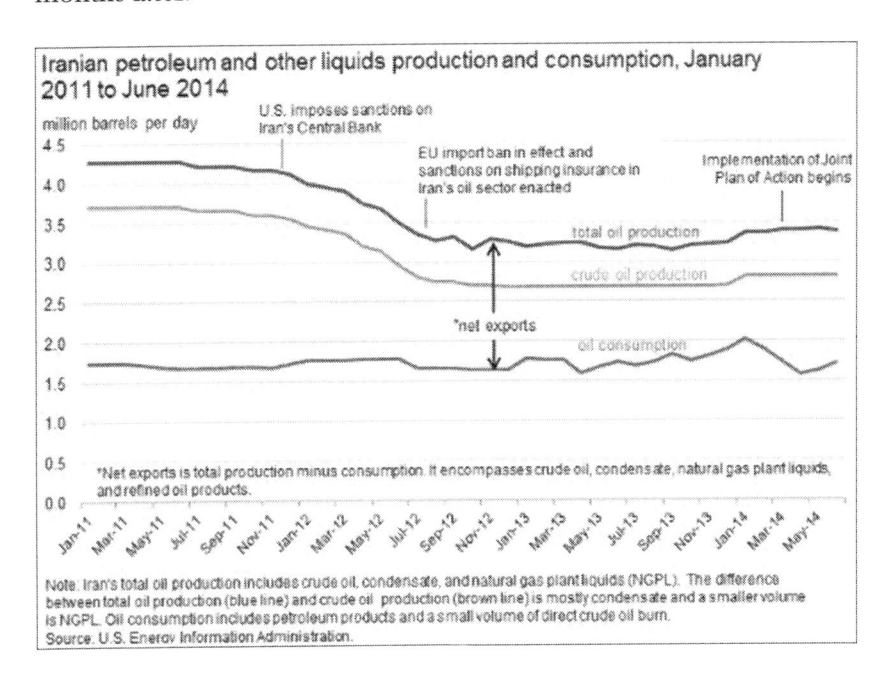

Iranian petroleum and other liquids production and consumption, January 2011 to June 2014

The key sea-change in this regard, that should have been noticed, came in the shape of revelations by Edward Snowden that Germany was extensively spied on by US intelligence agencies, which led to a complete breakdown of trust on the German side and with that an increasing unwillingness to simply toe the US line on all major geopolitical decisions. Indeed, a prime example of this new-found German independence from US global policies was the widely-reported deal struck personally between German Chancellor Angela Merkel and Russia President Vladimir Putin. This envisaged Moscow's annexation of Crimea officially being recognised in exchange for a USD1billion compensation package for the Ukraine government (for rent it used to pay for basing its navy at the port of Sevastopol), plus an agreement from Putin not to interfere with Ukraine's new trade relations with the EU and to offer Kiev a long-term contract for future gas supplies with Russian hydrocarbons behemoth, Gazprom, in addition to the EU withdrawing its support for rebels fighting in eastern Ukraine.

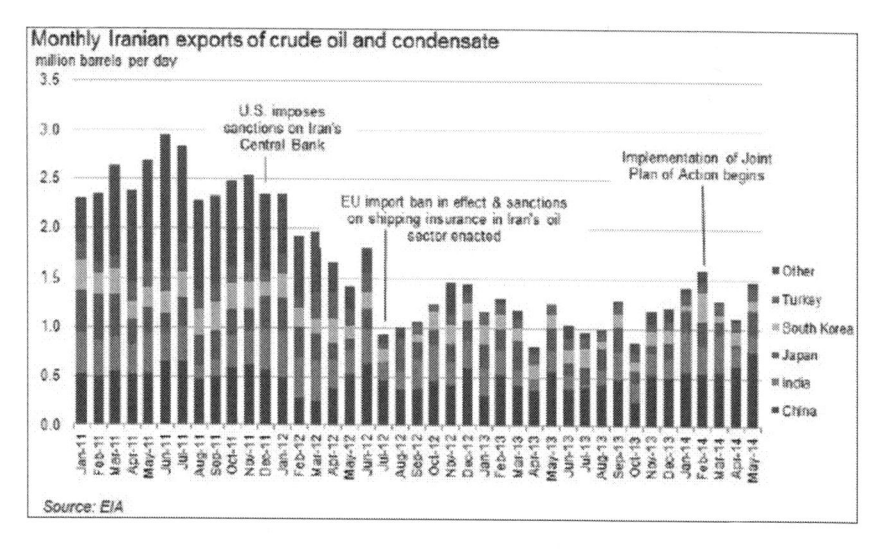

Although this deal was put on hold due to the shooting down of the Malaysian airliner MH17 over east Ukraine, supposedly by Russian-backed rebels, the Merkel-sponsored initiative still remained on the table, according to sources on both sides. It is hardly surprising that Merkel was so infuriated by the US spying on every level of the German government, given that she was brought up in the former East Germany, in which spying, even by those one trusted, was endemic. As an adjunct to this, and to Germany's energy needs (35% of its gas is imported from Russia) and to its export markets (Germany sold about EUR36 billion – USD48 billion – of goods to Russia last year, and some 6,200 German firms are active there with EUR20 billion of investment), **Merkel had no interest anymore in automatically aligning itself with the US if it entailed either damaging its relationship with Russia, or with any of its geopolitical allies, which, of course, includes its number one power proxy in the Middle East, Iran. As such, Germany led the move in the EU towards abandoning all of the sanctions against Iran.**

Although at time of writing some USD-centric sanctions remain in place, these are likely to be removed soon enough, but in the interim, Iran offers huge opportunities as it seeks to build out both is bond and stock markets, despite its not being a well-established emerging market. In the case of the former, which feeds into and from the latter, shortly after the statement that sanctions would be lifted Iran made a low-key, and largely overlooked, announcement that it is to issue IRR50 trillion (USD1.7 billion) in local currency-denominated bonds in that Iranian calendar year (ending in March 2016). However, it was not that the proceeds of the issue were to be primarily used to help fund enhanced recovery and preservation projects with focus on the giant South Pars gas field that should have been of interest to global financial market players. Rather, it is what the issue itself signalled about Iran's plans on how to finance its overall development once sanctions had been removed that should have been seen as momentous. This type of good-sized local currency issuance is precisely what countries do when they are looking to re-enter the global sovereign bond market after a notable absence. It allows them to gauge the buzz that is generated once the news is fully absorbed by potential global investors and also to get the engine of its capital markets infrastructure back into gear.

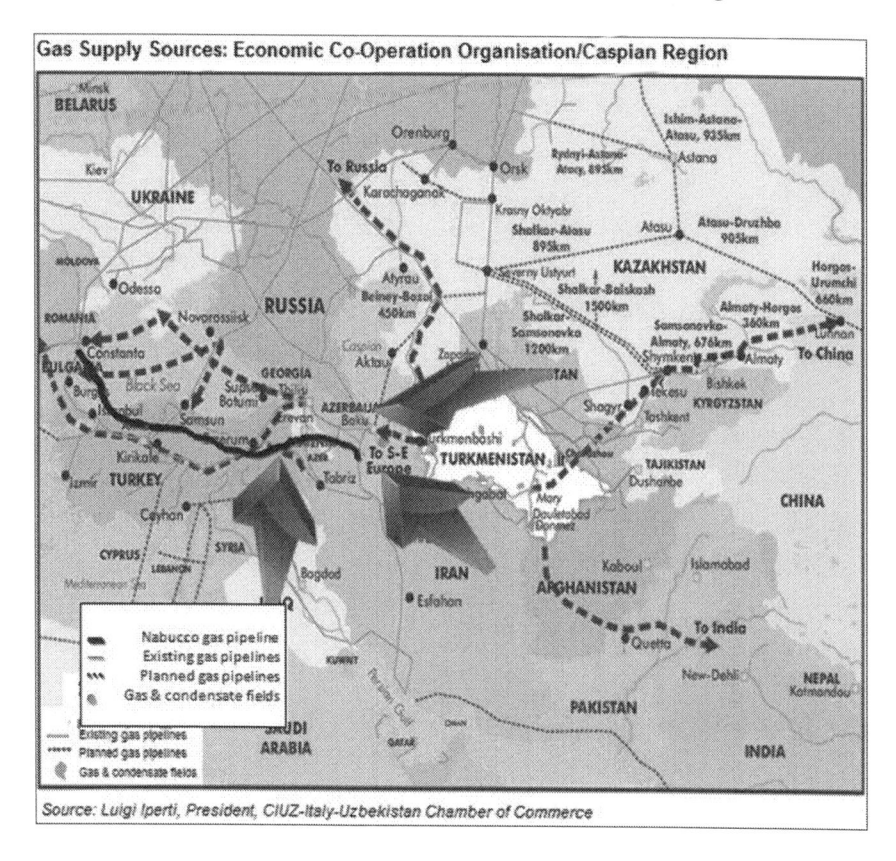

Gas Supply Sources: Economic Co-Operation Organisation/Caspian Region

Source: Luigi Iperti, President, CIUZ-Italy-Uzbekistan Chamber of Commerce

In fact, ever since the realisation grew in Tehran's corridors of power that, with the new Western-friendly President Hassan Rouhani in place, the West's longstanding sanctions against Iran over its nuclear programme may soon be removed, plans to resuscitate Iran's capital markets moved quickly. **The key catalyst for Iran was when Rouhani received that first phone call from US President Barack Obama on 27 September 2013, the first time that a US leader had spoken with an Iranian president since the Islamic Revolution threw out the US-backed Shah in 1979.** From that point onwards, Iran was gearing up to ensure that it returned to the global oil and gas markets at good capacity, generating working cashflow from boosting its petrochemicals output and working out how to broaden and deepen its capital markets in order to ensure that there is a big pool of private finance available to realise all of its plans over time. With targets of increasing crude oil production to at least 3 mbpd by the end of March 2016 and then to 5.7 mbpd by 2018, natural gas production up to 1 billion cubic metres per day by 2018, and annual petrochemical production to 180 million tons by the end of 2022, **it is estimated that Iran will require between USD150 billion to USD550 billion in new capital to achieve these (the amount varying according to timeframes for completing key projects).**

Given this, investing in local currency bonds issued by either of the big state hydrocarbons firms – the National Iranian Oil Company (NIOC) or the National Iranian Gas Company (NIGC), with the implicit government guarantee that the paper would carry – was likely to appeal both to those international oil companies (IOCs) who are eyeing bigger, direct investment into Iran's oil and gas fields and to those who want to take a more limited risk exposure to Iran in the early days of its post-sanctions recovery. Getting involved early on, as well, in whatever size, would also allow firms to judge how efficiently the resultant bond funds were utilised by the government towards their original intended purpose – or whether they would wind up being frittered away on a range of non-oil and gas projects, as happened with Venezuela's PDVSA – and, at least as important, would afford participating firms preferred bidding status for future offers, be they local currency- or foreign currency-denominated.

World's Largest Proved Reserve Holders Of Crude Oil, Current (billion barrels)

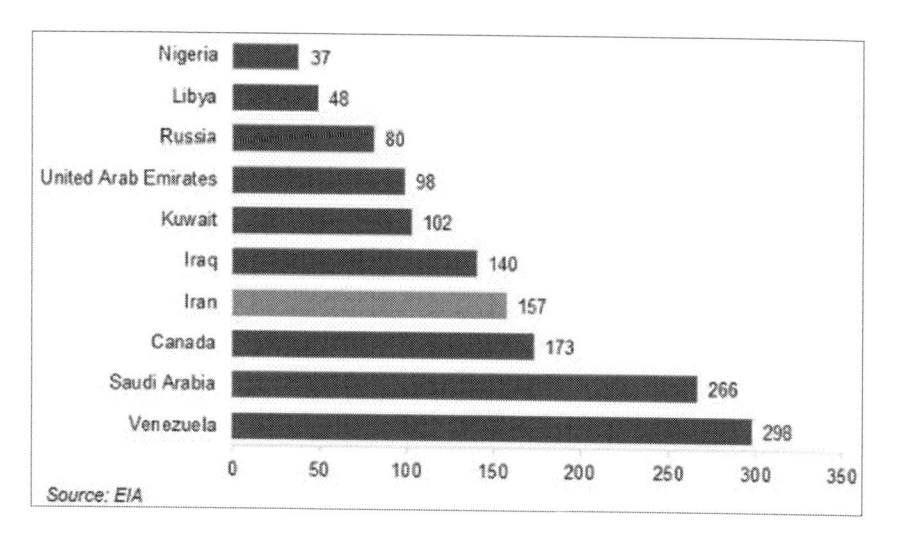

Nigeria	37
Libya	48
Russia	80
United Arab Emirates	98
Kuwait	102
Iraq	140
Iran	157
Canada	173
Saudi Arabia	266
Venezuela	298

Source: EIA

Given Iran's lack of a sovereign debt credit rating over the past few years, it might have seemed that the chances of it launching any successful bond issues would be slim at best, but the Iranians have been working on three strategies to ensure that any such landmark issues would meet with extraordinary investor demand, initially from the Far East and then from the major EU countries. The first of these is to ensure that for issues denominated in rials the return is guaranteed at a suitably high coupon rate, over and above that which might be expected to be offered from a B/B+ rated sovereign (which Iran was just prior to its ratings being removed due to sanctions).

Strategy two is the issuing of bonds, also in rials, but – crucially for potential foreign buyers – carrying with them the option not only to be redeemed in rials but in any major currency (US dollars, euros, Japanese yen, British sterling and Swiss francs) that a buyer prefers at the prevailing spot rate of the day the buyer decides to redeem the paper. Finally, and perhaps even more astonishing than the multiple currency option idea, not only that one of the currencies on offer for redemption will be the Chinese renminbi, but also that several major international bond issues are planned by Iran, with the Peoples Bank of China (PBOC) in Beijing acting as sole lead underwriter and principal distributor of the bonds. The structure will be that the Iranian government, or state vehicle, will issue a bond through the PBOC, which will be backed by the Chinese central bank, either in renminbi or another currency pegged at a specific rate to the renminbi, and the PBOC will then distribute them simultaneously to the Central Bank of the Republic of China (Taiwan) in Taipei and the Monetary Authority of Macao.

On the one hand, the risk for the Chinese in this structure will be minimal, as all of the international sovereign issues will be backed fundamentally by some of the world's largest hydrocarbons reserves, while, on the other hand, the upside is huge, as it will promote the use of the renminbi as one of the world's truly international currencies, which China regards as befitting its standing on the world stage. For expected big investor Russia there would be multiple benefits. For a start, it is already heavily involved in Iran's oil and gas fields anyway so it knows the underlying assets are excellent. Second, it has massive renminbi-based receipts and obligations that relate to its ongoing gas supply deal to Beijing (Russia is paid for supplied gas in renminbi, which it could then use to buy renminbi-denominated bonds to secure stakes in its key target of Iran's oil and gas assets). Finally it would remove more of Russia's balance sheet away from US dollars and euros, which are subject to sanctions.

The point here is that these types of announcements are critical in spotting such paradigmatic changes in a country way before they happen. Then, there is the question of how to invest. In Iran's case, the easy way is through the stock market. **Extremely positive as well in this regard is that, on demographics alone,** the investment fundamentals of Iran are at least as attractive as any emerging market in the world, with **a population of around 80 million – about the same as former premier investor darling Turkey until IS-related security issues emerged last year – and more than any of the long-running investment favourites in**

Eastern Europe (and around three times that of Saudi Arabia). Iran also has a large middle class, easily comparable to both Turkey and Saudi, with an 88% overall literacy rate comparable to the 95% each in Turkey and Saudi, and total internet usership of 15% in between the two neighbours. Basically, Iran has everything Turkey had when it was top of all global emerging markets investor lists before the security troubles kicked in, but with the added bonus of having 10% of the world's oil reserves and nearly 20% of its gas reserves to boot.

Moreover, despite – or because of – hydrocarbons-related sanctions, **Iran's economy has been forced into becoming significantly more diversified than any of its Middle East neighbours.** Indeed, Iran's GDP of USD440 billion or so is the 27th largest in the world, on the same scale as much-vaunted emerging markets of Argentina, Taiwan and Thailand, and ahead of developed EU Western power, Austria. **It may surprise a lot of people how diversified Iran's economy actually is, but in reality it exports in every single category of the IMF's 'breakdown of exports' list bar none, including – by the way – alcohol, albeit for industrial use, and it is absolutely the case that no other country in the Middle East has such a diversified economy as Iran.** Additionally, it will benefit enormously from its prime geographical location, sandwiched between the 500 million population of the EU trading bloc and the ongoing booming markets of Asia as well. Geopolitically as well, the Republic already enjoys very close political and business relationships with China and Russia, with sanctions lifting having completed the set in adding the EU and the US (aside from some ongoing financial sanctions) to the mix of its global power partnerships.

Brent Oil Prices Required To Meet Various Fiscal Sustainability Thresholds (US$/bbl)

	GS primary deficit breakeven (2015 production)	Debt / GDP	Price needed to keep Debt/GDP constant After 1 year	After 2 years	Price needed to reach 40% Debt/GDP ratio in 3 years	Reserves / Public Debt
Kuwait	$60	11%	$63	$69	$64	102.2
UAE	$64	12%	$71	$86	$38	17.0
Qatar	$68	35%	$71	$80	$77	3.0
Saudi	$83	3%	$85	$88	$79	35.8
Russia	$101	10%	$104	$108	$92	2.9
Algeria	$106	9%	$108	$109	$92	14.1
Angola	$117	39%	$128	$145	$142	1.9
Iraq	$126	31%	$131	$136	$133	1.3
Iran	$133	11%	$139	$141	$98	3.3
Nigeria	$144	10%	$158	$182	$129	6.6
Libya	$185	5%	$204	$230	$180	

*Reserves include SWF where applicable. Total production includes crude, NGLs and nonconventional oils.
Source: IEA, IMF, World Bank, African Development Bank, Goldman Sachs*

From a technical markets' perspective, Tehran Stock Exchange is also at a number of advantages both to many emerging markets' bourses in general and to those of the Middle East in particular. Crucially for global investors in light of the subconscious jitteriness left over from the global financial markets rout after the 2007/08 Global Financial Crisis, the level of market volatility for Tehran's exchange is likely to remain considerably more moderate than investors in emerging markets might usually expect. In this respect, many emerging market bourses are characterised by having a heavy presence of small investors, and these tend to chop in and out of the market often and quickly and get spooked very easily, which leads to wild market moves – just as was seen in China's stock markets in 1Q2016, but Iran has a completely different investor base.

The key to building this less volatile investor base lay in the way Iran went about its privatisation process, targeting this towards two principal types of target investors: the pension funds of civil servants and the military, and 'Justice shares' to be held by major domestic funds that could then be distributed amongst the wider population, as a means to make them feel personally invested in the country's economic future. The pension funds, as mentioned, are very long-term investors, as they tend to be anywhere in the world and will hold onto stocks through thick and thin for ten, twenty, thirty years, and the funds that hold the 'Justice shares' are beholden to keep them for the people for the duration so, again unlike the indigenous participants in many emerging market bourses, Iran's core investor base is in it for the long term, which means very limited volatility.

Finally, the infrastructure for Iran's bourse is already in place to accommodate much greater expansion. The Tehran Stock Exchange already has a daily turnover of around USD100 million and a wide range of companies in different sectors constituting a market capitalisation of around USD100 billion on an average price to earnings ratio of only around 5 or 6 times. With the price to earnings ratio being the key metric highlighting investor activity on speculation as to future gains, in itself a function of the weight of opportunity for a company to increase its earnings going forward, it can be expected that the Tehran Stock Exchange's P/E ratio, and its total market capitalisation, will increase exponentially in the coming months.

Technical Analysis

Candlesticks

For those readers who bought my previous three books – *Everything You Need To Know About Making Serious Money Trading The Financial Markets, How To Make Big Money Trading In All Financial Conditions* and *The Great Oil Price Fixes And How To Trade Them* – you may wish to skip this section as it is largely a reiteration of what can be found in those books, unless you have been losing money, in which case it would probably bear reading again. **The reason why Technical Analysis appears in all of the books is that without fully understanding it any meaningful risk management cannot be achieved, and this is the fundamental reason why retail traders go bust.**

Many traders believe that, in and of itself, Technical Analysis reveals certain key truths about how the markets have worked in the past, work currently and will work in the future. More specifically, these traders believe that by looking at how markets have performed in the past their future performance can be predicted, in that key patterns from the past will recur and inform market movements going forward. Having worked as a trader and salesman at major investment banks, I do not subscribe to this view, except in so far as, because so many people do believe in Technical Analysis, it often becomes a self-fulfilling prophecy. This is even truer now in the age of automated trading when the programs involved use key support and resistance levels to execute massive sell or buy orders, thus triggering other stop loss orders centred around these levels. So, whilst economic fundamentals, political shocks, moves in bonds, equities and commodities, general trading tricks, psychology and plain old rumours are essential to predicting market movements, it is also essential now to know everything one can about Technical Analysis, simply because everyone else looks at it too.

Key to Technical Analysis is the **candlestick method of charting. This is particularly useful as it not only shows simply whether the market has largely bought the base currency** (typically shown in green or white) or sold it (typically shown in red or black) but also how strong these buys or sells were (indicated by the length of the lines above each candle, 'wick', for buying or below, 'shadow', for selling).

Candlestick Structure

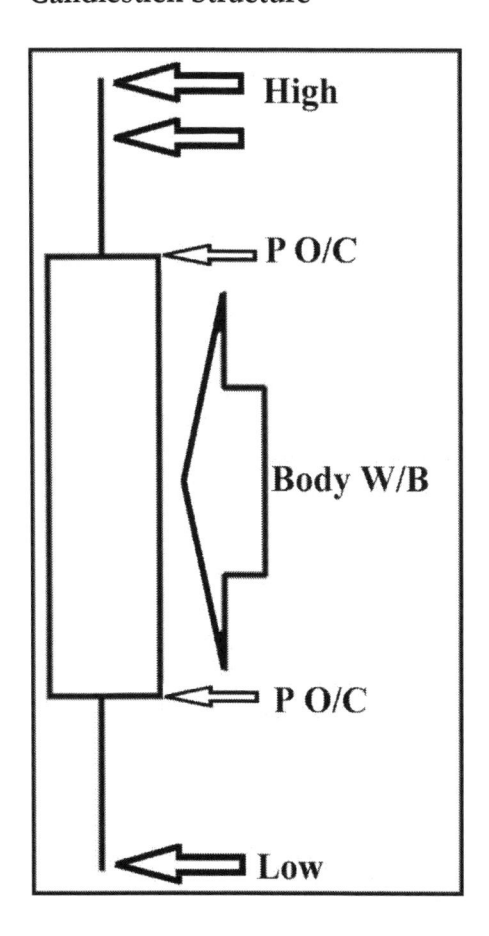

[Key:
High = Highest price during trading time period
P O/C = Trading time period open or close price
Body W/B = Real body is white (or green) if currency closed higher over the trading period or black (or red) if it closed lower
P O/C = Trading time period open or close price
Low = Lowest price during trading time period]

If a market is undecided as to where it views the direction of a pair then the candlestick will have no substantial body, wick or shadow (**'doji'**), reflecting that the price closed the day where it opened and that neither buyers ('bulls') nor sellers ('bears') prevailed in moving the pair their way over the course of the trading hours.

A similar inference can be taken from the **'Spinning Top'** pattern, although not to quite the same degree, as some intra-day movement will have taken place. In either event, both can be viewed as **marking possibly the end of the previous trend**, as it has run out of steam. These patterns make ideal places to enter new trades or exit existing ones.

Doji   **Spinning Top**   **Hammer**

Hanging Man   **Inverted Hammer**   **Shooting Star**

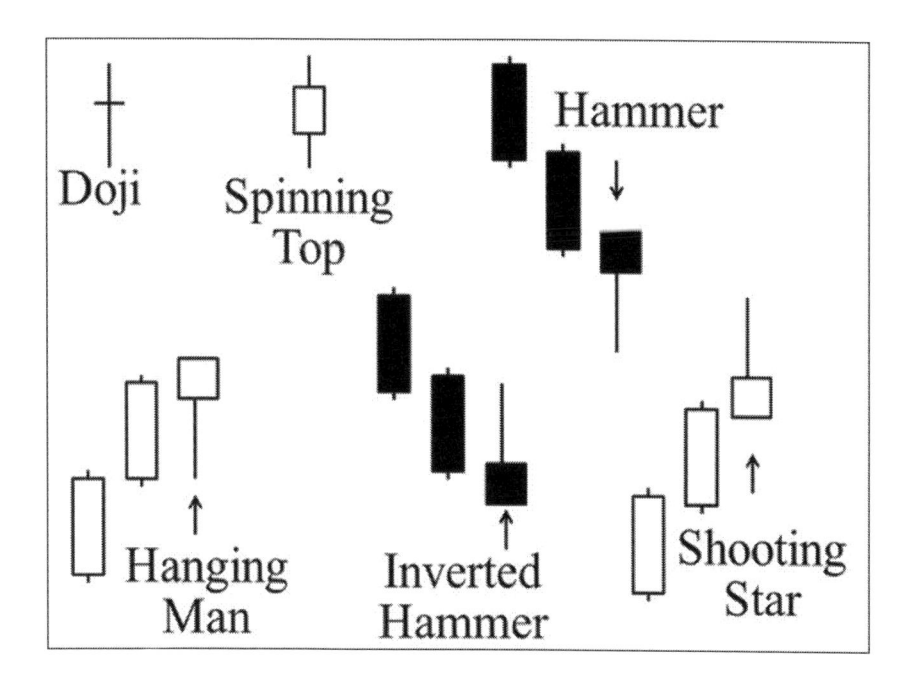

The '**Hammer**' pattern appears after a previous move to the downside and indicates that a move to the upside is on the cards. The long shadow shows that, despite it trading substantially lower during the day, the weight of selling was not sufficient for it to stay at depressed trading levels. Consequently, the inference is that major buyers have stepped in at these levels and may well continue buying overnight or as the new Western trading period properly commences.

The same can be said for the '**Inverted Hammer**', although to a lesser degree, as although buyers have stepped into the market, they have failed on this occasion to reverse the downtrend entirely.

Conversely, the '**Shooting Star**' should be read as a sign that a move to the downside is on the cards, after a previous move to the upside, with bulls having failed to continue to push the pair higher and substantial bears having now entered the market.

The same can be said for the '**Hanging Man**' although to a lesser degree, as although sellers have stepped into the market, they have failed on this occasion to reverse the uptrend entirely.

Bullish Engulfing   **Bearish Engulfing**

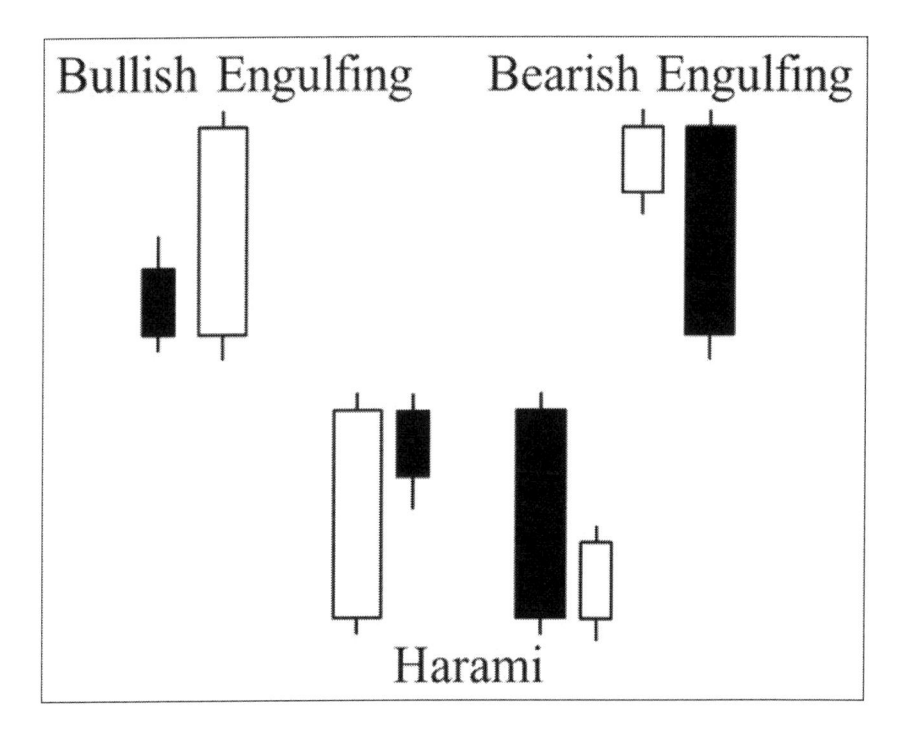

Harami

A '**Bullish Engulfing**' pattern is a clear indication that the signs of reversal of a previous trend (either through a Shooting Star or Hanging Man) have gained momentum, and the reverse is true of the '**Bearish Engulfing**' pattern (either through the Hammer or Inverted Hammer).

The '**Harami**' pattern, though, which can occur after a move either up or down, can be taken again as a sign of uncertain price follow-through and may mark the beginning of a change of trend direction.

USDCAD (Historical)

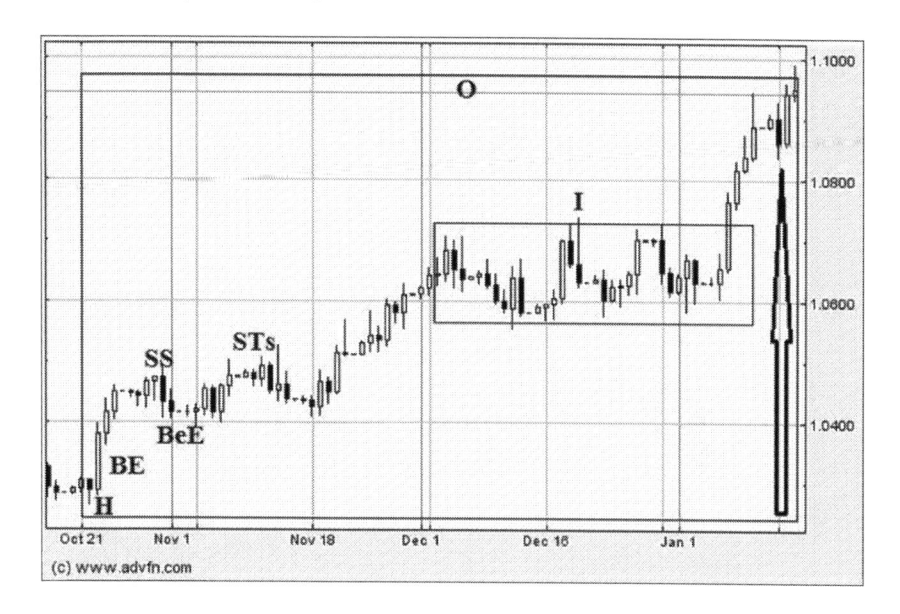

[Key:
H = Hammer
BE = Bullish engulfing
SS = Shooting star
BeE = Bearish engulfing
STs = Spinning tops
O = Overall uptrend
I = Indecision of the market]

In all of the above cases, the **weight that should be attached to these patterns should be increased when additional confirmations are found.**

These can be where they occur at **major resistance and support levels, Fibonacci levels** (key mathematical ratios of an original number, representing a move up or down: 23.6%, 38.2%, 50% and 61.8%) or **Moving Average** levels (simply, each day's price added together and then divided by a certain number of days: 20, 50 and 100 are the most used), including selected oscillators.

In the above chart, for instance, aside from a few moves down (which fail to gather momentum, as indicated by the Spinning Top patterns) all of the significant moves have been to the upside (as indicated by the rolling Hammer patterns).

Resistance And Support Levels

Support levels (where the market has overwhelmingly bought the base currency in the past, once it has been in decline) will invariably be found **below the current market price**, whilst **resistance levels** (where the market has overwhelmingly sold the base currency in the past, once it has been on the rise) will be found **above the current market price**.

In other words, in chart terms, support levels can be found where selling turns to buying (denoted on candlestick charts, see below, as a red bar turning to green), whilst resistance levels can be found where buying turns to selling (denoted on candlestick stick charts as a green bar turning to red). R1 is the first resistance level and so on, whilst S1 is the first support level, with the current market price indicated in the black box.

EURUSD (Historical)

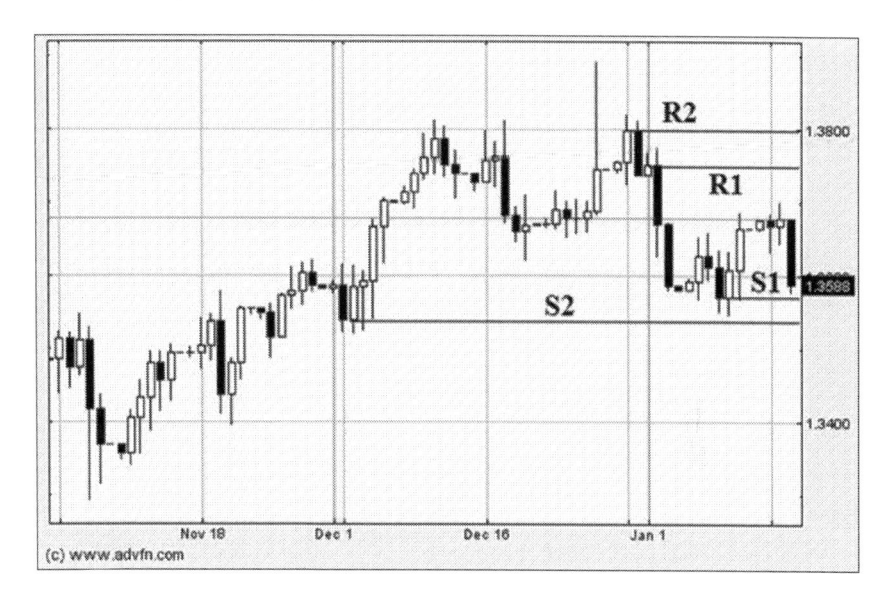

[Chart showing EURUSD price action from Nov 18 to Jan 1, with levels marked R2 (~1.3800), R1, S1 (~1.3598), S2, and price range 1.3400-1.3800]

[Key:
S1 = First support level
S2 = Second support level
R1 = First resistance level
R2 = Second resistance level]

These levels should be the cornerstones of all serious trading activity, as they act (together with other confirmations, discussed below) as signals to buy or sell into a new position or to exit existing ones.

To reiterate, though, **it is essential to note that resistance and support levels do not always coincide with any/all of these additional confirmation signals.** It may well be, for example, that a particular level has been **targeted by a country's central bank** as being essential for the advancement of its economic or monetary policy and that it will act decisively to ensure either that its currency weakens at a certain level (to encourage exports and boost economic growth, for instance) or strengthens (to discourage demand-led inflation, for instance).

The chart below, for example, shows the determination of the Bank of Japan (always one of the more active global central banks) stepping in to prevent the JPY from strengthening to such a degree that the country's exports would become even more uncompetitive in the world's markets than already was the case at the time.

USDJPY (Historical)

[Key:
R1 to R10 = The sequentially lower resistance levels hit by serious hedge funds and others, from longs taken out all the way down, before the Bank of Japan effectively set a floor]

Similarly, it may be that there are enormous **FX options** that would be triggered if a currency reached a certain level. In this case, whoever held the option would do everything cost-effective that they could to prevent it reaching the strike price for the option.

Often, one will see levels that apparently have little or no other obvious significance being resolutely defended up to a certain date (the expiration date for the option) and then dramatically going through that level once the option has lapsed, as shown below.

USDCAD (Historical)

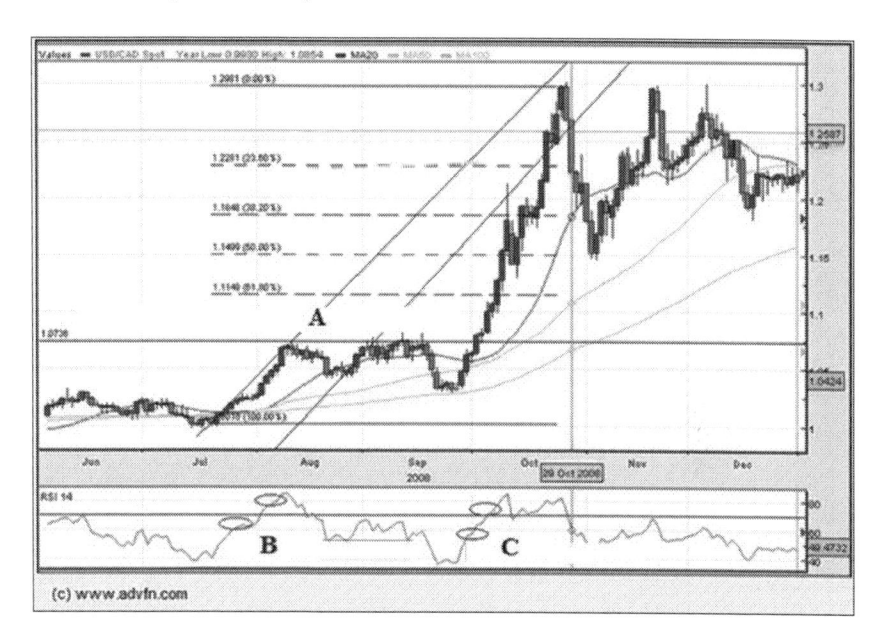

[Key:
A = USD call, CAD put option @ 1.0745
B = Big buying but capped
C = Big buying not capped]

Fibonacci Levels

These are key mathematical ratios of an original number (price), representing a move up or down: **23.6%, 38.2%, 50% (not actually a Fibonacci ratio, but most Fibonacci users include it anyhow), 61.8% and 100%**.

These can be overlaid on a chart, from the bottom of a trend to the top in a bullish market or from the top of a trend to the bottom in a bearish one.

As mentioned earlier, they can often mark resistance and support levels, as shown below.

USDJIA (Historical)

[Key:
A = 23.6% Fib level acts as support
B = 38.2% Fib level acts as resistance
C = 50% Fib level acts first as support and then as resistance]

In the above chart, we see clearly the **correlation between Fibonacci levels and those of support and resistance**. Interestingly here we also see that at the 50% level, initially this starts out as a resistance but then, as the cycle progresses, it acts as a support.

Moving Averages

These are particularly useful in determining short-term indications as to whether a market is set to continue in its current trend, reverse that trend or trade in a range. As mentioned earlier, MAs are simply each day's price added together and then divided by a certain number of days: 20, 50 and 100 are the most used.

As an additional confirmation (to established support and resistance levels, for instance) they offer a good idea of whether a currency is likely to break to the topside or the downside, as illustrated below.

USDJPY (Historical)

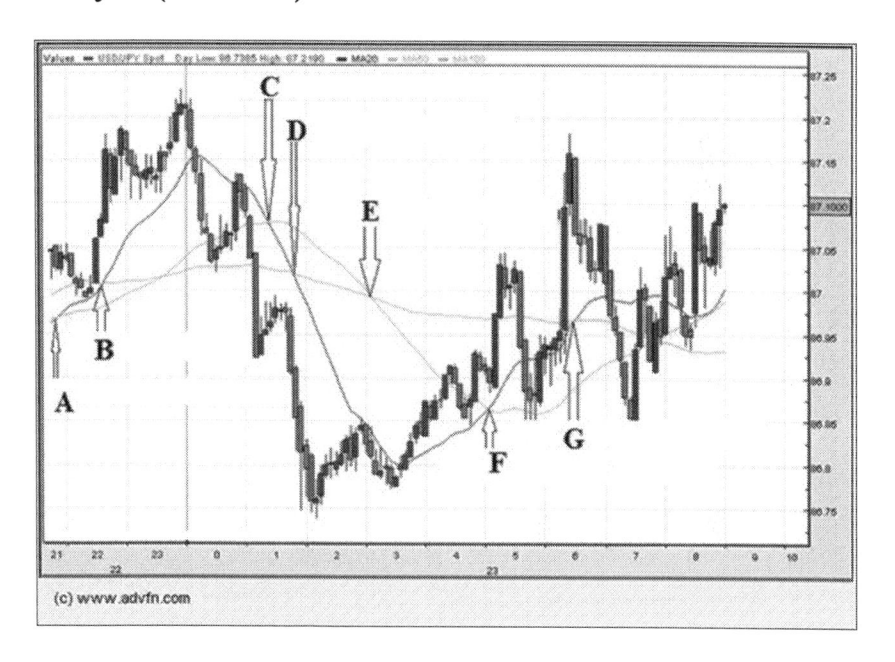

[Key:
A = MA20 up through MA50 = BUY
B = MA20 through MA100 = BUY
C = MA20 down through MA50 = SELL
D = MA20 down through MA 100 = SELL
E = MA50 down through MA100 = OVERSOLD
F = MA20 up through MA100 = BUY
G = MA20 through MA50 = BUY]

Broadly speaking, as shown above, if the short-term MA20 breaks through a longer-term MA then one might expect the currency pair to trade in whichever direction that break has occurred. More helpfully still, MAs can be used for earlier trading indications, using the **Moving Average Convergence-Divergence** (MACD) indicator, as shown below.

USDJPY (Historical)

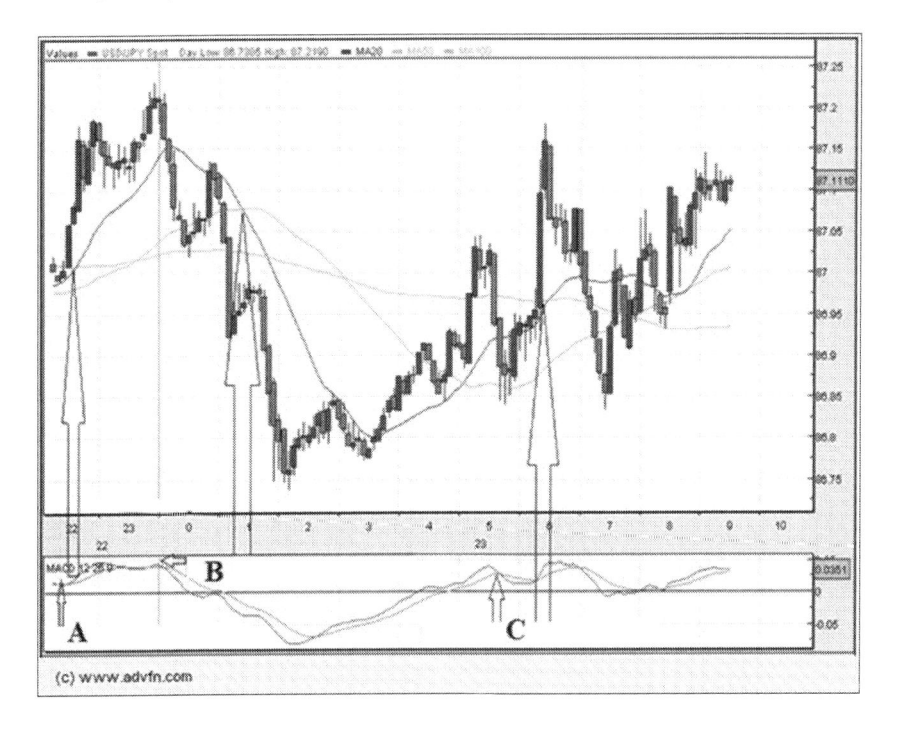

[Key:
A = Early signal for crossover = BUY
B = Early signal for crossover = SELL
C = Early warning for crossover = BUY]

MAs are also a vital part of determining the momentum of a price movement, in its application with the 3/10 Oscillator. This is a simple indicator constructed by subtracting the 10 day period

Exponential Moving Average from the 3 day period Exponential Moving Average (but do not fret, virtually all charting packages allow one to replicate this with the MACD by setting the short term parameter to 3, the long term parameter to 10 and the smoothing parameter to 1.

Dow Jones Price/Oscillator Convergence/Divergence Signals

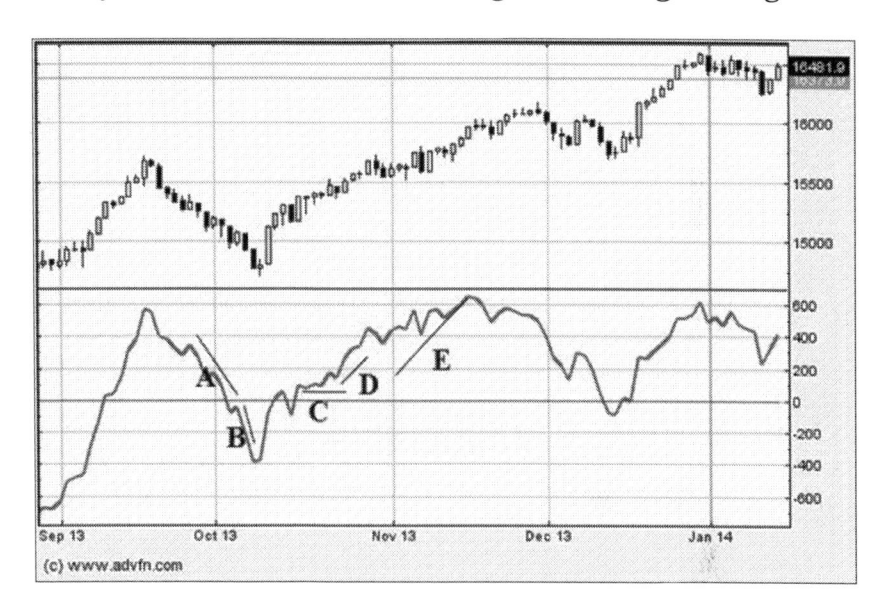

[Key:
A = Selling momentum gathers force
B = Selling momentum diverges = change of direction due
C = Range trading momentum
D = Buying momentum kicks in
E = Buying momentum gathers force]

Anyhow, the concept underlying this indicator (similar in theory to the RSI) is that if a price moves up or down and is expected to be sustained then one would anticipate that, along with a range of higher highs (for an upmove) or lower lows (for a downmove), the momentum (or force) behind each of these would also be sustained.

If not, one would have to question whether the move can have the strength (more buyers than sellers or the other way around) to continue.

Dow Jones Bearish Regular Divergence Of Price/Oscillator

= *Although the price is rising, momentum is going down* = *bearish divergence*

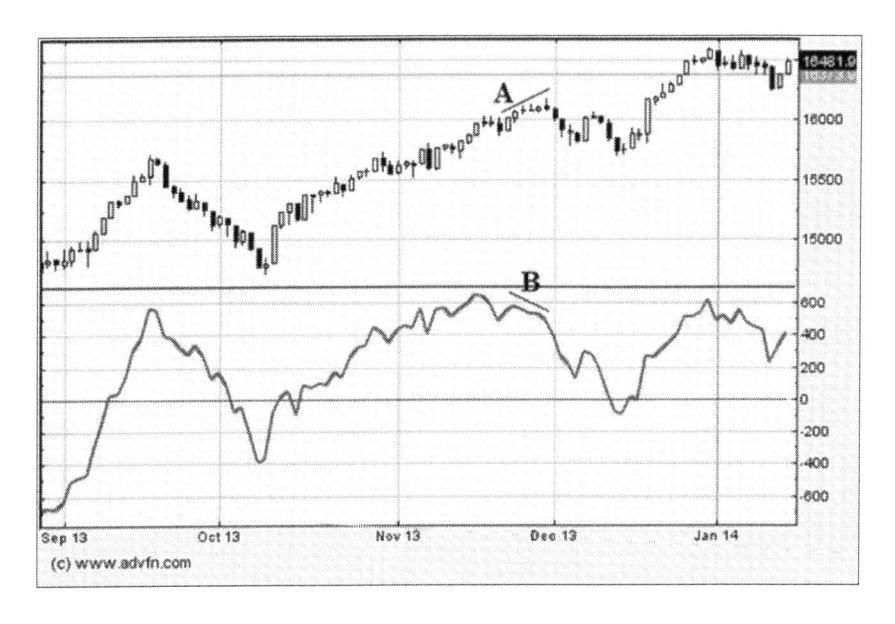

[Key:
A = Higher high
B= Lower high]

Dow Jones Bearish Hidden Divergence Of Price/Oscillator

= *The price is still bid, but at a lower level, and momentum is gaining at lower prices*

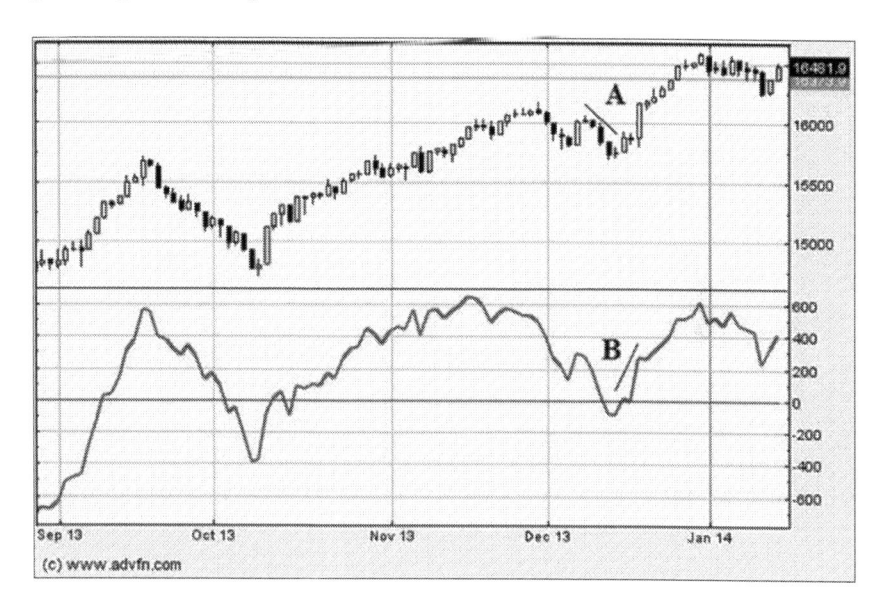

[Key:
A = Lower high
B = Higher high]

Dow Jones Bullish Regular Divergence Of Price/Oscillator

= *Although the price is falling, there is less momentum pushing it down*

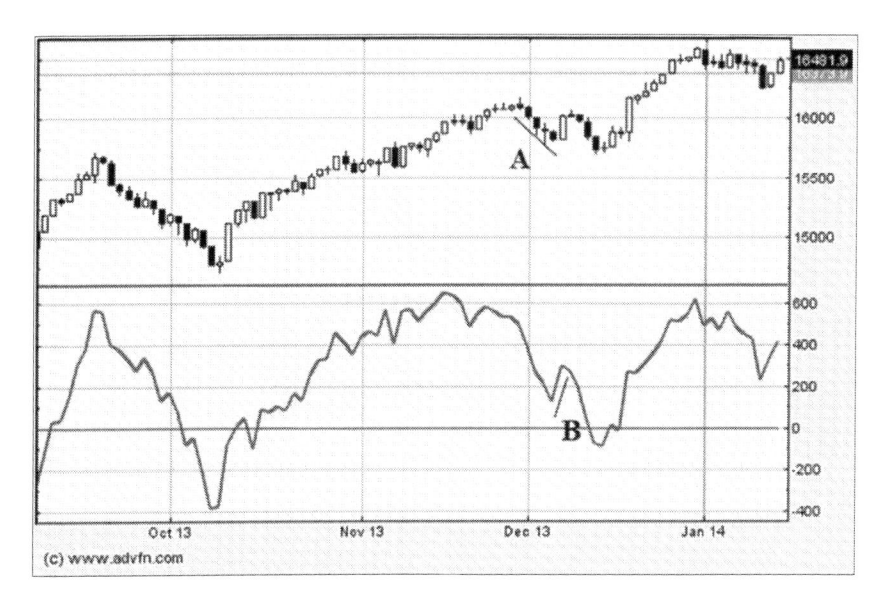

[Key:
A = Lower low
B = Higher low]

Dow Jones Bullish Hidden Divergence Of Price/Oscillator

= *Although it is still offered, the momentum gains as the price rises relatively*

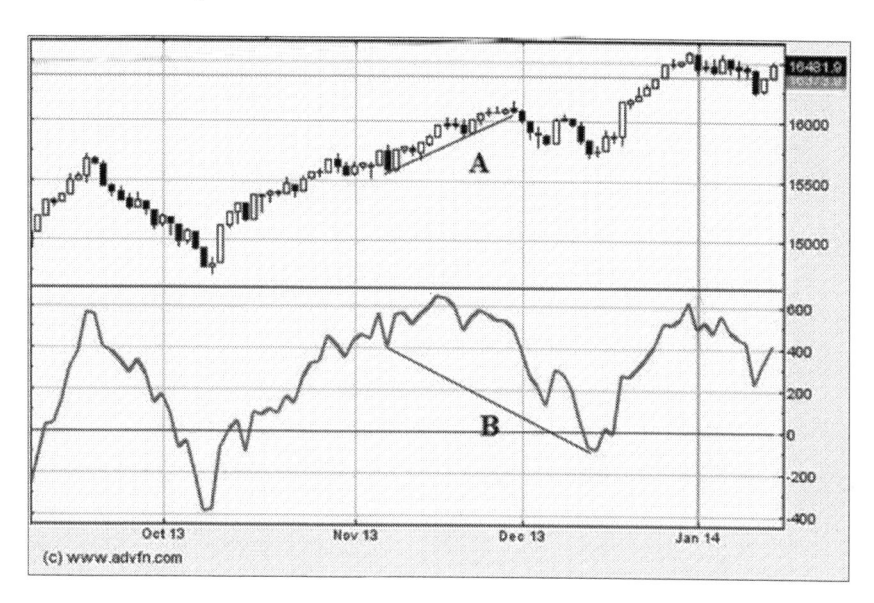

[Key:
A = Higher low
B = Lower low]

Relative Strength Index (RSI)

RSI is another extremely useful oscillator indicator. **In general terms, the RSI shows the momentum of a pair's trading – in effect, the degree of market participation in its current price movement – and can act as a valuable pre-emptive indicator showing a potential reversal of trend.**

For example, even if a pair appears to be rising quickly, if the RSI is showing that negative momentum is occurring then it might be time to look at the other indicators that signalled a long position and look to either exit an existing long or establish a new short.

Conversely, as shown in the chart below, there is a very notable shift upwards in RSI higher before the actual market price follows it.

EURUSD (Historical)

= RSI confirms upward trend before actual price turns higher

[Key:
A = RSI rises sharply higher, in advance of the price movement
B = Actual market price catches up with bullish momentum on RSI]

More specifically, the RSI moves between a scale of 0 to 100, with 100 showing that every participant in the market is buying the base currency of a pair and 0 showing the opposite. **As a rule of thumb, any reading of 70 and above indicates that the pair is overbought, with a possible reversal on the cards, and any reading under 30 showing it is oversold and that the opposite is true.** This, together with the formations of usual double top/bottom patterns, can show up even before they do in the actual price movement ('Divergence').

Similarly, areas of support and resistance show up very clearly on RSI patterns, as shown below.

EURUSD (Historical)

= RSI confirms strong resistance before actual price turns lower

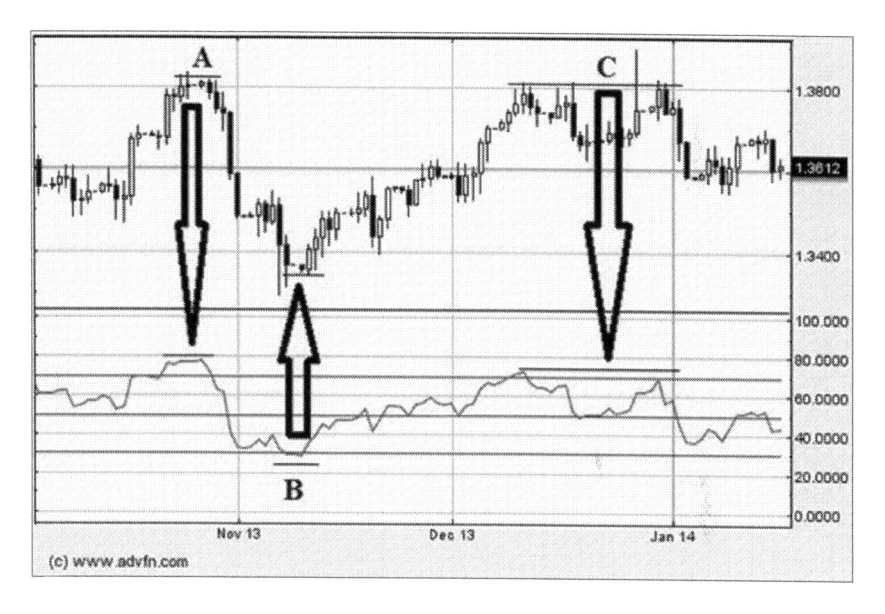

[Key:
A = RSI shows genuine resistance level in the price, in advance
B = RSI shows genuine support level in the price, in advance
C = RSI shows genuine rolling resistance level]

As is evident from the above, RSI's principal use is not in already trending markets, in which it can be used as a confirmation of direction or as an early warning indicator of a change of direction (if above 70 or below 30) but rather in range-bound markets looking for direction.

Here, as shown above, it can act as a proxy for volume interest in particular positions, so that, for example, a sharp spike up in RSI in a market trading around the mid-level could be taken as an early signal of a bullish move and vice-versa.

Bollinger Bands

Bollinger bands are plotted an equal distance either side of a simple moving average. The default settings on trading programmes use a 20 period simple moving average with the upper band (UB) plotted 2 standard deviations above the moving average and the lower band (LB) plotted 2 standard deviations below it.

In periods of low price volatility, these standard deviations become smaller (this process is called a 'squeeze' in Bollinger parlance) than in periods of high volatility and vice-versa (a 'bubble').

Given this, there is undoubtedly money to be made from anticipating/participating in such a breakout/breakdown to the existing bands.

EURUSD (Historical)

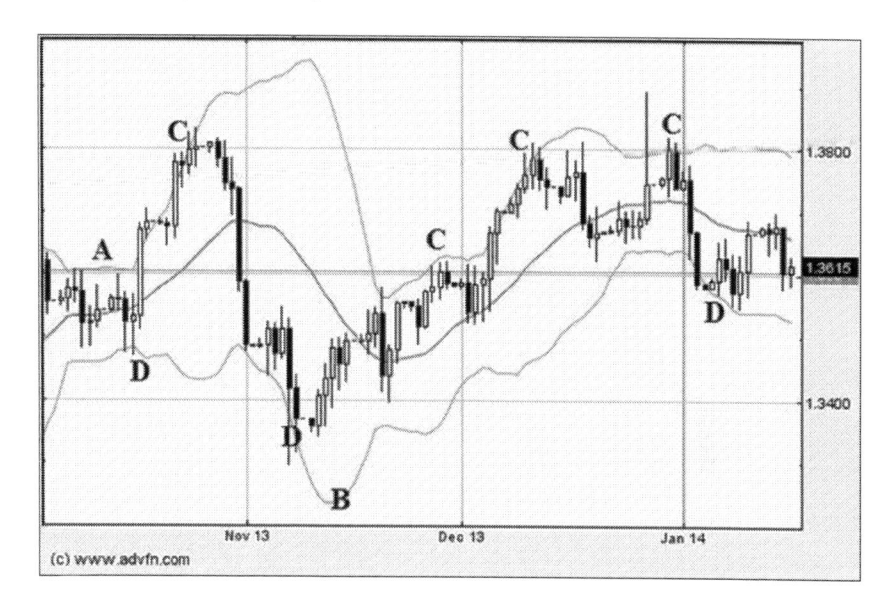

[Key:
A = Squeeze
B = Bubble
C = Upper band acts as resistance level
D = Lower band acts as support level]

More appositely, it is better to use Bollinger bands together with other firmer indicators such as support and resistance levels, Fibonacci levels and so forth, and to use them in such a way as to modify the results with what the Bollinger bands tell you about the probability of a move continuing/reversing.

If the price is moving towards the top of a band then beware longs, and if it is moving towards the bottom of a band then beware shorts. But don't get too hung up on what Bollinger Bands say in and of themselves.

Elliott Wave Theory

Elliot Wave Theory is particularly useful as it shows major moves and minor ones, with the former likely to be caused by institutional investors (and well worth following, if they are not spoofs) and the latter likely to be caused by retail investors playing catch-up (normally a good time to start thinking about exiting a trade).

In its most basic form, Elliott Waves show that the market does not move in a completely chaotic fashion but rather is a product of patterns that repeat themselves over time. These patterns ('waves') define a trend, which can be the basis for predictive trading.

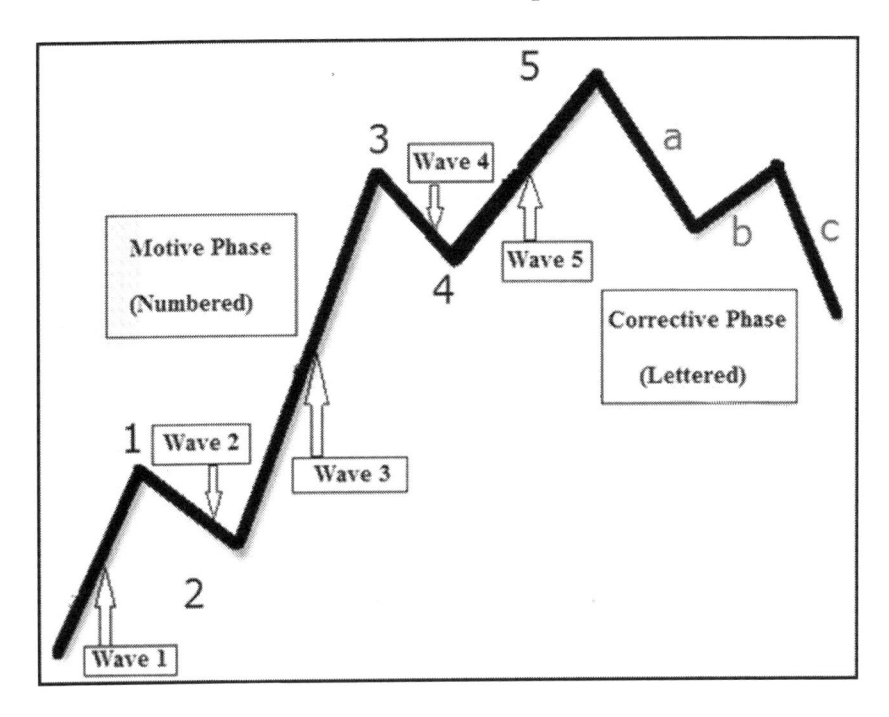

More specifically, according to Elliott (Ralph Nelson Elliott, just in case you were wondering, who posited his theory in around 1934), a trending market moves in a **five-three wave** pattern, where the first five waves ('motive waves') move in the direction of the larger trend. Following the completion of the five waves in one direction, a larger corrective move takes place in three consecutive waves ('corrective waves'), as illustrated in the above chart.

Interestingly, **the patterns identified by Elliott occur across multiple time frames**: that is, a completed five wave sequence on a small time frame (5 minutes, for instance) may well be just the first wave of a longer temporal sequence (in a daily chart, for example) and so on and so forth.

Elliott Waves On EURUSD (Historical)

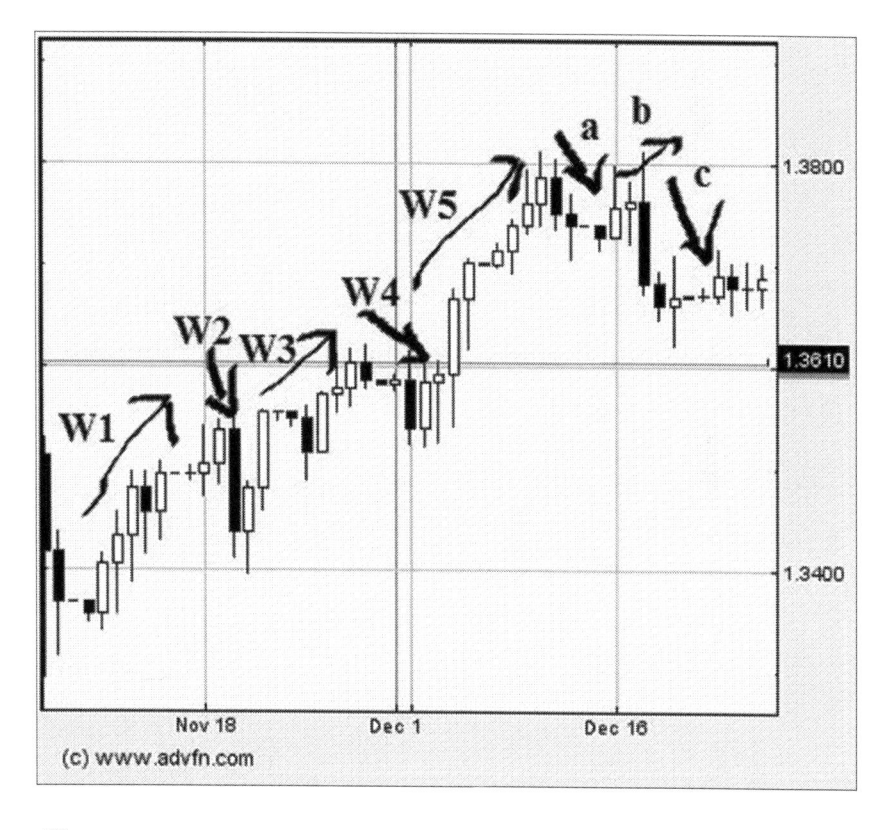

[Key:
W1 to W5 = Motive phase waves
a to c = Corrective phase waves]

The **combination of Elliott Waves and Fibonacci ratios is particularly useful in trading into new positions or trading out of existing ones for a number of reasons**, outlined as follows: Fibonacci ratios are usually important levels of supply and demand (i.e., support and resistance).

The motive and corrective levels are often measured by percentages of the previous wave length, with the most common levels being the Fibonacci ones of 38%, 50%, 61.8% and 100%; timings with a distance of 13, 21, 34, 55, 89 and 144 periods should be particularly monitored (e.g., if you find a crucial reversal or an unfolding of a pattern on a daily chart then expect another crucial unfolding at the above daily points thereafter); a corrective move that follows a motive move from a significant low or high usually retraces 50% to 61.8% of the preceding impulse; wave 4 usually corrects as far as 38.2% of wave 3; given that wave 2 generally does not overlap the start of wave 1 (i.e., the 100% of it), the start of wave 1 is an ideal level to place stops; and the target of wave 5 can be calculated by multiplying the length of wave 1 by 3.236 (2 X 1.618).

It is also interesting to note, as we touched on in Long-Term Economic Patterns sub-section earlier, that we could regard the nature of these cycles in Elliot Waves' terms. That is, that at the onset of a long-term economic cycle there is likely to be a lack of confidence and a fear of falling back into slump or depression, before inflation, interest rates and credit slowly start to rise as confidence in the new age increases (you might say, Elliot Wave 1).

As the economy expands (indicated in this instance by inflation) and interest rates increase as an adjunct to this, then so business and consumer confidence grows further and credit is extended more (Elliot Wave 3 correlation).

As we enter into the final up-phase of the move, confidence levels morph into over-exuberance and extraordinary loose 'bubble-like' credit conditions, with interest rates also declining (Elliot Wave 5 correlation).

Finally, rising concerns over loose credit, inflationary upward spiral and bad debt causes business and consumer reticence to embark on new projects (in business terms, expansion and in consumer terms, new purchases), default rates increase, credit is squeezed, the economic outlook turns negative, unemployment rises, disinflation turns into deflation and we have a negative world view.

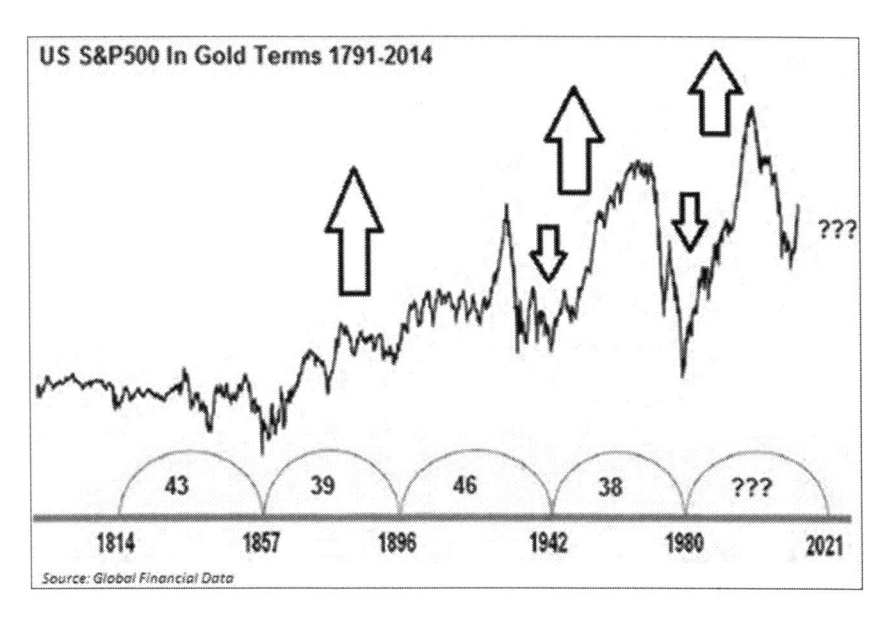

[US S&P500 In Gold Terms 1791-2014. Cycles: 43 (1814), 39 (1857), 46 (1896), 38 (1942), ??? (1980-2021). Source: Global Financial Data]

Consequently, it would be fair to say that based on this time set the **US stock market, and for that matter the UK one and those of the major northern European countries, are currently in an overall cyclical downturn and that, for the time being, the overall trend – economically and in terms of asset prices, interest rates and volatility – may be net down over the next few years.**

Continuation Patterns

These patterns allow the trader not only to understand from where the price action and momentum has come but also to anticipate where and to what degree it is headed. Thus, as these patterns are also watched by thousands of other traders around the globe, they allow an RT to obtain an ongoing record of the sentiment surrounding a currency pair at any given time and consequently allow the trader to manage his order placing better as well.

Ascending And Descending Triangles

Triangles basically allow the trader to gauge which of the myriad support and resistance levels on a chart are the ones he should be watching most carefully in determining false or genuine breakouts.

An **ascending triangle** is formed by a combination of diagonal support and horizontal resistance, implying that the bulls are gaining the upper hand in the ongoing trading dynamic of the pair and buying at higher and higher levels, while the bears are merely trying to defend an established level of resistance.

EURGBP (Historical) Ascending Triangle

[Key:
A = Horizontal resistance level
B = Inclining support]

Clearly, in the above example, the trader has advance warning that the pair is more likely to break up through the resistance level than down through the support one. Also, of course, by anticipating the formation of the triangle the trader can gain/not lose further points, depending on his position, as currency pairs often trend, consolidate and then re-trend.

In the case of a **descending triangle**, the bears are gaining strength and selling at lower and lower levels, while the bulls are merely trying to defend an established level of support.

AUDUSD (Historical) Descending Triangle

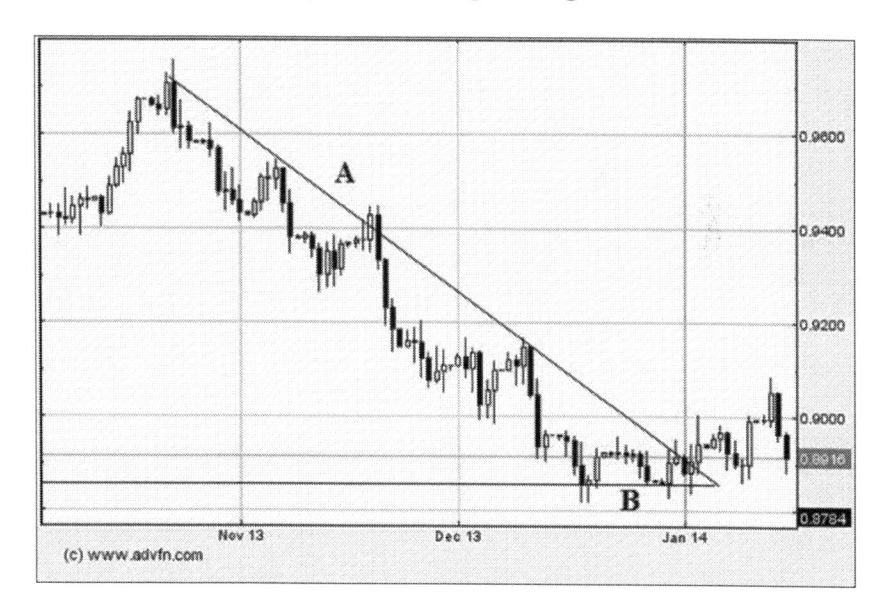

[Key:
A = Declining resistance
B = Horizontal support]

Given these two scenarios, it is easy to see that one can make money riding the principal wave up or down respectively and also to see that triangles make the placement of stop loss orders relatively simple as well; in the ascending triangle example, they would be placed just under the inclining support line at a level that accorded with one's own risk/reward ratio for a rolling long position.

Conversely, in the descending triangle example, they would be placed at a point above the declining resistance level that accorded with one's own risk/reward ratio for a rolling short.

In the cases of both ascending and descending triangles, **any true break (more than one spoof break-out) of its direction (up for descending triangles, down for ascending ones) should be taken seriously by traders to consider exiting trades made on the trend until that point (taking profit) and reversing positions.**

Flags

Flags and pennants generally represent a pause in trend and can be used either to take profits on a position going with that trend or to add to that trending position, if one is feeling particularly aggressive (and, preferably, has one's confidence bolstered by other factors meriting an increase in position size – for example, more favourable than expected fundamental or political developments).

The example below is of a downward trending USDJPY, which pauses for consolidation in a flag pattern before resuming its downward trajectory. Often one can expect pretty much the same number of pips in the second part of the downtrend (labelled 'Downtrend 2' on the chart, appositely enough) as in the first part of the downtrend (you can work out what this one is labelled), but in the chart below, it seems on cursory glance that this is not the case.

However, looking further into the distance and going on the basis of a longer-term trade, it becomes apparent that, in fact, the real second wave (or you could term it 'Downtrend 2, Part 2) makes up the entire pips expected as a result of Downtrend 1.

USDJPY (Historical) Flag In A Downtrend

[Key:
A = Downtrend 1 = 723 pips
F = Flag
B = Downtrend 2 = 348 pips, OR DOES IT? See below]

In fact, this flag and many similar presage a much sharper move down, as can be seen below.

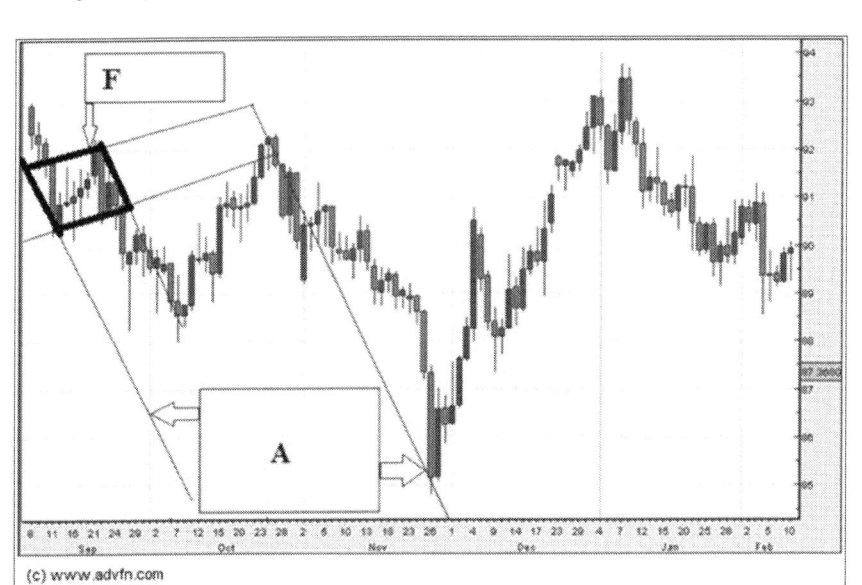

USDJPY (Historical) Continuation In A Downtrend

[Key:
F = Flag from previous chart
A = Logical conclusion of the original downtrend 1 = 700 pips had the trade been stuck with]

Trend Reversals

Double Top And Double Bottom

Given that the market has a way of generally correcting any untoward excessive movements one way or another in asset prices over time, spotting a real reversal in a trend from just a shimmering mirage is key to making money on a long-term basis.

In this respect, we have already covered a lot of ground, but there are a couple of other, more basic patterns that a trader should look out for.

A **Double Top is, as it sounds, when prices stop rising at the same point twice in a short sequence of time**, as shown below. In order for a real reversal of trend to be indicated, the pair must break down through the key support level as indicated on the chart. This is sometimes the result, as we have also touched on, of a central bank looking to halt the appreciation of its currency to such a degree that its export revenue is damaged (or, indeed, of financial institutions guarding a level in order not to be hit by an option being exercised).

GBPUSD (Historical) Double Top

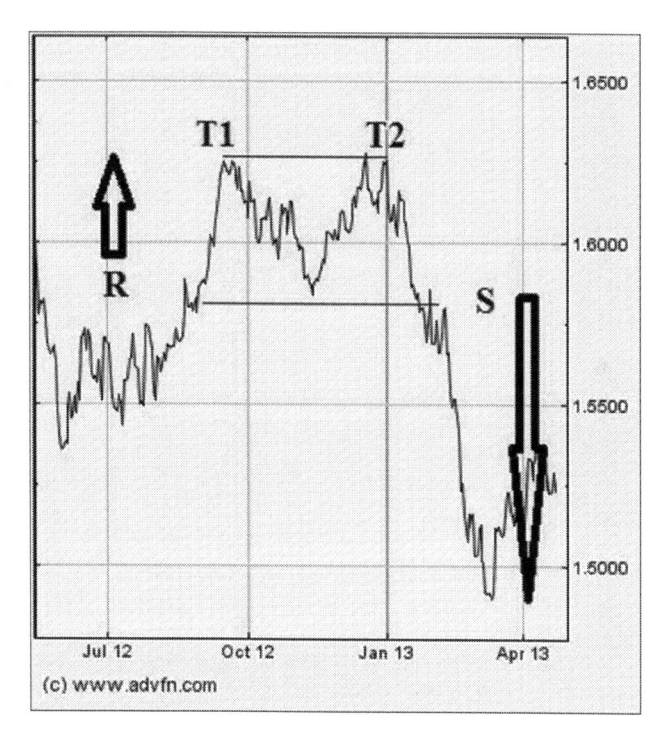

[Key:
R = *Rising trend*
T1 = *First top*
T2 = *Second (double) top*
S = *Break below this double support level here implies downtrend]*

A double bottom is the same principle, only reversed.

Head And Shoulders Patterns

In the meantime, a head and shoulders pattern, as illustrated below, develops with the exchange rate trending up and forming the left shoulder on a reversal. Then the market trends higher to form the head and falls back to the same support of the first shoulder to form the right shoulder. The neckline is thus the line connecting the troughs between the peaks. If it is broken, expect a downside move to occur.

AUDUSD (Historical) Head And Shoulders Trend Reversal Pattern

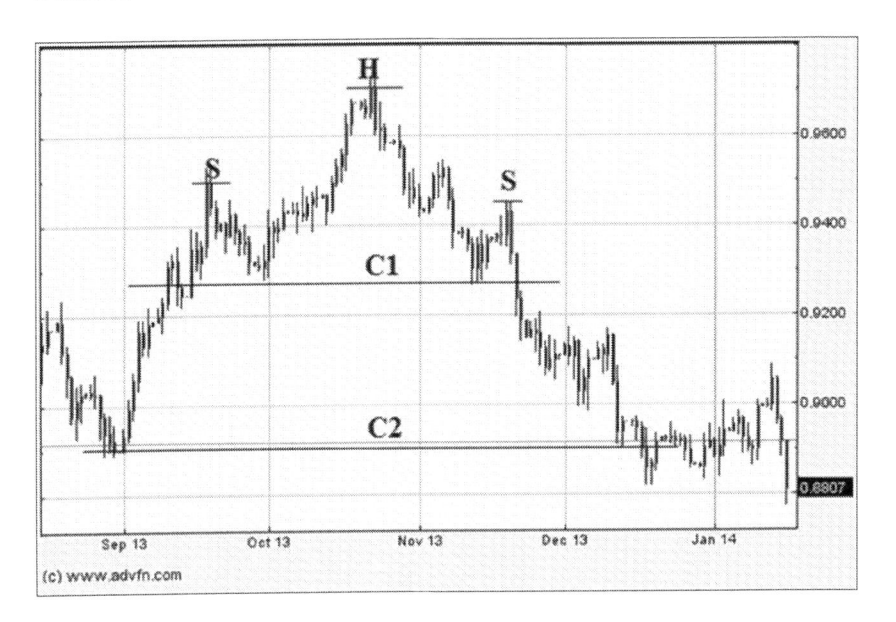

[Key:
S = Shoulder
H = Head
C1 = Confirmation of breakdown 1
C2 = Confirmation of further breakdown 2]

Risk/Reward Management And Hedging

The Nature Of Risk

Ultimately, money goes to where it is best rewarded (yielded in the first instance from interest rates but later additionally from capital gains) for the concomitant risks involved (indicated broadly by credit ratings but also from more specific shock geopolitical, market and systemic risks) and this is, broadly speaking, the definition of the 'risk curve'. **Traders, in order to be successful over time, need to be constantly aware of this risk curve and also to manage the risk/reward ratio of their own investment portfolio in a logical, sensible and emotionless fashion, otherwise they will go broke; it is as simple as that.**

In the case of **in-the-money (ITM) positions (those that are running in the profit zone),** bad traders (i.e. those not managing their risk properly) exit at the wrong time, either getting out once the peak profit-taking opportunity has passed (through misplaced greed) or getting nervous and taking profit way before they should. In the case of **out-of-the-money (OTM) positions (those that are losing money),** they hang on to bad positions hoping that they will turn around. The key guiding principle here is: **do not run losses past a comfortable stop-loss point (with the order having gone in at the same time as the entry trade), only run profits.**

By far the best way for a retail trader to avoid being one of the 90% of this type that loses all his money within 90 days of starting to trade is by utilising – and religiously sticking to – **orders (both stop-loss and take-profit) when trading,** and we look at this in depth below.

The Risk Curve

The more risk involved in an asset, the more reward is required. Hence, the worse an economy is perceived to be doing, the more reward investors will want as compensation to holding an asset in that country. By extension, if that interest rate does not increase then that asset will be unpopular and thus weak.

Having said that, there is a major difference between probability and a risk/reward profile, in trading terms. The law of probability (more accurately, the *Law of Large Numbers*) is:

"If the probability of a given outcome to an event is P and the event is repeated N times then the larger N becomes, so the likelihood increases that the closer, in proportion, will be the occurrence of the given outcome to N*P."

In practical terms, this means really that if a two-sided coin is tossed a sufficient number of times then the distribution of the results between heads coming up and tails coming up will be exactly the same.

There is an evident problem here for the trader: there is a 50/50 chance on the first toss that heads will come up and, therefore, according to the logical extension of what many 'trader training companies' say, it would be perfectly reasonably to put half your money on heads but – having put money on this outcome – it instead comes up tails. Nonetheless, according to the aforementioned rationale, the trader then puts everything on heads coming up, as given that tails came up first time and the probability of heads coming up was 50% (1 in 2) heads is bound to come up next time but it does not and, continuing to pursue this rationale, the trader will go broke. **The fact is that probability only goes a part of the way to explaining sequences of numbers.**

There is also the random walk theory, in which followers believe that market prices follow a completely random path up and down, without any influence being exerted on them by past price action, making it impossible to predict with any accuracy which direction the market will move at any point or indeed to what degree. However, as has been proven repeatedly, this is incorrect, as patterns of all sorts manifest themselves daily, indeed hourly, and all that is required is to know what to look for: risk/reward ratios are what a trader needs to know.

Risk/Reward Ratios And Effective Order Management

Knowing accurate support and resistance levels is pivotal in determining the risk/reward ratio of a particular trade and in placing orders to capitalise on favourable movements (take-profit orders) or to limit the downside potential of a trade (stop-loss orders).

Technical Analysis (please see *Technical Analysis* section) is a bit of a self-fulfilling prophecy as whether or not there is any real empirical value in the levels that its classical application produces – the most basic cornerstones being support and resistance levels, as mentioned earlier – the fact that lots of other people believe in it means that these levels take on a trading significance.

One distinct advantage of this collective belief in key levels – exacerbated by their use as triggers for trades in many 'black box' programs run by many investment outfits – is that on a day to day basis, **once a trader has worked out where the key support and resistance levels really are – and this is a pretty straightforward process – and he has set his risk parameters according to his risk appetite (in the early days of trading to go for at least a 1 to 4 risk/reward ratio) then he should place his stop-loss orders appropriately and stop messing around with his trades.** The exception to this is if something major happens that invalidates the original hypotheses for undertaking the trades in the first place, or – as with the example above – means that he should add to his position (or scale it back).

More money has been lost by people messing around with their trades or trading through boredom, than has ever been lost in rogue trading operations. **If the trader did all of the other things that he should have done before entering a trade and nothing extraordinary changes – political, economic, technical, Acts of God – then he should relax, and the best way of relaxing in a trade is to put on a stop-loss order and, indeed, a take-profit order, at the same time as putting on every new trade.**

USDCAD (Historical)

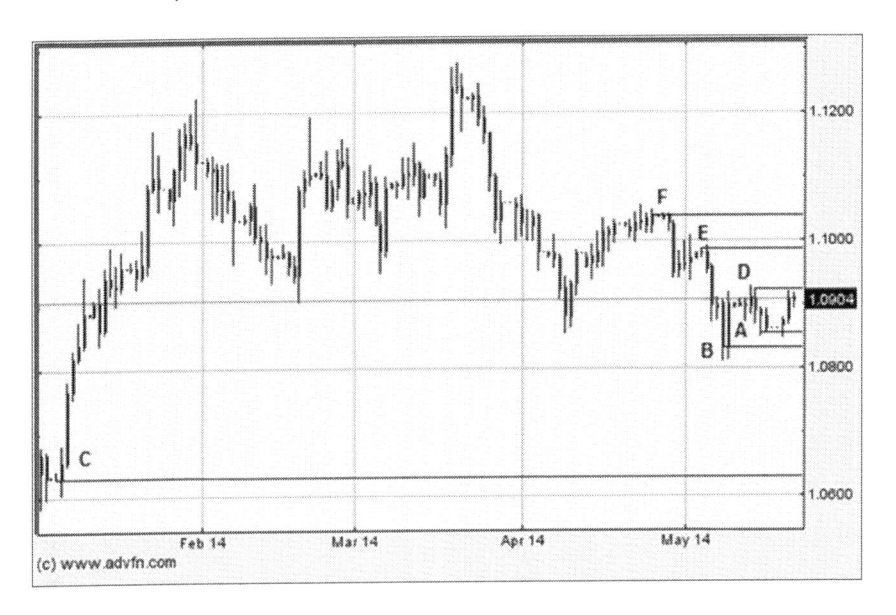

[Key:
A = *First support level*
B = *Second support level*
C = *Third support level*
D = *First resistance level*
E = *Second resistance level*

F = *Third resistance level]*

Net Margin/Trading Requirement (NMR/NTR)

When trading on any platform, a **retail trader will find that his room for manoeuvre in trading is not only limited by the total amount of capital that he has in his trading account but also by the NMR/NTR of that particular platform**, according to the platform's judgement of the risk involved in any particular asset that he is trading.

For example, even if not trading on any leverage at all (instead, trading GBP1 per pip meaning GBP1 gained/lost for each pip gained/lost), one will find that for each GBP1 traded the platform will reduce one's available account balance by anywhere from GBP100 to GBP200 or more, depending upon the type of contract that one has entered into (depending on how risky/volatile the platform assesses each contract to be).

Not only will this eat into available capital but additionally any losses that a trade occurs as it is ongoing will also be deducted from available capital. So, let us say that a trader sold EURUSD at 1.1400 at GBP4 per pip. Even before the pair has moved the retail trader's platform capital account will be showing that he is down on available capital by, perhaps, GBP800. If he had available capital before trading of GBP1,000 then he could only afford to have the position go 200 pips against him before he is automatically closed out of the position by the trading platform (and thus wiped out entirely).

Moreover, it affords no opportunity for hedging positions as they run (see below). Conversely, of course, if the position makes money from the off then your available capital will increase (although this will not affect the amount that the platform has set aside for your risk margin).

Account Size And Setting Targets

In order to have any peace of mind as a trader, **it is necessary to have an account with sufficient capital for one's trading ambitions. Or, conversely, a trader needs to have trading ambitions that are cut according to his capital.** There cannot have an imbalance here.

It is true, theoretically, that with a GBP500 initial stake in an account, a trader can become a millionaire within just over five years (see chart below), if he doubles his money every six months, as the table below illustrates:

Capital Accumulation Over Six Years From An Initial £500 Investment	
Months	Capital
0	500
6	1000
12	2000
18	4000
24	8000
30	16000
36	32000
42	64000
48	128000
54	256000
60	512000
66	1024000
72	2048000

This, though, requires a high degree of self-discipline, rigorous order management, excellent market knowledge and contacts and highly developed skills of technical analysis.

In terms of self-discipline first, cut your profit target according to your account balance. **At minimum, a risk/reward ratio of 4:1 in the first few years of trading should be set – that is, for every GBP1 a trader might lose he could make GBP4, based on where the key support and resistance levels are.**

Second, if trying to double funds over the 0-6 month period then a trader must make GBP500 during that first half year period. This amount split down into weeks implies a weekly profit target of GBP19 per week.

Concomitant with this, a trader will need to work out how much is the maximum that he can place on any one trade. Professional bank and fund management traders will typically risk anywhere between 1-5% of their capital on any single trade, but, to begin with for the relatively inexperienced retail trader, no more than 1% of total capital should be risked on any one trade. Therefore, on any single trade, a trader could risk no more than GBP5 in total.

This is clearly not much, if doing GBP1 per pip, which is why this becoming a millionaire with just GBP500 in just over five years is unlikely, as it allows no real room for error, as the spread alone (the difference between a trading platform's bid and offer prices for the base currency in a currency pair) is often at least 3 pips.

Therefore, a sensible **minimum amount to have in a trading account to begin with is at least GBP10,000.** This allows flexibility in hedging ongoing positions that are not performing well in the very short-term but that a trader believes (based on empirical evidence) will come good in the slightly longer term. And, of course, the doubling process outlined in the earlier chart is still the same.

In order to make GBP10,000 within the first six months, a trader must make a weekly profit of GBP385 per week over six months: 1% of GBP10,000 is obviously GBP100, which means that this amount should be the stop-loss level on every single order, and these should be placed at exactly the same time as the entry trade. At GBP1 per pip that is a 100 pip movement against a trader, which is relatively reasonable in a market of average volatility. Indeed, it may be that, under these conditions, a trader might consider putting GBP2 per pip on the trade, whilst simultaneously cutting his stop-loss to 50 pips from the point of trade entry. As such, it is fairly straightforward and realistic to make the required sum in the target period and even more quickly if using weightings across different asset classes, given proper risk management.

Straight Averaging Up

Given the premise that the aim of trading is to minimise any losses and to maximise any wins, averaging up – if done well – is a good way of achieving the latter.

The basic averaging technique is pretty self-explanatory: it involves **adding to a winning position as the trade continues into profitable territory.** So, for example, in the chart below, a position had been entered by buying EUR against the USD (selling USD) at 1.3000 (this is an historical example, but the point is the same for any time period). After completing the technical analysis, it was clear that a break of this key resistance level would indicate a move higher, and it had been decided to add GBP1 per pip at every 50 pip upwards increment. Having done this three times, there was an average long position of GBP3 per pip at EURUSD1.3050.

EURUSD (Historical)

[Key:
A = Buy EURUSD at 1.3000, GBP1 per pip
B = Buy again at 1.3050, GBP 1 per pip
C = Buy again at 1.3100, GBP 1 per pip
D = Therefore, average long price at GBP 3 per pip is 1.3050]

On GBP1 per pip at 1.3000, a trader would have made GBP250 as the EURUSD hit 1.3250. Another GBP1 per pip at 1.3050 would have netted a further GBP200 and the final GBP1 per pip at 1.3100 a further GBP150. The total, therefore, would have been GBP600. Of course, had the trader put on GBP3 per pip in the first trade, the profit would have been GBP750. Additionally the break-even on the trade has now moved up to 1.3050 rather than 1.3000.

If the trader had not sold at the top of that particular move and the pair had traded down to 1.3100 then he might have lost the third leg profit of GBP150, which would have resulted in a net profit of just GBP150. Also, if the pair had traded back down through the

1.3050 area then the trader would have incurred a loss on the third long, together with no profit on the second, which would have resulted in a net profit of nothing at all.

Layered Averaging Up

Another way of averaging up that tends against the above phenomenon of being averaged out of any profit is to **add to a long position on pullbacks to the preferred entry level, or the other way around if a net seller.** So, if a trader decides to go long as above then he simply adds GBP1 per pip on any move back towards the 1.3000 level, if he is expecting a sustained move upwards over time.

Such tactics are particularly useful if there is an ongoing struggle between a central bank and a fund on two sides of the trade. For example in USDJPY, after the new Prime Minister Shinzo Abe came to power at the end of 2012, the Bank of Japan was buying USD and selling JPY very aggressively in order to support its export market (and thus aid broader economic recovery) from around the USD85.50 level, whilst certain funds – especially hedge funds – were selling USD and buying JPY anywhere above 87.00.

Once Abe was more firmly ensconced as PM, this battle moved up the values on USDJPY, as the Bank of Japan was given a much broader policy mandate than before. This was in line with those given to the US Fed and the Bank of England, which included looking at employment rates, interest rates and inflation. In this vein, the banks used quantitative easing where necessary together with direct currency intervention and forward guidance as a means of manipulating their respective currencies.

It was only when, in fact, the Bank of Japan was tasked with ensuring a broad-based policy strategy – engineering sustained nominal annual economic growth of 3% (there had been no average annual nominal GDP growth for 15 years) and at least a 2% annual inflation rate every year from 2015, as well as commencing a massive domestic bond-buying QE programme (Fed-style) – that the JPY managed sustained depreciation of the sort wanted by Abe and moved through the key USDJPY100 resistance level.

Alternately, **adding smaller amounts to the initial position is also a better way to take advantage of further moves** (in the aforementioned case) whilst also limiting the potential – as shown above – for all profits to be eradicated (or even to start making a loss). The converse of this, of course, is averaging down, in which a trader adds to losing positions in the hopes of making money back quicker as the original position reverses.

Value Averaging

As a natural corollary of the above, value averaging is another added value way of managing positions, this time by **constantly readjusting the risk/reward exposure to a pre-determined level.** Therefore, in practical terms, a trader sets an amount that falls within his risk/reward parameters.

For example, he may decide that he wishes to have a total exposure per day of GBP100 in EURUSD, at GBP1 per pip. In this event, if the position makes GBP10 in one day then next day he takes the GBP10 out and still has GBP100 riding on the position (at the original price). Conversely, if the position loses GBP10 in one day then the following day he would add another GBP10 at whatever the new price is to compensate. Thus, he has now spent GBP110 on the long, albeit at a more favourable average, given a down-trading market.

Trailing Stops

As a position turns into profit, the available amount of Net Margin Requirement (NMR)/Net Trading Requirement (NTR) that a trader has in his account increases, which can be used either for reinvestment in one of the methods detailed above or can be left where it is, depending on the nature of the market at the time. Nonetheless, depending upon how he manages his position, **there is no point in keeping the stop loss exit order at its original point, but rather it should move it up as the profit margin increases**. This is the notion of trailing stops.

So, basically, if a position increases profit by 10 pips the stop loss should be moved up by 10 pips and so on.

Hedging

A perfect hedge means one in which no risk whatsoever is taken. As a corollary of this, it means that there will also be no reward. The perfect hedge would be, for instance, buying EURUSD 1 million and simultaneously selling EURUSD 1 million. Thus, perfect hedging is a pointless exercise.

Instead, broader hedging can either help to reduce overall net losses in a bad position (by making offsetting gains in other related areas) or help to add to overall net profits (whilst not actually proportionately increasing the risk involved). In this sense, then, hedging is a method of dynamically managing the risk/reward profile for the trader and knowing how to do it properly and quickly in any situation is vital.

Cross-Currency Hedging

Beginning with the obvious, all currency trades involve buying one currency and selling another and, because of this duality, hedging currency exposures is actually fairly straightforward.

For example, a trader is long the EUR, which means he is also short USD: in market code +EURUSD. The position should always be marked in terms of the base currency first, then the amount (EUR1 million) and then the price (here, 1.5063). Therefore, in market terms, it should be written: +EURUSD1 @1.5063.

EURUSD (Historical)

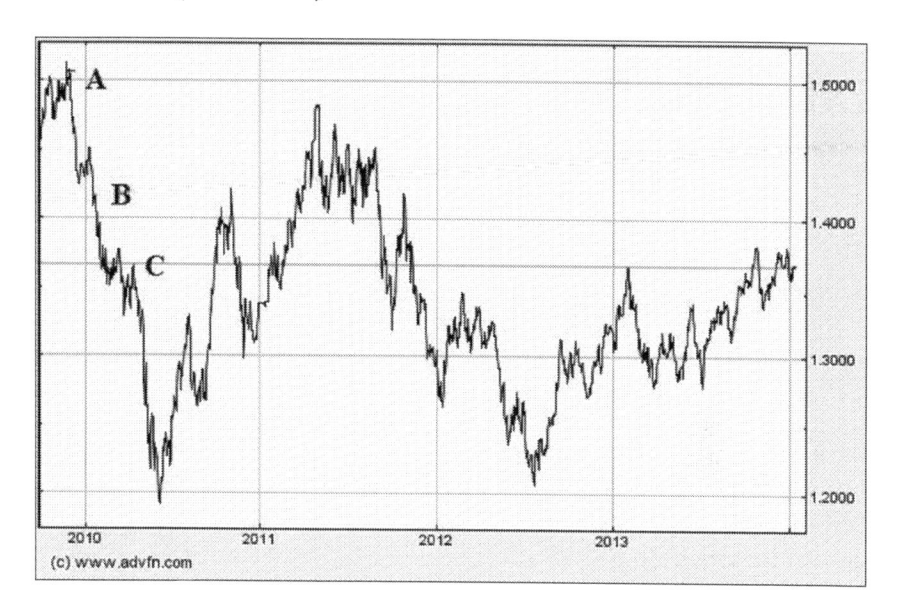

[Key:

A= Buy euros, 1 million and sell US dollars at 1.5063

B = Getting nervous about the euro story, so **buy US dollars, 1.5 million and sell Swiss francs at 1.0262**

C = The trader now has options – he is long EURUSD, long USDCHF; making money on the latter going up as the former goes down. Additionally, he can re-weight positions, depending on how each pairing performs (he can, for example, add to his long USDCHF position or reduce his long EURUSD position) or simply sell EURCHF, as he is effectively net long of that, or he can do counter-balancing stock indices trades]

The market is going against the trader but he believes that the EUR will go up soon. However, he is not exactly sure when and how much the swing against him might be. He knows that, by definition, if the EUR element of this pair is going down then the USD element of it is going up. Therefore, he can go long the USD against something else to attempt to make money on the rising USD as the EUR goes down, so he goes long USDCHF1.5 million as EURUSD breaks through the 1.4750 level.

USDCHF (Historical)

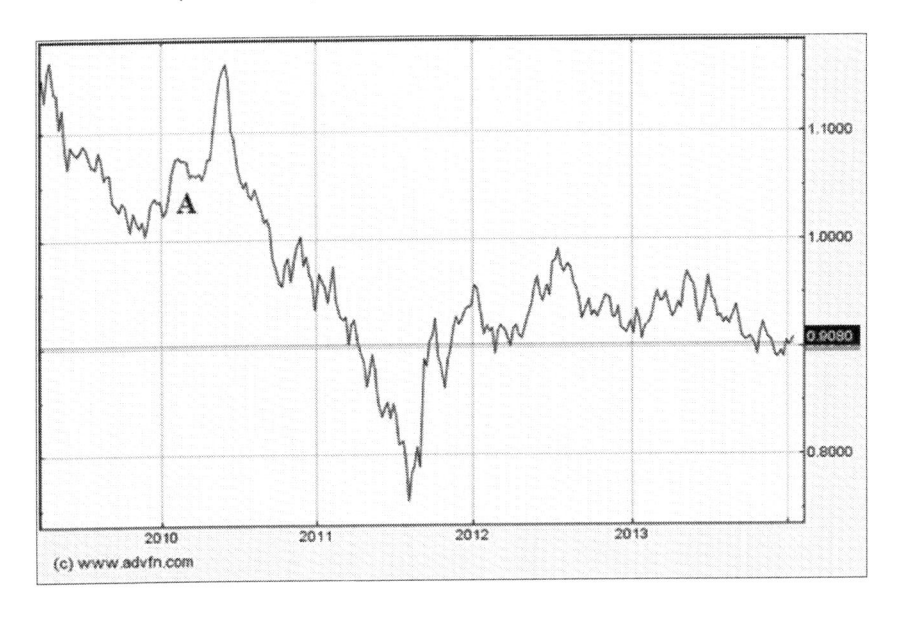

[Key:
A = Buy USD/sell CHF1.5 million at 1.0262]

Now things are looking up, as one trade is counterbalancing the other almost perfectly, as can be seen from the chart below, given that **he is essentially long EURCHF.**

As the EUR continues in its downward trend, the trader can use some of the averaging techniques described above to help loss turn into profit. This is simply a question of re-weighting each trade. As it stands, he has the same overall capital involved in each trade (EUR1 million, or around USD1.5 million) but as the EURUSD continues to trade down, he can add to his long USDCHF position. Let us say that he doubles it, at 1.0400 to USD3 million for the entire duration of the downtrend in EURUSD.

Looking at these trades in P&L terms then:

+EURUSD1 million @ 1.5063, liquidate at 1.1800 = total loss of EUR326,300 (= USD at the new rate = USD385,034).

+USDCHF1 million @ 1.0262, liquidate at 1.1700 = USD143,800

and +USDCHF2 million @ 1.0400, liquidate at 1.1700 = USD260,000.

Therefore, the **total profit for the venture (which did not start out well) was USD77,500**.

EURCHF (Historical)

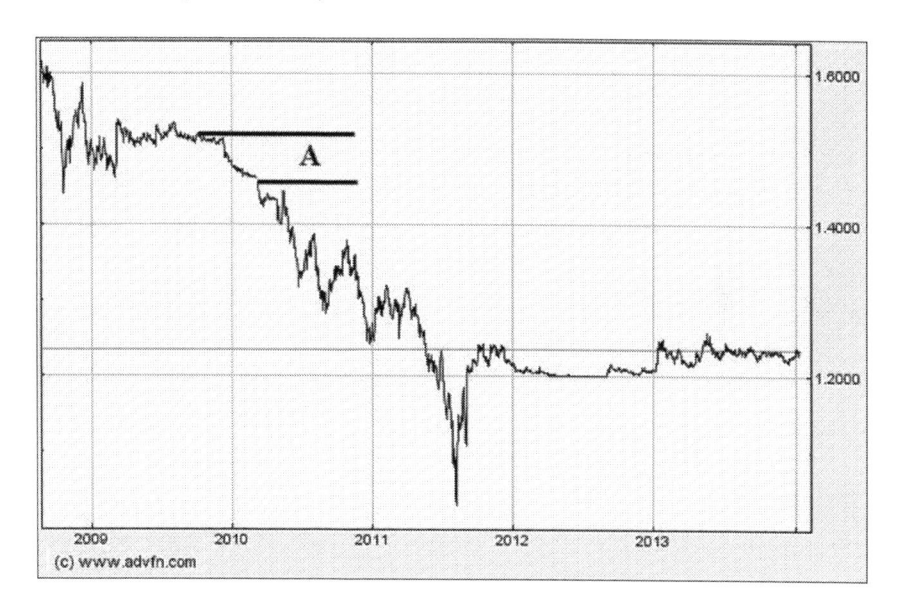

[Key:
A = *Overall, with just a flat long EURCHF position the trader is only down 250-300 pips but he can get rid of this entirely by re-weighting*]

In the above example, **he could also have sold EURCHF,** which would have given him a flat position, as:

1. +EUR -USD

2. +USD -CHF

3. Therefore, net long EURCHF

4. Therefore, sell EURCHF = flat.

However, there were **many other options available whilst he was long EURUSD and long USDCHF**:

1. Increase the relative weighting of the long USDCHF position (as described above) or he could think more laterally still and buy the USD against something else as well.

2. This would have increased his net long USD position but also it would have allowed him to insulate himself against any CHF-specific good news that might cause it to rally and thus lose him money on his long USDCHF position – for example, if the central bank of Switzerland (SNB) raised interest rates unexpectedly.

3. Therefore, he would have looked around for other currencies where the outlook was grim and good news was not expected on the horizon. At the time, GBP looked especially ropey, so he could have sold GBP and bought USD.

4. This again could be reweighted in terms of amount.

5. And so the process goes on.

Cross-Asset Hedging

Sticking with the failing long EURUSD position example for the time being, the trader need not have just hedged his bets with currencies.

Let us recap on the basic situation: he had gone long EUR, expecting some turnaround in the fortunes of the currency, based perhaps on the notion that future figures might show that the weaker Eurozone members (Greece, Spain, Portugal, Italy, Ireland) might be turning themselves around.

So, what else could he do to capitalise on the continued poor performance of the Eurozone that was crucifying his long EURUSD position?

1. Sell the major stock indices associated with the individual countries performing especially badly in the EUR region (as shown above).

Greece Athens Stock Exchange (Historical)

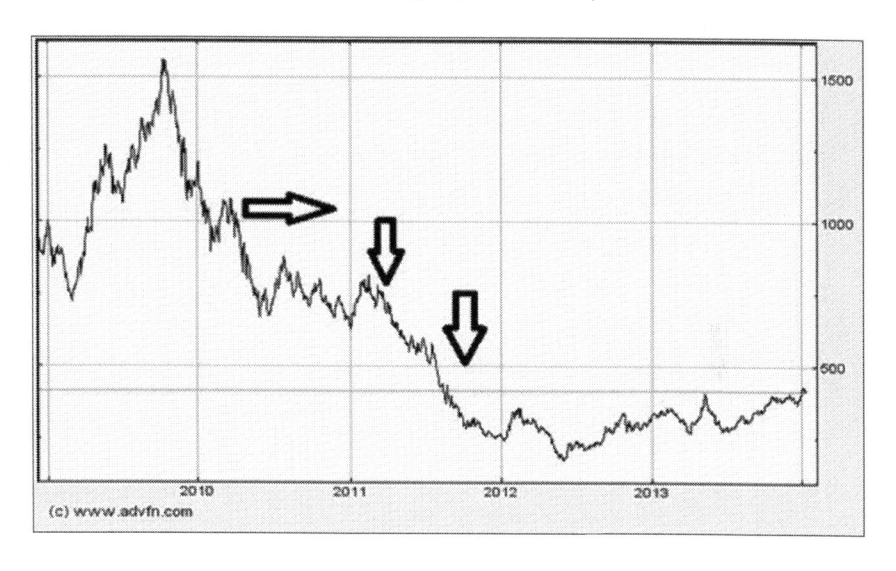

Had he sold the ASE as above, say another USD1 million worth, his entry price at the time would have been around 2250 and falling fast. He could also have sold the other major indices of troubled Eurozone countries.

2. Looking at it another way, he could have bought US stock indices instead/as well as.

Dow Jones Industrial Average (Historical)

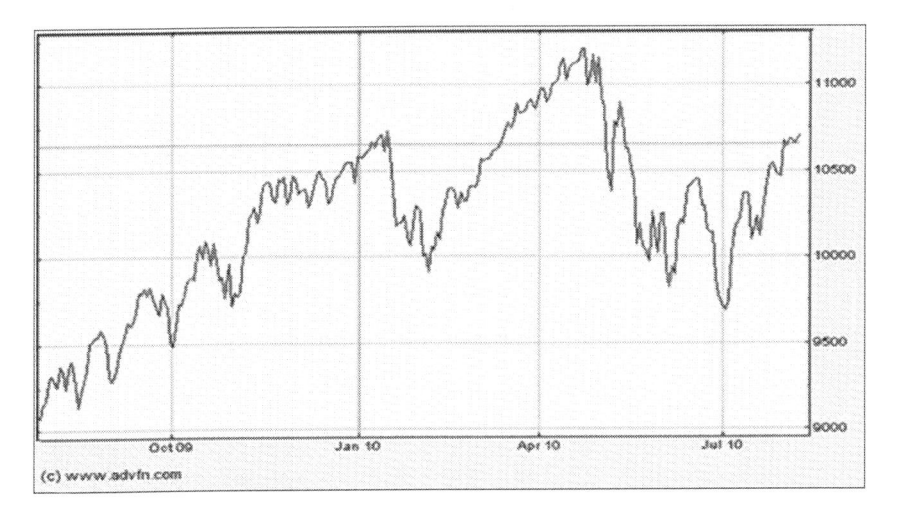

3. If he was, in the meantime, suddenly concerned about his net short CHF position then he could hedge out the CHF risk, by buying the major Swiss stock index.

4. He could have done a currency option to hedge risks either side (we will discuss options later on).

Cross-Sovereign/Credit Rating Hedging

Given that the credit risk for the troubled Eurozone members was increasing over the period when the EUR was falling out of bed, the trader could have bought credit default swaps (CDS) on the countries worst affected. CDS are basically like insurance policies on entities going bankrupt (for example, companies or, in this case, countries). The more technical definition is: CDS pay the buyer face value in exchange for the underlying securities or the cash equivalent should a government or company fail to adhere to its debt agreements; the higher the likelihood, the higher the price of the CDS.

Again, this would have hedged the EUR exposure as, broadly speaking, the more money that was lost on being long EUR, the more money was made on being long Greek CDS (that is, in essence, buying the likelihood of Greece defaulting on its debt).

Options

It should be pointed out at this juncture that trading options is an exceptionally risky business and one which I would strongly recommend no retail trader does in his first five or so years of trading, at minimum. The reason I am including a sub-section on this is specifically for the reason that options positions sometimes have a significant effect on the overall trading patterns of a market, so a trader needs to know what they are when they read market reports stating that x and y options are weighing on/supporting key levels.

Key Types

An option is the right, but not the obligation, to buy or sell an asset at a particular price (the 'exercise price') on or before a specific future date (the 'exercise date').

The two most common types of option are called an **American style option** (which can be exercised at any point up to the option expiration date) and a **European style option** (which can only be exercised on an exact exercise date).

For the more 'exotic' **Asian options** the payoff is determined by the average underlying price over some pre-set period of time, conceptually different from both the American and European option types in which in both cases the payoff of the option contract depends on the price of the underlying instrument at exercise.

Barrier options, meanwhile, that often have a significant effect on market trading patterns, are a type of option whose payoff depends on whether or not the underlying asset has reached or exceeded a predetermined price. A barrier option can be a knock-out, meaning it can expire worthless if the underlying exceeds a certain price, limiting profits for the holder but limiting losses for the writer. It can also be a knock-in, meaning it has no value until the underlying reaches a certain price.

Key Terms

An **option to buy an asset is called a 'call' option and an option to sell one is called a 'put' option. You can buy or sell either type of option (that is, you can buy the right to sell or buy, and you can sell the right to sell or buy)**. If you sell an option then you receive a premium from the buyer (a bit like an insurance premium), however, you are obligated as the seller to pay out to the buyer in the event that the option is exercised (and these payouts can be limitless, depending on how the option has moved). If you buy an option then you receive these premiums.

Options are extremely useful as hedging tools (this was their original purpose, as a type of insurance against unforeseen movements in asset prices) but, as with all financial assets, they can also be used for purely aggressive speculative purposes.

In a currency option, then – let us stick with the EURUSD example that we have been predominantly using in the last few pages – if you bought a EURUSD call then you would be buying the right (but not the obligation) to buy EUR and sell USD, and if you bought a EURUSD put then you would be buying the right (but not the obligation) to sell EUR and buy USD. And vice-versa if you were selling a call or put; you have a liability then to meet the obligation implied in the option if the buyer decides to exercise it.

Although we are not going to go into huge details about the pricing of options, one thing that it is useful to be aware of is that the premium paid to buy an option is a reflection both of the exercise price of the option (and whether it is currently in profit, ITM or out of profit, OTM, see above) and also the volatility of the market for the currency pair.

Looking at options in terms of them being insurance policies is quite helpful in a number of regards. Let us say that you have bought a house and you want to insure its contents against theft for GBP10,000. The insurance company has to decide on a range of factors in determining the level of your premiums. Have you got window and door locks, are you backing onto a secluded area, is it an area known for burglaries etc? So, let us say that the answers are: yes to locks, no to secluded area, no to burglaries. The insurance company decides that overall you will only have to pay them their GBP10,000 back over 20 years. This implies zero risk volatility or thereabouts.

One year into the policy and there are a spate of burglaries in the area, so your premiums go up, as there has been an increase in the risk and so on and so forth. You have a private security firm patrolling your grounds 24/7, so your premiums go down again due to lower risk.

In the EURUSD example, **the player had gone long EUR short USD at 1.5063 and the position had started to go against him almost from the off. The near-perfect hedge here would have been to buy a EURUSD put (the right but not the obligation to sell EUR and buy USD) at a strike price of 1.5063** although the price would have to be adjusted slightly to take into account the premium that the player would have paid to the seller of the option, but basically that is the idea.

He could, conversely, have banked money in advance if he had sold a EURUSD call option (giving someone the right but not the obligation to buy EUR from the player, therefore the player is selling them and buying USD) also at 1.5063.

Key Legislation

A key part of why more investors in general are now looking at options (and futures) investment than they were before the new swathe of market regulations (Basel III, Mifid, Dodd-Frank etc), of course, is that they appear to fall outside the confusion of precisely what will and will not be actively managed within the scope of the new FX regulatory environment.

For example, one key idea was that the traditionally bilaterally-traded over-the-counter (OTC) FX derivatives markets would be migrated into a mandatory electronically-executed environment, all under the auspices of central counterparties (CCPs) that act as middlemen between the trading parties and the central clearinghouses. Moreover, participants would be obliged to post initial and variation margin to the CCPs on a daily or intra-day basis, so the need for easily accessible capital to enable such trading would also increase dramatically.

However, timing remains a problem for the futures markets, given that the dates of the contracts are much more specific than those of spot and forward outright contracts, which are completely flexible, and liquidity is also a problem for the futures markets, which are very small compared to the global FX markets.

The massive risk in writing options was highlighted in the Nick Leeson case. Leeson was in charge of both Barings Bank's front office dealing operations on the Singapore International Monetary Exchange (SIMEX) and its back-office function so that when a trade went wrong at the front end he personally could simply rubber-stamp it at the back end. He continued to do so until he lost Barings around GBP830 million, bringing the bank down in the process; this being a reminder of over-confidence in one's abilities.

And second, in order to cover his mounting trading losses he decided to write vast numbers of options essentially betting on the Nikkei stock market rising. He had pocketed millions of dollars in 'insurance options' from others and all was looking good as Japan boomed, until the Kobe earthquake hit Japan in January 1995, whereupon the Nikkei fell like a stone and his customers wanted their insurance payments back; this illustrating that markets are not always predictable.

Basic Structures (Long-Only Options)

Buying a call option: This is used most simply by those who believe that an asset is going up in value (it is buying the option to buy a certain asset). If the asset price is higher than the strike price plus the premium paid then the trader makes a profit. The only risk here, as with all options bought, is that the trader loses the premium paid.

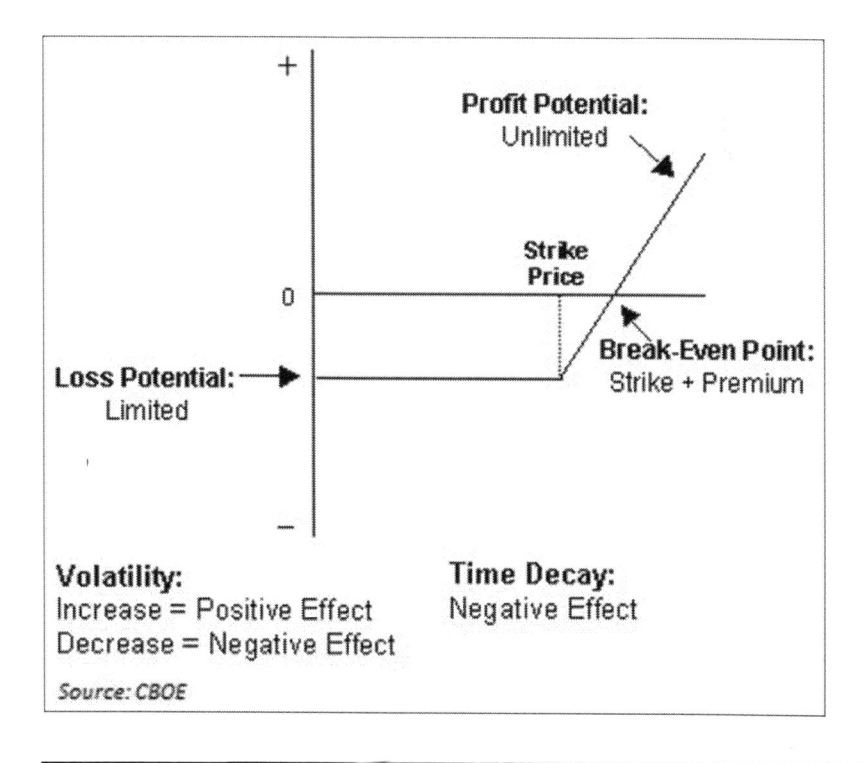

```
                              +
                                       Profit Potential:
                                       Unlimited
                                                   ↘
                                                     ▲
                                       Strike
                                       Price        /
                         0                         /
                    ─────────────────────────────/────
                                                ▶
                                       Break-Even Point:
Loss Potential: ──▶                    Strike + Premium
Limited

                              ─

Volatility:                   Time Decay:
Increase = Positive Effect    Negative Effect
Decrease = Negative Effect

Source: CBOE
```

203

Buying a put option: This is used by those who believe that an asset is going down in value (it is buying the option to sell a certain asset). If the asset price is lower than the strike price plus the premium paid then the trader makes a profit. The only risk here, as with all options bought, is that the trader loses the premium paid.

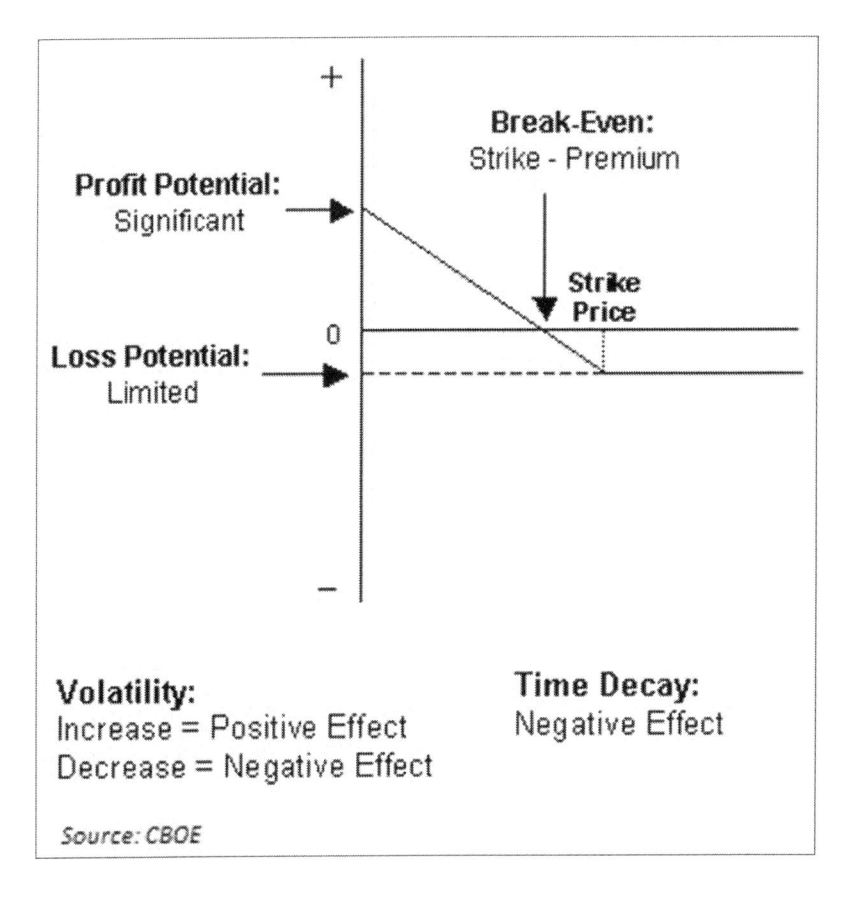

Profit Potential: Significant

Loss Potential: Limited

Break-Even: Strike - Premium

Strike Price

Volatility:
Increase = Positive Effect
Decrease = Negative Effect

Time Decay: Negative Effect

Source: CBOE

Long Straddle: This is used by investors who think an asset is going a long way in one direction, but is unsure as to which direction that might be. It involves buying both a put and a call option at the same strike price and the same expiration date. This offers unlimited potential upside but limited downside.

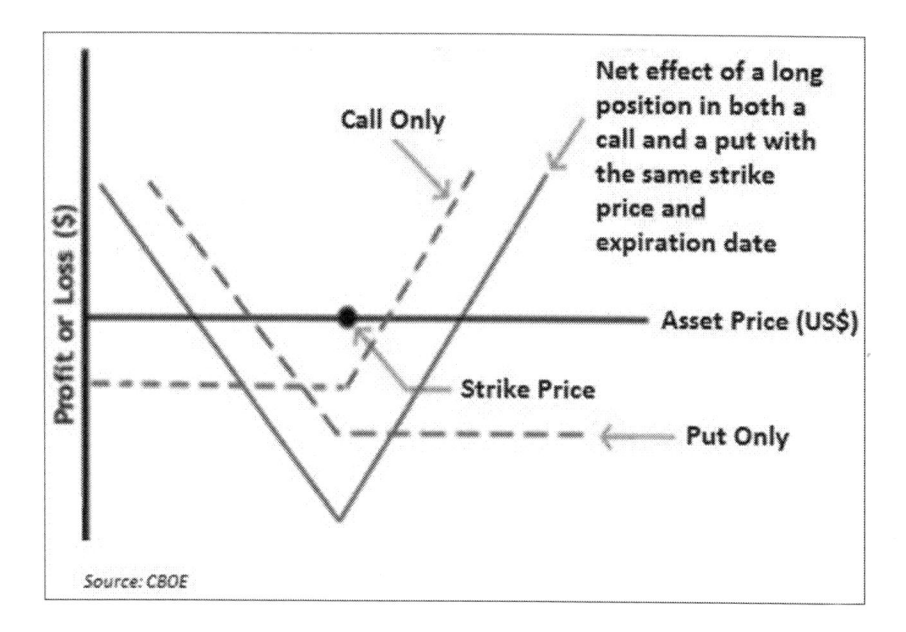

Long Strangle: This is for investors similar to those in the Long Straddle strategy, but with the differences that both are usually some way out of the money and the call option and put option elements have different strike prices (but the same expiration date).

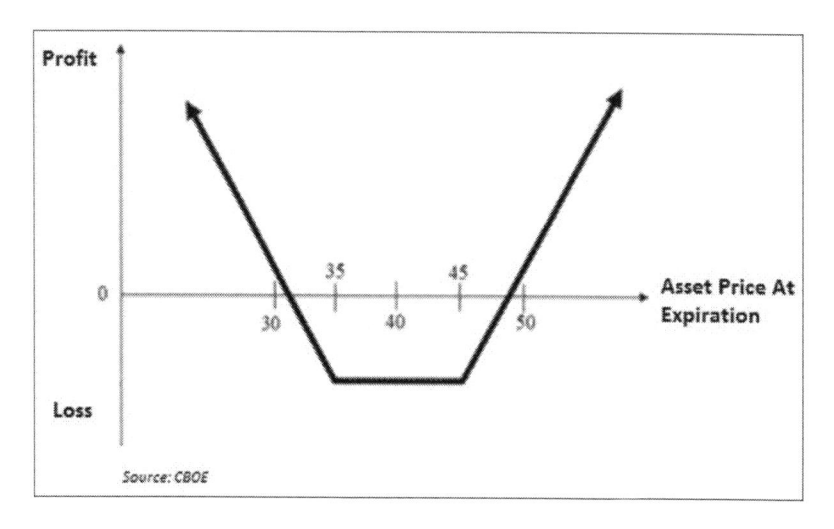

As mentioned, sometimes big options positions (generally, those sold by financial institutions) have a major effect on markets. This occurs as those who have sold them understandably attempt to avoid an asset reaching the exercise price of the option, at which point they would face massive payouts to those who have bought them. In practical terms, the level of these exercise prices are often located just below key support levels or just above key resistance levels respectively, and protective buying or selling in order to avoid option exercises often reinforce the strength of these support and resistance levels.

About the Author

After graduating from Oxford University with BA (Hons) and MA (Hons) degrees, Simon Watkins worked for a number of years as a senior Forex trader and salesman, ultimately achieving the positions of **Director of Forex at Bank of Montreal and Head of Forex Institutional Sales for Credit Lyonnais**. He has since become a **financial journalist, being Head of Weekly Publications And Managing Editor and Chief Writer of Business Monitor International, Head of Global Fuel Oil Products for Platts, Global Managing Editor of Research for Renaissance Capital** (Moscow) and **Head of Developed Market Bond Analysis for Bond Radar**.

He has written extensively on Forex, equities, bonds and commodities for many publications, including: *The Financial Times, Euromoney, FT Capital Insights, FX-MM, CFO Insight, The Edge Middle East Finance, International Commerce Magazine, The Securities And Investment Review, Accountancy Magazine, The Emerging Markets Monitor, Asia Economic Alert, Latin America Economic Alert, Eastern Europe Economic Alert, Oil And Gas Middle East, European CEO, Global Finance*

Magazine, World Finance Magazine, The Emerging Markets Report, FTSE Global Markets, VM Group Energy Monthly, VM Group Metals Monthly, Islamic Investor Magazine, Finance Europe, Finance Emerging Europe and *CIMA Financial Management.*

In addition, he has worked as an investment consultant for major hedge funds in London, Moscow and the Middle East.

This is Simon's fourth book for ADVFN Books. Turn over for details of his other three.

Also by Simon Watkins

The Great Oil Price Fixes and How to Trade Them

The oil market has been manipulated to an extremely high degree for decades, both overtly and covertly, and given its enduring geopolitical importance that is likely to continue.

Traders need to understand the essential dynamics that drive the global oil market, offering as it does unparalleled opportunities to make returns over and above those of other markets. The oil market is also an essential part of trading FX, equities, bonds and other commodities.

Simon Watkins' book *The Great Oil Price Fixes And How To Trade Them* offers you the knowledge you need. It covers the history of the market, gives you an understanding of the players in the oil game and provides a solid grounding in the market-specific trading nuances required in this particular field.

The essential elements of the general trading methodology, strategies and tactics that underpin top professional traders are covered with reference to how they can be used to trade in the oil market.

Available in paperback and for the Kindle from Amazon.

How to Make Big Money Trading in All Financial Conditions

The markets are going through a period of turbulence right now, but even in periods of low market volatility there's always some asset, somewhere in the world, that oscillates in price sufficiently to offer traders opportunities to make big money. The trick is to know what the asset is, to identify whether it's trading higher or lower than it should be and to have the skill, speed of thought and tenacity to take advantage of it.

In the follow up to his book *Everything You Need To Know About Making Serious Money Trading The Financial Markets*, Simon Watkins covers changing volatility patterns, risk-on/risk-off trading, how to find value in emerging markets and long-term global economic cycles. He outlines more fundamental principles that should guide your trades and trading methodologies to help you succeed.

Fully illustrated with detailed charts, the book shows how you can use technical analysis to make your decisions, how to manage your risk and how to take out hedge positions to offset possible losses.

Available in paperback and for the Kindle from Amazon.

Everything You Need To Know About Making Serious Money Trading The Financial Markets

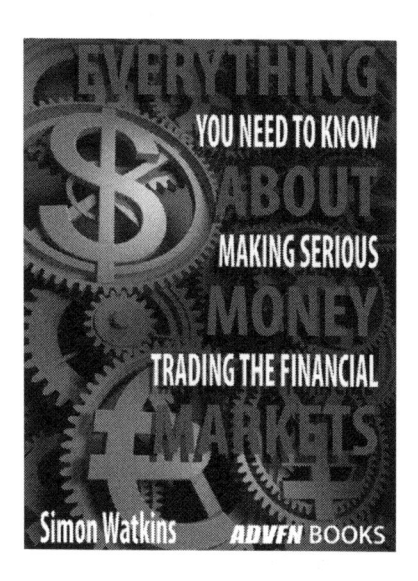

All over the world, people are trading on the financial markets. Some of them make a fortune – and many more lose their shirts. This book tells you how to be one of the winners.

It's a stark and sobering fact that around 90% of retail traders lose all of their trading money within about 90 days. That's because they have little grasp of the realities, technicalities, psychology and nature of the financial markets. In short, they don't know what they are doing.

Everything You Need To Know About Making Serious Money Trading The Financial Markets teaches you how to avoid being one of the 90%, and explains how to stack the odds firmly in your favour so you can become one of the 10% that make life-changing money trading. It's a trading bible that covers all aspects of the subject, from the psychology of trading and the mindset you need to succeed, through the fundamental principles that should guide your trades, to the trading methodologies that will help you succeed.

Fully illustrated with detailed charts, the book shows how you can use technical analysis to make your decisions, how to manage your risk and how to take out hedge positions to offset possible losses.

Available in paperback and for the Kindle from Amazon.

More Books from ADVFN

18 Smart Ways to Improve Your Trading

by Maria Psarra

Any trader or investor that says they have never lost money in the markets is too young, too stupid, too inexperienced, or just plain lying to you. Everyone makes mistakes, particularly when starting out as a trader. It's part of the learning curve.

What matters is that you learn from your mistakes. Even better, learn from the mistakes others have made to avoid making them yourself.

18 Smart Ways to Improve Your Trading explains some of the common mistakes traders make and the routines that winning traders use to avoid those errors. The author draws on her many years' experience of trading, both on institutional proprietary trading desks and for herself, and the knowledge she has gained advising professional clients.

In this book she shares her expertise with you. The *18 Smart Ways* include the habits that separate winning traders from losing ones, the secrets to profitable trading and how to deal with the emotional hiccups that cause you to lose in the markets.

If you absorb these lessons then they should make you a better investor or trader.

Originally published as articles in Master Investor magazine.

Available in paperback and for the Kindle from Amazon.

101 Charts for Trading Success

by Zak Mir

Using insider knowledge to reveal the tricks of the trade, Zak Mir's *101 Charts for Trading Success* explains the most complex set ups in the stock market.

Providing a clear way of predicting price action, charting is a way of making money by delivering high probability percentage trades, whilst removing the need to trawl through company accounts and financial ratios.

Illustrated with easy to understand charts this is the accessible, essential guide on how to read, understand and use charts, to buy and sell stocks. *101 Charts* is a must for all future investment millionaires.

Available in paperback and for the Kindle from Amazon.

The Game in Wall Street

by Hoyle and Clem Chambers

As the new century dawned, Wall Street was a game and the stock market was fixed. Ordinary investors were fleeced by big institutions that manipulated the markets to their own advantage and they had no comeback.

The Game in Wall Street shows the ways that the titans of rampant capitalism operated to make money from any source they could control. Their accumulated funds gave the titans enormous power over the market and allowed them to ensure they won the game.

Traders joining the game without knowing the rules are on a road to ruin. It's like gambling without knowing the rules and with no idea of the odds.

The Game in Wall Street sets out in detail exactly how this market manipulation works and shows how to ride the price movements and make a profit.

And guess what? The rules of the game haven't changed since the book was first published in 1898. You can apply the same strategies in your own investing and avoid losing your shirt by gambling against the professionals.

Illustrated with the very first stock charts ever published, the book contains a new preface and a conclusion by stock market guru Clem Chambers which put the text in the context of how Wall Street operates today.

Available in paperback and for the Kindle from Amazon.

For more information go to the ADVFN Books website at www.advfnbooks.com.

ADVFN BOOKS

Printed in Great Britain
by Amazon